# Changemakers

A 'how to' guide to designing, adapting and delivering effective physical education

Phil Mathe

CHANGEMAKERS

First published in 2024 by Scholary

The Dutch Barn, Bremhill Grove Farm, Chippenham, Wiltshire,
SN15 4LX, United Kingdom
Scholary is an imprint of Scholary Ltd

© 2024 Phil Mathe

All rights reserved. No part of this book may be reprinted or reproduced or utilised in any form or by electronic, mechanical, or other means, now known or hereafter invented, including photocopying and recording, or in any information storage or retrieval system, without permission in writing from the publishers.

British Library Cataloguing in Publication Data.
A catalogue record for this book is available from the British Library.

ISBN: 978-1-0687095-3-1 (pbk)
ISBN: 978-1-0687095-4-8 (hbk)
ISBN: 978-1-0687095-5-5 (ebk)

# Overview

**The world of PE is ever changing. More and more PE departments and PE teachers are reflecting on what PE looks and functions like within their schools and looking to make meaningful change or adaptation to benefit their pupils. This is always a good thing.**

*Changemakers* is your go-to guide for facilitating meaningful and long-lasting change within your PE curriculum, as well as wider curricula development within schools.

Taking the expertise of PE teachers globally as well as industry experts in change management, *Changemakers* will provide you with ideas of the structure, processes and practice to ensure the changes we make within PE address the needs of our pupils and the requirements of our schools.

Whatever the changes you are considering, *Changemakers* will support you through the process, from inception to delivery and assessing the impact of your project and will help you structure your developments to be as effective as possible.

With real life examples of tried and tested approaches, from around the world, *Changemakers* gives teachers the confidence to consider change as an opportunity rather than something to be nervous or wary of.

There are many books about what PE could or should be like, available to teachers. *Changemakers* is not a book in that mould, rather it's a useful guide, providing PE departments with the knowledge and tools to make the changes that will really benefit their pupils, in their own context.

**We are *Changemakers*.**

# Contents

| | |
|---|---|
| Overview | 3 |
| Acknowledgements | 6 |
| Foreword | 7 |
| Introduction | 10 |
| **Chapter 1 - Not A PE Book!** | **12** |
| *Changemaker Reflection: Martin Wragg* | *16* |
| **Chapter 2 - But We've Always Done It This Way** | **18** |
| *Changemaker Reflection: Tom Manley* | *22* |
| **Chapter 3 - Making Change Happen In Physical Education** | **24** |
| *Changemaker Reflection: Tommi Charlish* | *30* |
| **Chapter 4 - Think Of The Children!** | **33** |
| *Changemaker Reflection: Mathew Jones* | *38* |
| **Chapter 5 - The Power Of 3** | **40** |
| *Changemaker Reflection: Kayali* | *52* |
| **Chapter 6 - Process For Progress** | **54** |
| *Changemaker Reflection: Jon Campbell & Matthew Trowbridge* | *65* |
| **Chapter 7 - Research And Reflection** | **70** |
| *Changemaker Reflection: Aaron Davey* | *75* |
| *Changemaker Reflection: Charlotte Roxburgh* | *78* |
| *Changemaker Reflection: Shrehan Lynch* | *81* |
| **Chapter 8 - Let's Go!** | **83** |
| *Changemaker Reflection: Louis Fearn* | *86* |

# CONTENTS

**Chapter 9 - What Are You Doing?** — **88**
*Changemaker Reflection: Anna Power* — *90*
*Changemaker Reflection: Helen Battelley* — *93*
*Changemaker Reflection: Christopher Jackson* — *95*

**Chapter 10 - Nuts And Bolts** — **97**
*Changemaker Reflection: Phil Mathe* — *98*
*Changemaker Reflection: Neil Moggan* — *121*
*Changemaker Reflection: Hannah Crawley* — *151*

**Chapter 11 - Who And How?** — **155**
*Changemaker Reflection: Ellie Woodcock* — *156*
*Changemaker Reflection: Matthew Kelly* — *167*

**Chapter 12 - Solid Foundations** — **170**
*Changemaker Reflection: Anna Sheppard* — *180*

**Chapter 13 - How Change Happens In Your Context** — **184**
*Changemaker Reflection: Alan Dunstan* — *186*

**Chapter 14 - Make It So** — **188**
*Changemaker Reflection: Gary Spink* — *191*

**Chapter 15 - And Then** — **194**
*Changemaker Reflection: David Wallace* — *196*

**Chapter 16 - So What?** — **198**
*Changemaker Reflection: Lee Sullivan* — *202*

**Chapter 17 - Be The Change** — **204**

References — 208

# Acknowledgements

The difficult second book. Following up on Happiness Factories was something I debated long and hard within myself. I had originally said I wouldn't do it again, but clearly, I didn't mean it! The more I thought about it, about what else I had to say, I kept coming back to the idea that ideas, principles, visions, believes and perspectives are all important, critical in fact, but no more so than structure, plans, experience, knowledge and skills. The golden ticket for PE provision is an ambitious, effective and meaningful programme, delivered with efficiency, accuracy and impact. If there was anything else worth writing about, it was about how rather than what.

As before, I've been supported throughout this process by more people I could ever hope to name individually, but if you've ever given me some advice, some support or some guidance, during my time as a PE teacher and leader, then the chances are your impact is reflected somewhere in these pages.

My family, Emma, Aaron, Finley and Rosie, who have shared my International PE adventure and always been my anchor in life. Without you all, none of this would have happened.

Pete and Sean, my business advisors, who explained how the real world works and the intricacies of project management outside of education and mum, for just telling me to get on with it!

My publishers, Scholary. Liz, Tim, Will, Lee and the PE Scholar team, who have backed me and supported me throughout. Tracey, our amazing editor who took my rambling writing and turned it into this amazing final version. Thank you all, I will not forget your support and enthusiasm for this project.

But ultimately, this book is dedicated to my Dad. The most influential person I know. Someone who can make a plan, and stick to it, regardless of what life throws in his way. I've seen you build and create, plan and deliver, over and over again through your business life, always with structure and purpose. The lessons within this book, are testament to the lessons I learnt from you. I don't tell you enough, but thank you, and I love you.

# Foreword

For at least ten years in my teaching and leadership career, I viewed change as something that happened to me – something that I was expected to do and to follow. Whether it was policy, performance or pay, my own ability to exert change where it mattered seemed limited. The more I learned and developed myself professionally, the more I began to realise that change isn't something that just happens to you – it's something that you can also be part of, in its design, implementation and outcome.

For the next five years that followed, I set about trying to instigate change and make change happen to myself and those around me. What followed was a remarkable journey that saw me start a business, write several books, travel the world and in doing so, bring people, their purpose and pleasure together for the greater good.

The Chinese have a wonderful saying when it comes to change: 'When the winds of change blow, some people build walls and others build windmills'. Ask yourself whether you are the person who builds walls and resists change, or whether you build windmills and use the force and power of change to adapt your practices and ride in the slipstream of positivity.

Many of you reading this are likely to be highly experienced, skilled and talented PE professionals who are highly appreciated by your schools in the value you add to your school and its holistic educational programme. It is well noted that PE Teachers often go on to make good school leaders. They are versatile, can handle pressure and are resilient when faced with personal and professional challenges. They are strong advocates of change. Think about how our warm-ups have developed, how learning to swim has moved on and, critically, how approaches to health and safety have advanced. The future lies right in front of you and starts with recognising the need for change and the courage to embrace it.

When Dick Frosby had the courage to finally change the way that high jumpers attempted to clear the bar at the Olympics in Mexico City in 1968, few had ever seen anything like it in their lives. A change so radical, so unbelievably different – to be almost alien, that people genuinely resisted. Those who did resist however, found themselves in a darkened room, without light and no window of opportunity. Our PE curriculum and its lessons are in need of change. The United World College network and its shared commitment to an 'alternative' sustainable curriculum path based around increasing global needs and through an increasingly practical pathway, cannot be overlooked. Change has to happen.

As you will read in this book, when developing any kind of change mandate – especially in PE, the students should be front and centre of your thinking. Most importantly, ask yourself 'if we continue on this path and do nothing, what is likely to be the outcome?'.

I am sure that like I have, you will enjoy the tireless effort that has gone into the compilation of this book. Its title and content are incredibly original and unique. Bridging people's ideas, writing styles and personal values systems is by no means easy. A glowing testament to Phil and his vivacious personal journey of self-improvement which so many of us now find ourselves on.

Enjoy this book as much as I have. Use it as a foundation for discussion and collaboration among your own school PE and wider leadership teams and in doing so share your feedback with its author, who will be only too happy to reply.

Whatever journey you are on, I wish you well.

**André Double**
*Founder and CEO, Leading Your International School*

---

Albert Einstein once said 'The world as we have created it, is a process of our thinking. It cannot be changed without changing our thinking'. As I reflect upon my career in physical education, and where it began at the start of the Millennium, it is hard to imagine or quantify the changes that have taken place - personally, professionally, and globally. In just the last few years alone, the transformative journey that education has been on has been both profound and unprecedented. Who could have foreseen a global pandemic; the rapid changes we would have to make as a physical education community and the impact it would have on all our lives.

We constantly stand on the cusp of new eras, new beginnings, and uncertainty. We are marked by technological advancements, shifting societal paradigms, and a global community. Indeed, nothing has ever been certain. It is hard to imagine that the teacher I was all those years ago could still think about physical education in the same way I do now. Back in the early 00s, the only other physical education professionals I knew and could reach out to were in my department. Opportunities occasionally emerged to work locally with other schools, and I felt lucky to have maintained a close-knit group of teacher friends who I had trained with. I did not know what PE looked like in other countries. My resources were limited to what I could photocopy (and store in a ring bound folder) and professional development was once a year when I was able to attend a local course.

Fast forward 25 years and we are now a rich and diverse evidenced-based profession. We know more than ever before about physical education pedagogy, curriculum design, health, movement, social and emotional aspects of learning. Unquestionably we have become a more informed and knowledgeable physical education profession.

And yet, in so many ways, physical education has hardly changed at all.

Have we changed, or have we just got better at what we have always done?

If you are reading this book, you are likely to be a passionate and committed teacher, possibly seeking inspiration for change and ways to create change within your setting. Embracing other perspectives is a powerful way to think about what is possible. The collection of voices in this book is an important start. Each voice represents a unique context, perspective, and position. Making meaningful change is hard, but through this book, Phil has brought together a supportive and inspiring community of '*Changemakers*' to encourage us to take those steps. It is now tasked to all of us to create the change we are seeking and ensure that the next 25 years of PE is Positive and Exciting. Wherever that journey may take us.

## Dr Vicky Randall
*Teacher Educator, Researcher and Consultant*

# Introduction

**'In any given moment we have two options: to step forward into growth or step back into safety.'**
*Abraham Maslow*

Before I retrained as a teacher in 2008, I worked in sales. I sold a random range of different things in my career, from eLearning to paper (you cannot think of anything duller to sell to people than paper!). Regardless of who I was working for, where I was based and what I was selling, there was always one constant, across all my jobs. That was Change. Change happened all the time, whether enforced by the economics of business, the transitory nature of sales teams or the competitive environment in which teams operate. Things changed around me all the time, and businesses were set up and prepared not just to embrace change, when necessary, but to thrive as a result of it. Vast sums of money were spent on preparing and upskilling staff, (like me), to accept, confront and view change as a positive thing. Change management was a term used in every office I ever worked in. We were given books on how to cope with change, before redundancies were made. We were given training on change facilitation before company ownership transitioned. We were told that change was not just necessary but beneficial, even if the change that subsequently occurred didn't always feel positive to us as employees. Change was, and still is, a constant, ever-present reality within business environments and as such, I learnt to accept change as a natural part of the life cycle of any role I ever took on.

Fast forward to my teaching career and change is often viewed very differently. Change is scary, change isn't always positive, change hurts and change is something dictated to us by others and is often perceived as unnecessary, and negative. The truth, however, is that just like in business, educational contexts experience the constant influence and impact of change all the time.

Change is a natural and necessary factor in the development and progress of education and as such something we all need to embrace. We've all heard the terms radiators and drains and have sat through CPD where we've been told about the difference between those of us who radiate positivity and those who suck it from their surroundings, but the reality is far more nuanced than that. Every one of us is different, unique in our values, experience, motivations, and character. No one reacts to change in the same way and as a result we can never be totally sure how our colleagues, students, parents or even ourselves will react when it happens. What we can do is think, reflect, plan, discuss, collaborate and structure change, to ensure that everyone feels considered. The most important thing, when we think about change, is the sense of being in control. Without control we get scared, worried, anxious and less effective. When we are given some control over the things that happen to us, around us or through us, then we are more able to feel positive about the change that will occur. If there is one thing that my career selling paper taught me it is that change is something to be embraced, faced and controlled. If this book helps you with only one thing, then I hope it is to understand that change, however inevitable, can always be positive, when considered and shared. This is a book about change, but it's also a book about collaboration, teamwork, personal ambition and team dynamics. PE departments are some of the most exciting, positive places I have ever worked, and if we can embrace that positivity in our approach to change, together, we can do amazing things.

### Reflective Questions: Initial thinking

Try and think about something that has changed for you recently, either professionally or personally:

- How do you feel about that experience?
- What went well. Do you think others would agree?
- What could have been better? Do you think others would agree with that too?
- What could you have done differently?
- If you had to describe, in only a few words, what time of changemaker you think you are, what would you say?

We're going to return to these questions, at the very end of *Changemakers*. I wonder if your perspectives will have changed?

# Chapter 1 - Not A PE Book!

*'All great changes are preceded by chaos.'*
*Deepak Chopra*

This is not specifically a book about what PE is. This book will not tell you what PE was, can be, should be or could be. It's not really going to tell you anything about what PE looks like, how it should work, what should be included with our PE provision, or indeed give you many of my opinions about PE at all!

This book will not give you any real help in deciding what your PE curriculum should look like, but it will, however, support your curriculum development in whatever approach and model you decide to adopt, and as such, *Changemakers* should be relevant to every single PE department across the world, who will, inevitably, one day, change something they do.

We are, however, going to explore the concept of change within the context of PE because, as a PE teacher, it's what I know. It's been my world for twenty plus years and as such it makes sense that most of my experience, examples and ideas come from the sphere of PE teaching. Whenever I have looked for change it has been within the scope of PE in my schools and as such my knowledge is all linked back to the provision of PE for my pupils. The reality is however, that what follows can be equally applied to any subject area within education. This book will be relatable to teachers across the whole spectrum of subjects, geographical locations or contexts, who have faced the challenge of change. Whilst I will inevitably refer back to my experiences within PE, I hope that the concepts, ideas and approaches will make sense and provide value to everyone, regardless of the subject they teach.

# CHAPTER 1 - NOT A PE BOOK!

This book is about change. An inevitable constant within education. Change happens all the time, all around us, both consciously and subconsciously. Sometimes it is organic and other times it is revolutionary. Sometimes change is sought and desired and other times it is enforced. Change can take many forms and be approached in many ways.

| Unfamiliar | Lack of clarity | Cannot see benefits |
| Fear | | Lack of trust |
| Loss of control | Don't know why | Means more work |

Change is often seen negatively. Many of us fear change, avoid change, challenge change. Change can be scary and unsettling. For something so common in our professional and personal lives, it is strange that we see it as something to be wary of and we often see it as a personal affront to our professionalism or capability as educators. Change and the idea of change is all around us, but we avoid talking about it. This book will attempt to support you as you consider, reflect and plan for change, as well as demystify some of the challenge and apprehension that change within PE, or any other aspect of education, so regularly brings.

The best way to approach this book is alongside an existing idea of what change might look like within your context. You may already have an idea of what you think your PE curriculum should or could look like, but equally you may have no idea at this point. You may not even know yet whether change is needed. You may have read a PE book that has suggested a different approach that you think might work for you, or you may still be searching for that spark. Wherever you are in your journey towards meaningful change, the fact that you have decided to read *Changemakers* suggests that you think there might be something that needs to develop within your provision and I sincerely hope that this book provides you with a supportive and useful guide to the exciting and rewarding process you are about to engage with.

Some of you will read this book alone. Some will share it with your departments. Regardless of whether you choose to make your change process part of a collaborative exercise or a personal one, I believe that fundamentally change within education is a process best shared. Discuss with trusted colleagues or peers, the questions and reflections that arise as you work your way through *Changemakers*. Focus your planning on the fundamental principles set out in the coming sections and really explore what change will look and feel like within your own context. Don't be afraid to reach out to those support networks within your educational community. See what has worked for colleagues in other subject areas, seek ideas and thoughts of fellow PE departments within your region. Ask questions of your community and use their experiences to shape your own.

Throughout this book I've attempted to include the ideas and experiences of fellow PE teachers and PE leaders who are on their own journey of change. Some are further ahead than others and each has their own unique context in which they are facilitating change. All, however, have one critical thing in common. Their change process is aimed at providing the very best opportunities for the pupils they serve. Fundamentally change occurs because we want to do the very best we can, for the children we teach. Always remember that you are the expert in your own context. No one knows your pupils as well as you do, and no one wants your pupils to experience the very best version of PE more than you do. Trust in yourself and your department and always keep your pupils at the very heart of every decision you make moving forward.

There are many models designed to explain and demonstrate the process we go through when facilitating change. Some of them will appear in the coming pages. Some will tell you about specific steps that occur as we move through a change process, and some will identify key moments during the change management process that indicate a change of phase or the successful completion of a step in your journey. Whilst these are useful, they are often generic in nature and as such not directly applicable to the world of PE and education that we inhabit. Essentially change will look different depending on a wide range of factors that make your provision unique. Whilst we can use generic models to quality assure our own progress, we need to understand that the journey we are on will not look like the one from the model creators perspective, nor anyone else's. Here in *Changemakers* I have tried to keep the process as simple as possible, step by step, whilst always remembering that you will modify, adapt and revise the process to suit you, your department, and your pupils. That is my hope.

*Changemakers* start by looking at the potential reasons why we're considering change. Those very initial reflective moments that provide the catalyst for considering doing something different. It is at this point that much of our future progress is formed. We will look at why we might want to change the way we provide PE. We will look at the resources and research that can support our exploration of change within PE and reflect on the ways to justify if change is really needed.

*Changemakers* goes on to explore change from the perspective of three key stakeholders:

- Yourself as the changemaker
- Your colleagues and department as the changers
- Your pupils as the recipients of change.

Change looks and feels different to each of these three groups. The reasons for change will be different. The feelings and emotions regarding change will vary between them and the challenges faced by change are not the same.

We will explore how change might work, within your context. We will discuss what change might look like, how we facilitate change in the dynamic environment of a PE department and then explore what tools and methods we can use to assess how impactful and effective our change has been. Finally, we will reflect on why change is so important, and how much impact we can have when we make the decision to make change happen. We will explore what difference we can make through the changes we have adopt and we will explore how we review changes within physical education to recognise whether any adaptions we have made have had the desired impact we were looking for.

It is important, at this early stage, to remember that change is not a finite entity. We don't just make changes, then stop. Change is ongoing, evolving and ever growing. When you think you're reaching an end point to a change management process, you will discover new ways in which change is needed, or desired. You'll start the process again. Good PE, and good education is an ever-evolving entity. Organic you could say. We work in dynamic, humanist environments which are never static. Pupils come and go; pupils grow and develop. Teachers join and leave, are promoted or shifted around. Facilities grow, modernise and change. Budgets ebb and flow and a million other things change all the time around us. To consider change as a finite action is too simplistic and does not really reflect the reality of our world.

The other, critical thing to remember, is that we are already experts in change. Whether we are the most or the least resistant to change we are, by our very nature, experts in coping and managing change. We deal with change every day in a myriad of ways, often without even realising it. As teachers we often suffer from an inability to give ourselves credit, but when it comes to change, we are particularly lacking. You are likely to recognise yourself in many of the situations that we will go on to discuss in *Changemakers* and I would encourage you to believe in yourself and your ability to make positive, meaningful change happen, because you are already an expert changemaker.

### Reflective Questions:

- Why did you buy this book?
- Why does change matter to you?
- Is change more important to you, than those colleagues around you?

### Changemaker Reflection: Martin Wragg
*Head of PE, The English School, Kuwait*

Curriculum innovation and change management are facets of our profession that are not for the faint of heart. As teachers, we often go above and beyond daily, simply just to satisfy the requirements of our multidimensional roles. Thus, following the status quo, and choosing to replicate 'what has worked before' in terms of curriculum delivery, can understandably bring a welcome feeling of ease and consistency, within a workload and culture that is well-documented to be causing an increase in teacher burnout. However, anything worth having doesn't come easy, and if you are able to manage change effectively, resulting in an improved curriculum, then your school stakeholders will be dining off the fruits of your labour, and your legacy will be woven into the fabric of the school and the memories of your pupils.

I have led physical education in international schools for over a decade and have successfully exercised a simple and effective approach when managing curriculum change which focuses on 'selling' your PE vision to school stakeholders. Essentially, I use the everyday opportunities I have at my disposal (parents' drop-off, assemblies, break times, lessons, after-school clubs) to talk with people about PE and my view of it. I have found that doing this with a big smile on my face, and showing a genuine enthusiasm about why my ideas for curriculum change are going to benefit the lives of pupils, has sparked many positive, engaging and exciting discussions. Naturally, people are very much interested in what benefits them, and thus I have found that if I clearly explain how my changes will directly benefit them (or their children) and offer some real-world examples to support these, then the take-up and acceptance towards my ideology is far more positive.

I have found that making a clear distinction between PE and school sport has helped me to promote 21st century skills in PE. In our PE lessons, I will use phrases like 'there are no outs in PE' meaning that games are designed for maximum participation, and that 'you are unlikely to become a professional bench ball player when you are older, however no matter what you choose to do, you will need to collaborate confidently with others in competitive environments, and this PE lesson will help you develop these skills'. I have found that using statements such as these (and others along the same vein) consistently across all units of PE, has helped me to promote my intended change of enhancing 21st century life skills through a holistic PE curriculum.

Now that pupils understand the underlying themes within PE lessons, I have recently experienced success with using my more able pupils to coach the less experienced. The more able understand that 'winning' is not the main objective with PE lessons, and thus are more relaxed and inclined to offer meaningful support to their peers. More able pupils do get plenty of opportunities to compete with games lessons and our extensive extracurricular programme, which helps them focus on the educational aspects of our PE lessons.

# Chapter 2 - But We've Always Done It This Way

## Why PE And Education Is Always Changing

*'The measure of intelligence is the ability to change.'*
*Albert Einstein*

I'm sitting on the beach, at Sandbanks, in Bournemouth. It's windy, but not cold. It's busy but not too busy. It's a Saturday, but that isn't relevant as it's always busy here. It's one of my family's favourite spots on the English South Coast and a great way to spend a summer holiday weekend.

Spread across the beach is all manner of activity and a real cross section of society. From large party groups with their gazebos and cool boxes to families digging sand and couples lazing in the sunshine and all around me I can observe humans going through their normal, everyday actions and interactions.

When you watch people, you see just how much goes on in the day of anyone's life. Today is no exception. I can see the whole range of human characteristics at play all around me. Choices being made, over where to place themselves so they're near the sea but not too close to anyone else. Discussion and negotiation about the position of windbreaks or blankets. Arguments and disagreements about sandcastles and buckets and spades and decision-making taking place over what to do, when to buy ice creams, whether to play, snooze, read or swim. Every type of human action at play all at once and everything requires careful (or perhaps not so careful) observation, reflection, analysis, decision-making and reaction. We make decisions and take actions at every moment of every day throughout our lives and more often than not, those decisions and choices are needed as a result of changes happening around us.

Change is everywhere, all the time. Everything in our lives is constantly changing in a multitude of subtle and obvious ways and progress, in every aspect of our individual lives and the wider evolution and expansion of humanity, comes from the constant drive of change occurring all the time. As humans, evolved through thousands of years we are engineered to recognise, react and benefit from change and yet, it's not something we really take the time to consider.

With change being such a significant part of evolution, it is of little surprise that change influences and dictates much of what happens within our working lives as well. For those of us working within PE this comes in many forms and always requires a combination of reactionary and proactive action on our part. Change is everywhere, and everything changes. How we react, adapt, drive and encourage change, says a lot about us as an individual.

I've worked in physical education for 20 odd years, first as an unqualified and then qualified teacher. Progressing onto Head of Section then Head of Department, then Director of Sport, onto leadership. I've seen PE delivered in a huge variety of ways, in many different regions of the world, by a vastly diverse set of PE professionals, to vastly different demographics of pupils. I've seen the good, then bad and then unbelievable and I've seen the consequence of excellent, and terrible PE provision on pupils.

The one thing that every environment I've worked in, or connected with and explored, has had in common is that they were always changing. I've never worked in a department, or spoken to a PE teacher colleague, who hasn't felt their provision was evolving or developing. Today we find ourselves in what is probably the most exciting and dynamic period in our subject's history, certainly in the time that I have been involved in it.

Discussion about what PE is, what it could, should, might be are taking place all around the world and there has never been a more research driven, evidence-based period in the evolution of our subject. If ever there was a time in which change should be embraced and supported, it is now. To a greater, or lesser extent, every PE department, from the single PE teacher teams to the sprawling departments of sporting behemoths, is evolving and changing. The world of PE is shrinking as connections across social media and through technology expose us to more examples of excellent and more diverse approaches than ever before, and as a result, our perception of the provision we give in our own context, comes under wider and deeper scrutiny. We are all asking ourselves the same type of questions:

- 'What does PE look like in our school?'
- 'Is what we are doing the best it can be?'
- 'Are we doing the very best for our pupils?
- 'How do we know we're doing the best for our pupils'?
- 'What can we do better/differently/additionally?'
- Do we need to change anything?

When we start asking ourselves these types of searching, reflective questions, then a process of change is often the inevitable outcome. The fact that we are asking these questions is the most obvious indicator we can ask for, that we believe there is scope for our provision to evolve. If we genuinely believed that what we offer is the finished article, we wouldn't see so many examples of critical analysis of provision as we currently do. Whilst we can identify areas that we do really well, even the most experienced and longstanding PE departments are now looking at the world in which their PE is provided and questioning whether we are really offering the very best fit for today's modern pupil demographic.

PE is without question, the most debated subject within education. Historically PE has always been at the mercy of political, socio-cultural or cultural change as identified by Sallis et al, (2000), Dishman, (1985), Jaeschke et al, (2017), Caspersen et al, (1985) and many others. I don't believe it is a coincidence that PE finds itself the topic of such heated and divisive discussion about its place within education, within our schools and across the wider societies in which it is provided. PE is often used as a catch-all for individual, school-wide or even societal or historical challenges that individual nations or communities have faced throughout time. Whether it's activity levels or lack of, obesity, holistic development, provision of competitive sporting opportunity, life skills or any other current issue, PE is subjective (Ekberg, 2021). It's seen through different lenses by different people. It is stalked by negativity from prior experience (Brown, 2014), it is the marmite of education. When you look at PE through this lens is it really surprising that the lack of consensus leads to a fluid environment where change is an inevitability? (Doolittle, 2007)

As I said at the start, this isn't a book about what PE is, however, so I'm not going to continue for much longer about different aspects of PE. We all know that there is vast discussion and debate currently ongoing about what PE looks, feels, and functions like and there are many different versions of PE being provided across the world. Different offerings, for different communities, in different geographical locations, with wildly different objectives, have created a melting pot of ideas, creativity and opinion. Whatever your version of PE looks like it is likely determined by a set of criteria specific to your school and therefore unique. For the past fifty years research has explored the question of what PE should be, (Beni et al, 2017). We could and probably will debate for generations of PE teachers to come, over what PE 'should' look like, but I am not sure we will ever reach genuine consensus, nor am I sure we ever should, or need to. Whilst there are fundamental underpinning elements, such as movement, activity, passion for lifelong love of participating, which no PE teacher would argue against, how and why these are imparted onto our pupils, is always going to be the subject of discussion and debate.

What I am sure about however, is that PE will forever evolve, as new priorities, pressures and possibilities manifest themselves in our thinking. It is this evolution that means the discussion on 'how' is often more critical than the discussion about 'what' in our day to day interactions with our subject. The conversations about 'why' we do what we do often precede the more extended conversations about 'how' we create an environment and programme that allows us to ensure our 'why' happens well, with meaning and effect. I think, across any aspect of curriculum development in any context, time spent on 'how' is of equal or even more importance if we are to move our provision forward.

### Reflective Questions:

- What are your professional priorities right now?
- Have they changed recently?
- What do you think they will be, in 6 months' time?
- Do you think you have the same priorities as your colleagues?

## Changemaker Reflection: Tom Manley

*Head of PE/Curriculum Lead, Initio Learning Trust, St Michael's School, Wimborne, Dorset, UK*

My story of change began in 2017 when I experienced what Tripp (1993) would term a critical incident. A student in my care was experiencing physical sickness prior to school owing to the anxiety they felt competing in intra-school fixtures. This incident made me question my ideologies. Why was I driven by short-term goals of winning? Why was I making every child play in competitive fixtures? Why were the most-able children in receipt of the best coaches and resources? These questions marked the beginning of a journey.

As suggested by Sinek (2011), I started with why. I undertook research reflecting on the purpose of PE and sport. Furthermore, I engaged with student voices, something I had not done previously. Ennis (2017) advocates the importance of teachers and students working together to set goals and activities within a flexible student-centred curriculum. Furthermore, Sport England (2014) highlights that students may want to challenge themselves but are cautious of embarrassment. On reflection, I realised that I had caused students embarrassment, for example, insisting that they run in cross-country events by selling these as 'character building' without any evidence.

I implemented student voice by introducing online questionnaires and focus groups, encompassing a wide pupil demographic. Feedback from 'sporty' pupils was positive; from those identified as non-sporty it was scathing. The latter stated that the PE programme was boring and disengaging with a sport-centred competitive mentality. A change of culture was clearly needed, one which valued mastery and enjoyment over outcomes, one in which all would strive earnestly, and some would excel, but, crucially, both would be celebrated. Its success criteria must include retainment and joy. A culture and vision that embraces meaningfulness for all needed to be championed.

My next challenge was to change colleagues' perceptions by using the Meaningful PE framework which encompasses motor competence, challenge, fun, delight, personal relevant learning and social interaction as a filter for pedagogical decision making (Fletcher et al, 2021). To create a sense of urgency for change, I used the feedback from student voices, presenting this to the department. I showed that the current sport technique curriculum and grouping systems prompted inequalities and unfairness. As a leader, I ensured that I took responsibility for these failings. This allowed staff to accept the need for change towards a more holistic, student-centred curriculum.

Having realised that our focus was limited to technical sport-oriented assessment and feedback, we reflected on the need to see the bigger picture. I asked staff to use Beckey's (2021) 'Equaliser' metaphor enabling teachers to stand back and make in-action adjustments to a lesson through the Meaningful PE lens. Department members reflected on our new centralised meaningful PE statements, co-created by staff and pupils. Department members scored each central theme out of 10. Next, they considered potential adaptations to increase or decrease specific features (for example, improve social interaction in lessons by allowing more paired and grouped problem solving; increase personal relevant learning by linking to ideas in wider society; improve 'just right' challenge by using differentiation and level challenges). This approach seems to have brought about short-term wins. In our most recent student survey pupils' overall rating of PE increased significantly.

# Chapter 3 - Making Change Happen In Physical Education

**'The secret of change is to focus all of your energy not on fighting the old, but on building the new.'**
*Socrates*

The story of 'Who moved my cheese' by Spencer Johnson, written in 1998, about two mice, 'Sniff' and 'Scurry,' and two little people, 'Hem' and 'Haw', took the business world by storm. (Spencer, 1999) It became the go-to book given to employees about facing business reorganisation', redundancies or cost-cutting. I was given a copy of 'Who moved my cheese' one Friday afternoon and half my team were made redundant the following Monday. It became so prevalent that it sold over 30 million copies worldwide and the appearance on a desk caused panic across a building within minutes.

The underlying message behind the parable is simple: change happens, we can anticipate change, prepare for it, adapt to it, embrace it positively and ultimately thrive as a result of it. Whilst the book terrifies people, the message should reassure us. Change is inevitable and whilst it can seem big and scary, the benefits to change can be profound, positive and permanent.

Change is a natural part of the evolutionary nature of education. Whether a direct or indirect consequence of major school level modification, such as leadership turnover, or the outcome of a more subtle set of factors over a longer period of time, change within education is an inevitable challenge that every school and school employee faces. How schools approach it is often directly linked to the way that it views itself as an evolutionary entity. Some schools have significant history and cultural stability that has not shifted for decades or longer. Often these foundations provide structure that means core aspects of vision, mission and processes are almost ingrained. Others are more dynamic in nature, shifting and flexing to suit the needs of changing pupil demographics or socio-economic environments. It would be fair to say that often schools within the tradition-based private sector are more inclined to avoid significant cultural or structural change than those working within state-controlled sectors, where political or economic factors more regularly come to bear. It is also fair to suggest that (whilst obviously not without exception), state schooling is a more volatile and dynamic platform upon which schools are asked to function.

Regardless of the context in which your school operates, the notion of progress through change is one that all those involved in education are used to. Change happens because progress is a natural part of the educational and pastoral development that drives standards within our schools. Significant volumes of research over a long period of time all identify the importance of change and development within schools and its influence on the educational outcomes for young people. Indeed, there is much evidence to suggest that schools that evolve, grow and change will provide a much more consistently positive pupil experience than those that remain more static in their approach to their procedures, their policies and their approach to education.

Change happens and change matters (Green, 2016). Without change schools would not be able to consistently and progressively grow their educational experiences. Inevitably, as school leadership teams, teacher cohorts and people demographics shift with the society in which they are based, change occurs organically. Today most schools operate on the understanding that change is inevitable and that changes are ongoing, viewing it as an ongoing consistent and permanent factor in their development plans. Change is good, full stop. Change drives standards up. Change allows schools to reflect, review and develop programs to better suit their current cohort of pupils. In fact, I would go as far as to say that without change schools would not be able to ensure that they are meeting the needs of their cohorts today and in the future. Without change schools become dormant, static environments in which progression is stifled and the culture of 'we've always done it this way' permeates through all aspects of their provision.

So, if we agree that change is an inevitable part of the educational process, (Shen, 2008) then you would think that school would be adept at facilitating it, in all its forms. And yet evidence shows that a fairly insignificant percentage of professional development is given over to building the skills and resilience needed to facilitate change in a positive manner. Most policymakers, curriculum designers, and experts on school reform agree that teachers play a critical role in the process of changing education. (Datnow, 2000; Fullan, 1998; Earl, Hargreaves, & Ryan, 1996; Hargreaves & Fullan, 1998; McLaughlin, 2001) and yet, change management training is often deemed as something that only those within senior leadership teams require. Most senior leadership qualifications whether they be UK based ones or International have some aspects of change management within their curricular. Most leadership CPD will provide aspects of learning based around the management of staff and pupil response to change which is a good thing. It could however be argued that the skills and knowledge required to facilitate change at senior leadership level are equally as important at other levels of school structures.

As a middle leader for most of my career I am a testament to the fact that change occurs at a variety of different levels within a school structure. In fact, the majority of curricular change does not occur at the senior leadership level with their more strategic focus, but at middle leadership level, driven by those responsible for curricular change and pupil experience. Indeed, it could be suggested that the majority of change that occurs within schools happens at this curricular level. It is often driven by subject leads and subject departments in an effort to develop their curriculum programs to better facilitate the needs of their current learners.

Often it is middle leaders that are the catalyst for change. Middle leaders tend to be the individuals researching the specifics of their subject area, identifying new opportunities to enhance or evolve their curriculum provision. They are the catalyst for the reflection of the success of their programmes and provision, and as a result often are the inspiration for new ideas and new practice within schools

*Changemakers* focus primarily on curriculum development and change within programme structures, but it is obviously fair to point out that change happens in many different ways within our schools. Change can and does occur everywhere within our schools. Any situation that supports the effective functioning of academic or pastoral provision is subject to the ever ongoing need to evolve and develop. Change is critical to the ongoing success of our schools and as such, must be a critical part of our thinking as we drive our provision forward.

## CHAPTER 3 - MAKING CHANGE HAPPEN IN PHYSICAL EDUCATION

For schools to function effectively in the medium to long term their programmes and processes must always be dynamic enough to change with the changing needs of staff, parents and students. Pastoral changes are a good example of this. As the needs of our young people change, usually linked to the world they are growing up in and societal and technological evolution, the pastoral and PSHE programmes we offer to support their development must change to support the needs of our students. This is inevitably something that every school places great focus on and much time is allocated to this in both departmental and whole school meetings and training.

Facilities development within the confines of an economic structure is another example of the consistent change management process that schools have to go through. Unlike curriculum change, however, this is often driven at a project level by senior leadership and therefore has less of an impact on subject specific areas day to day operations.

There are many examples of change occurring within schools, but for the purposes of this book we focus purely on curricular development and the impacts on our structures and provision. Whilst this is predominantly a book about change within physical education, the same principles can be applied across any curriculum subject area. Although PE is a very different physical environment to other departments, many of the processes that take place within PE departments going through a change management process are mirrored within the process undertaken by other subject areas.

Regardless of whether you're a PE teacher or not, reading this book I would hope that the strategies and structures processes and plans that appear within the following pages would be equally applicable across any subject area. Obviously it is fair to point out that PE has a set of factors that make change look and feel different within its boundaries however fundamentally change at the department level is something that occurs in similar ways across a school. What works for one department can equally work for another.

When we think about the work we do with our pupils within our schools, we often emphasise the importance of a positive attitude to challenge and progressive mindsets. This is no different to the way we should be approaching the need for change within our own activity area. The same positive attitude and progressive approach is critical if we are to drive the quality and scope of our provision, thus improving the experiences our students have. Fundamentally that is what we are always striving to achieve when we consider the reasons why change might be required and when we approach this in positive ways, the process is usually smoother, easier on every stakeholder, and more impactful.

When done well, change should be a hugely positive experience for everyone involved, and a beneficial process through which our vision and provision improves, however when rushed, ill thought through or poorly supported, change can be an incredibly stressful and negative experience. Much writing has been done about the importance of making sure everybody feels positive about change. The message presented in books such as 'Who moved my cheese' by Johnson in 1998, and 'Our Iceberg is melting' by Kotter and Rathgeber in 2006 focuses on the idea that change is not always perceived well or viewed in a positive manner and is an important one to consider. Not everybody will see your ideas for change as necessary, reasonable, positive or achievable. In fact there will be people within every department who see change through fearful eyes and it is for this exact reason that we must ensure that when we launch into a change process (whatever that looks like) we do so with the knowledge that a well-structured process of change and a collaborative cohesive approach is likely to provide far more positive experiences and outcomes for every stakeholder involved.

I hope that *Changemakers* will give you some ideas, knowledge, information and research that will support the positivity of your approach to change and support you with tools and ideas that you can use to help your teams understand how to view change positively as you decide what the change process may look like within your department. What this book will not do however, is provide you with a step-by-step guide to what change should look like within your context because as you will be aware every context is different.

Every school may face specifically unique challenges (Tamadoni et al, 2024). Every school is fundamentally different in its ethos, mission, values and culture (Fullan & Quinn, 2020) and it is for this very reason that every school needs to approach change in a different way. Careful consideration needs to be given to the environment and structures, the staff makeup and pupil experiences that will be impacted by the change throughout its evolution and progression.

Change is good and change is important however change must be managed like anything else within our schools, departments and curriculum plans. When change happens without due process and without a reflective approach, it can be disjointed and in turn can lead to conflict. I am not afraid to admit here that I have first-hand experience from early in my PE leadership journey, of the damage to team cohesiveness and motivation that can occur when we create changing environments in which colleagues feel the need to push back against change and question the decisions being made. You can believe with all your heart that the changes are right, just and meaningful but without the support and buy-in from your teams and stakeholders even the best ideas can be delayed or derailed regardless of the positive intent behind your work. I cannot stress enough that managing change is hard and as the leader or changemaker the task is infinitely harder if you do not achieve positivity towards your plans from the outset.

We will discuss later exactly how this buy-in can be gained but for now, an appreciation of its importance is sufficient. As long as we consider the views and opinions, fears and concerns of our fellow teachers from the very outset of a project, we are already more likely to succeed in our objectives.

### Reflective Questions:

- What are the biggest challenges facing you currently?
- What are the biggest challenges facing your department currently?
- What are the biggest challenges facing your school currently?
- What are the biggest challenges facing your pupils currently?
- Which is the real priority?

CHANGEMAKERS

**Changemaker Reflection: Tommi Charlish**
*MCCT, FSET, Course Director - Sport, West Suffolk College*

## Bridging the Gender Gap in physical education: Empowering Female Students and overcoming the Gender Gap in Student Cohorts

Physical education departments and teachers have long grappled with the challenge of bridging the gender gap in student cohorts. Encouraging equal participation in sports and physical activities among male and female students is crucial for fostering inclusivity and promoting a healthy lifestyle. At our sports department, we recognised this issue and set out to create a supportive environment that empowers female students to engage in sports.

To tackle this challenge, we devised a ground-breaking solution by deciding to run a dedicated course exclusively for female students following the ethos of the empowering campaign 'This Girl Can.' By tailoring the physical education curriculum specifically for girls, we aimed to dismantle the barriers that hindered their full participation in mainstream physical education classes.

Using the concept of 'This Girl Can' and government initiatives it enabled us to develop a pathway and steps towards achieving our objectives. Creating the dedicated course allows us to address the unique concerns and preferences of female students, promoting their self-confidence and overall physical well-being. Whilst creating a safe space for girls to exercise without fear of judgement or intimidation further encouraged their active participation.

Recognising the importance of representation, we plan to ensure that female instructors and coaches play a significant role in leading the course. It's noted that providing relatable role models will not only inspire girls to participate but also dismantled gender biases. Female instructors emphasise the importance of physical fitness, highlighting how it can positively impact various aspects of life, including mental health and self-esteem.

The success of this approach will be evident by the increasing number of female students actively involved in our physical education programmes. The hope is to inspire previously disengaged girls. In turn this would lead to newfound enthusiasm for sports, enhancing their physical and mental well-being. The positive impact is then hoped to be seen to extend to academic performance, as girls gain confidence and develop teamwork and leadership skills through their participation in sports.

## Tips and Ideas for Undertaking Change

Undertaking a change to bridge the gender gap in physical education requires careful planning and execution. Here are some tips and ideas for educators and departments looking to embark on a similar journey:

**Identify barriers:** Conduct a thorough analysis of the current physical education program and identify the factors hindering female participation. Understand the reasons behind the gender gap and tailor your approach accordingly.

**Promote inclusivity:** Create an inclusive environment where girls feel comfortable and supported. Collaborate with other teachers and departments to foster cross-curricular activities that promote gender equality and combat stereotypes.

**Tailor curriculum:** Design physical education courses that specifically address the needs and interests of female students. Incorporate activities that highlight the benefits of physical fitness, enhance self-confidence, and provide opportunities for skill development.

**Address concerns:** Communicate with female students to understand their concerns and challenges. Adapt the programme to address these concerns, ensuring that girls feel safe and respected during physical activities.

**Role models and mentorship:** Facilitate access to female mentors, instructors, or coaches who can inspire and guide female students. Representation plays a vital role in breaking down gender barriers and encouraging participation.

**Encourage teamwork and leadership:** Integrate team sports and leadership opportunities within the curriculum to develop valuable skills that extend beyond the physical education class. Emphasise cooperation, communication, and problem-solving through team-based activities.

## CHANGEMAKERS

Celebrate achievements: Highlight female students' accomplishments in physical education and provide platforms for recognition. This will motivate other girls to participate and showcase their talents.

Bridging the gender gap in physical education requires proactive efforts focused on empowering and engaging female students. By creating specifically designed courses, promoting inclusivity, and providing relatable role models, we can successfully drive positive change and empower girls to lead healthier and more active lives. Let's work together to break down stereotypes and inspire the next generation of women in sports.

Despite the program's pending launch, promising recruitment numbers signal an auspicious start in overcoming the gender gap in student cohorts, fantastic open event conversations and discussions have been truly promising.

Inspired by "This Girl Can," our tailored course aims to empower female students in sports and physical activities. We anticipate breaking down barriers and providing a supportive environment where girls can thrive. Our commitment remains unwavering in promoting inclusivity and holistic well-being among all our students.

# Chapter 4 - Think Of The Children!

## Who Is Important When Change Happens?

**'Change is inevitable. Growth is optional.'**
*John C. Maxwell*

When we consider beginning the process of change, or indeed even just collaborative reflection of our current provision with a view to evolution and development, it is critical that from the very start we consider what change may do to the atmosphere, the attitude and the emotional stability of the areas in which we work (Wang, Berry & Swearer, 2013). This includes colleagues, fellow teachers from other departments, pupils, parents, senior leaders and other stakeholders. Every change we make, will impact on all these important groups of people, and each rightly deserves our consideration at all stages of our change management plans and projects.

First and foremost, we must always consider our pupils. Every current model of curriculum available to you places pupils at the very heart of everything we do. Every book about PE or any other aspect of education will tell you that you must place the children at the heart of every decision you make. Any change, however big or small, needs to begin with an understanding that we are trying to do better for our students. Change for the sake of change is a worthless process (Lorenzi & Riley, 2000). Change for the sake of change can be time consuming and disruptive and if we aren't sure from the very outset of our planning that we are going to have a positive impact on our students or at the very least attempt to provide more positive experiences for our pupils then the whole plan needs to be reconsidered. Do not do things because somebody else is doing it, do not do things because social media tells you that you should, do not change things that are not broken. Ongoing, developmental and meaningful change and evolution is important, but not if it comes at the expense of the positivity within your student body, which has probably taken significant time and effort to develop.

Secondly, we must consider our colleagues. They are the people that will decide whether your plans are effective. If you can get your colleagues on board with change, your curriculum will benefit as a result. The more we collaborate and move together, the more likely our adaptations are to be adopted and supported and the more likely we are to be successful in our vision and mission.

I would encourage you to start your thinking by reflecting on what you do within your department area currently. I have no doubt that the experiences you are providing for your pupils are overwhelmingly positive ones. I have engaged with and researched enough PE departments globally to be confident that everybody is working for the betterment of their own pupils. I would be amazed if I ever come across a PE department who fundamentally doesn't care about the experiences, feelings, safety, security and sense of belonging that their pupils need and desire. I have no doubt that every department, regardless of the type or form PE takes within their school, ultimately functions to provide the very best opportunities it can for their pupils. I have no doubt that everything you do is done with positive intent, and I have no doubt that your pupils generally experience high quality and positive PE as a result of those efforts. Don't be afraid to acknowledge the great work you and your departments have done, are doing and are going to do for the benefit of your pupils. As teachers we are programmed to think critically and always look for the negatives, but I'm telling you not to. I'm telling you to be proud of the work you do, celebrate the excellence you have achieved and focus on the opportunities you have to grow and expand that excellence before identifying the things you want to do differently.

All that being said, I have no doubt that change and evolution is something that will have occurred to you. You may have viewed, listened to or researched things that have made you question whether what you do is the best it can be. This is human nature. We as a species are designed to change and whilst we find change challenging, we are designed to accept and cope with it as we know, either consciously or subconsciously, that change often brings adaptation and improvement. Fundamentally everybody's lives revolve around a constantly changing set of factors and we are designed by nature to be able to process, reflect and act upon those changing influences in order to grow. If you think about what pupils experience within your schools the same can be said. Pupil experiences within schools are designed around the idea that they will change and our teaching changes to ensure that we facilitate that change in positive ways. What is so different between that process we ask our pupils to undertake and the one we are talking about undertaking ourselves?

At school pupils' academic skills change, interactions with each other change. Their personal, social, moral, emotional balances change, their interactions and relationship with each other change and their physiological and biological development changes (National Academies of Sciences, Engineering, and Medicine, 2019). Consequently, we as teachers are adept at changing to meet the needs of individual pupils. Our schools change. As we've already said a school that does not change is a school that will not survive for very long. In fact, it could be argued they have no choice but to change. Adaptation to national curriculum structures change and we have to cope with the shifting frameworks within which our curriculum programs are delivered. The vision, mission, demographic, financial situation, staffing and leadership, parent engagement, pupil numbers and thousands of other factors all change, constantly, and each time, our schools have to adapt and evolve to ensure we continue to be able to facilitate great learning and teaching within those changing dynamics.

We have no choice but to change. All aspects of our lives, whether personally, professionally or socially are all subject to the shifting sands of change. As a result, often without even realising it, we become experts at change. We do it without thinking about it, and if you can take this mindset into your change management process you're starting from a far more positive foundation. Look around your next department meeting and understand that, whilst individuals will react to the process of change in different ways, we are all capable of, and experienced in, accepting, managing and processing change, possibly far more than we realise. We need to harness the power of that experience when change needs to happen. As we've already agreed, it happens best when it's done in collaborative ways. If we can engage with the natural positivity within our teams, which usually is linked to the positive experiences we have when interacting with young people, and utilise the experience, knowledge and skills within our teams we can discuss change in positive ways. When we start from positive places, we are in a far better position to ensure that the process is smooth, comfortable for all and ultimately more effective.

Change is good and a positive change process, where everyone is positive and supportive, is a much better experience. Indeed, change within curriculum is often the most collaborative experience we can have as PE teachers within PE departments. We learn so much about the people we work with when everybody engages within a change process and brings their own thoughts, research, experiences and knowledge to the table. The experience can be enlightening, enjoyable and rewarding; it can also be a catalyst for departmental cohesion (Schöttle & Tillmann, 2018).

We all want to work in departments that feel that they're pulling in the same direction and there's nothing better than a PE department that appears to get on with each other. Again, I am not afraid to admit that I have worked in, and led, departments where this collegiate and supportive atmosphere has sometimes been lacking, and the experience everyone in that department had as a result, was not always a positive one. No department can be one hundred percent positive and collaborative all the time, as much as we would like it to be. The challenges of teaching in general today, coupled with the strains of PE teaching in busy, pressurised and often competitive environments will mean there will occasionally be friction and disagreement, however avoiding this in times of change, is critical if we are to pull in the same direction.

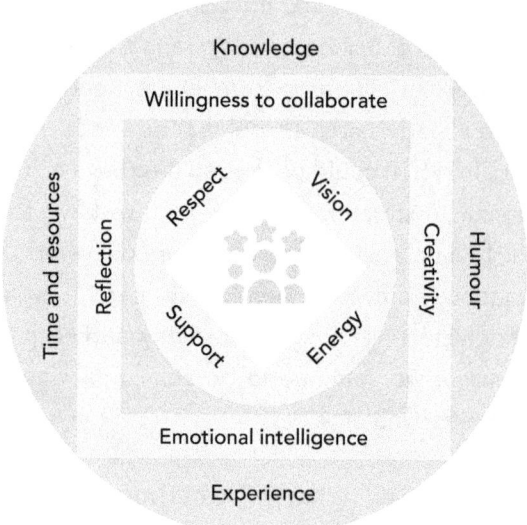

Foundations of a positive PE department

I believe that the stresses and the pressure placed on PE departments, the exact things that can cause friction between individual department members can in fact be just the things to pull a department closer during times of change. It's that 'All in it together' attitude that more often than not, leads to collaboration and powerful positivity to make something happen. Most importantly, curriculum change, when supported by all members of the department, can create a sense of unity around their provision that encourages the delivery of that collaboratively created curriculum in really positive ways.

Ultimately a department that has built a program together, that has reflected and considered every aspect of the provision together and feels collaborative ownership over the content and procedures is far more likely to deliver it with enthusiasm, excitement and a passionate belief that this is the best thing for their students. This collaboration can be an empowering process, especially if the initial impetus for change started with a colleague who perhaps hasn't 'stepped up' before, or a less experienced member of your team.

The success or failure of your curricular changes may hinge on your ability to ensure that every member of your department buys into the vision of the final outcomes you want for your pupils. The best, most effective way of making sure this happens is to focus on their engagement and inclusion and to value their input from the outset. This is where we will start on our journey together. We are going to look at what potential catalysts for change you may have already, or what they may be in the future. We're going to explore what looks good in your departments right now, and where the desire for change may come from. We're going to look at why departments or individuals within departments decide change might be something they want to consider and we're going to look at what that initial research and reflective process might look like within your department. We're also going to consider some of the sources of inspiration that might be influencing your desire to relook at your provision and how we can use the vast bank of resources at our disposal today, to reflect on what we could change, to do things even better.

Remember this is not a book about different types of PE. We are not going to discuss different types of PE provision and we're not really going to consider what it is that you are delivering to your students. If you want to know what your potential options are in terms of curriculum design there are plenty of books, many of which are referenced within this work, however this book does not consider what your PE will look like at the end of your process. You may be considering a concept-based PE programme, very holistic in nature looking at life skills, or you may be considering adopting a very traditional sport-based programme. You may be considering using a curriculum model such as 'ME in PE' (Tom Brush, 2016) or 'Head, Heart, Hands' (Frapwell 2014; Orr 1992; Sipos et al. 2008) or you might be designing your own. This does not matter in terms of the journey that you are going to go through within your department. Change and the process of change is effectively the same regardless. The only difference will be the focus of your reflections and of the topics you cover in your discussions, the resources and materials that you create and the curriculum programme you ultimately designed together. You will undoubtedly have ideas in your head already as to what you believe PE is or isn't in today's modern educational context. Keep those ideas close to the forefront of your thinking, but do not discount alternative options out of hand. Gather evidence and research in all its forms and store it away as it will come in useful later in your process. Remember that ultimately your values, beliefs and vision will determine what your PE provision looks and feels like, for the young people for whom you work so hard.

> **Reflective Questions: Think about your pupils**
>
> - What do the pupils in your school look like? - Not physically, but what 'type' of children occupy your hallways and sports facilities?
> - How much do you think about who your pupils are, when thinking about what PE you provide?
> - Could you categorise your pupils into those who benefit from your provision to those who perhaps don't, and reflect on why this might be?

## Changemaker Reflection: Mathew Jones
*Head of physical education, TASIS England*

When colleagues ask me about why I changed the PE curriculum, I always answer with 'to best suit the school and the students'. I have been fortunate enough to develop curricula in my last three schools with the view to make PE accessible to all. When considering if a change is needed, I look at trends of student engagement, gather student and colleague feedback and then use the data to decide if a change is needed. To change something that works well is not only time consuming but it's not going to have a big impact on student learning.

As PE teachers, we want our students to learn through movement, to create various pathways for student engagement and ultimately, create a passion for lifelong physical activity and a healthy lifestyle. The PE curriculum should meet the values and mission of the school, and these should be embedded within each lesson and unit.

At my current school, part of our mission is to create lifelong learners through connections, pathways and engagement. I looked at the old standards/outcomes and whilst they would suit many schools, I felt that they did not provide our students opportunities to create connections or experience various pathways for student achievement/growth. Whilst some would have flourished, not all students would have had an opportunity. Therefore, I spent a lot of time reading and making notes about various curricula from different countries with one eye on the students we had at the school and what would be best for them. It came down to conceptual units that are vertically aligned from Early Years to Grade 10 (we do not have exam-based PE-yet!). Our average student stays for 2 to 3 years so we have a highly mobile student body. Focusing on physical skills alone would not suit most of our students. With over 60 nationalities, we had to be mindful of various cultures and predisposed mindsets towards PE.

There is a common misconception that PE revolves around playing sports. We address this by emphasising the importance of physical performance, knowledge and understanding, health and wellbeing and leadership which are defined within assessment rubrics. These 4 criteria allow all students to showcase areas they can excel in and provide challenges to develop not only physical skills, but other transferable skills such as communication, conflict resolution, leadership and empathy whilst still learning about how their body moves and the benefits of physical fitness. Students are challenged to coach, referee, provide feedback on their own and other performances, provide meaningful feedback to peers and work together to improve in all areas of assessments.

The above is a brief overview of what we do but all planning is done using schemes of work, linked to the mission and the specific outcomes for the respective grades. When changing outcomes and standards, it is important to view it as a big picture but be able to break that into smaller jigsaw pieces to make sure it all fits and works as intended. If one piece is missing, the picture (curriculum) won't look as intended and therefore not meet the needs of the students and the school.

# Chapter 5 - The Power Of 3

## Three Reasons For Change

**'The price of doing the same old thing is far higher than the price of change.'**
*Bill Clinton*

Change can happen in many diverse ways and change is often a fluid and dynamic process that takes in many forms over the lifecycle of a project. There are however, three main reasons why change occurs. One or a combination of these influence every decision to review and adapt our provision.

1. **Redress** - What we do doesn't seem to be working.
2. **Recognise** - We see something we believe is better.
3. **Review** - Our context changes so must we.

I would challenge you to think of an example or scenario within your department when at least one of these three factors is not present in a process of change. There are not really any other reasons that change happens. You can elaborate or expand on the specifics of any of these three reasons but ultimately it will be because you or someone around you has identified at least one of these three things that needs to happen.

This makes the discussion around recognising the need for change, the decision making around making change happen, and the reasoning and justification for change, really quite simple. Let's look at each of the three reasons for change, in more detail.

## Redress - What we do, doesn't seem to be working

There are many reasons why the things that we do don't seem to be working. Often curriculum provision is based around a 'we've always done it this way' style acceptance that certain schools, with certain pupil demographics, do things in certain ways. This is nothing new, ever since the advent of national curricula there have been structures and procedures that have existed simply because they have never really been challenged, questioned or reflected on. Indeed, some of the key foundations of today's national curriculum in England could be said to exist for no other reason than 'it always has done'. Now I'm not suggesting that there is anything inherently wrong with doing things the way they always have been, as long as there has been regular reflection on whether the things we are doing are working. The problems occur when we identify that things aren't necessarily working the way we would want them to, but the pull of traditionalism and stability means the likelihood of change at this stage is minimal and often the barrier of 'always been' is quite a difficult one to overcome.

It becomes easier to overcome though, when we reflect on an aspect of our programmes, through the lens of our students, or more specifically, through the lens of our students' experiences. When we consider what we do, in relation to the experiences our pupils are being provided, then we can start to identify things that are offered 'to' our pupils rather than 'for' our pupils. Indeed, we can start to recognise when something is being offered 'to' our pupils regardless of whether we have any clear evidence that it is providing positive, meaningful learning opportunities 'for' them. In other words, it's easier to accept that something needs to change, when we recognise that it's not providing the best opportunities or experiences for our students. Once we look at things like this, then it doesn't matter how long we've been doing something, how steeped in tradition it is within our schools or how embedded it is within our provision. Once we know something doesn't work, we're almost professionally honour bound to seek an alternative direction. This makes life for us as *Changemakers* much easier, as we can apply simple and sound logic to a situation or aspect of our provision and make decisions without the emotion of tradition. If it doesn't work for your pupils, change it.

A good example of how challenging and potentially damaging 'we've always done it this way' can be to the evolution of our educational provision we offer our students can be seen in the adoption of traditional sport-specific curricula. Now obviously I'm not here to tell you that a sport-specific curriculum is neither right, or wrong. Indeed, it is not my role here to even provide opinion as to the practice. It's just an example of how, in the wrong context, it can stifle the creativity and evolution of our provision.

Hypothetically, if a school has always offered a very sport-specific, competitive by nature, game-based curriculum, whether as part of a wider 'sporting' programme or just as a result of a very 'sport' focused tradition, then it is likely that for a reasonable percentage of pupils, there will be a disconnect between the PE on offer and the PE desired. If, however, the school has a long and proud history of 'sport' it is unlikely to be very willing to instigate change that may end that tradition. Even when we can see that for a good number of pupils within the school, traditional sporting offerings aren't motivating them as once it did, the pressure to continue the honourable tradition of the school is inevitably strong.

Add into the mix the likelihood of long standing members of a PE department who have 'always done it this way', a culture associated with a specific type of provision, possibly community respect as a result of a historical reputation, possibly a marketing angle and many other non-pupil specific focuses, and you can start to see why these situations are amongst the most challenging within which change can be proposed, justified, encouraged and accepted.

Sometimes the needs of our pupils, which should always come first, just don't. Despite the best of intentions, despite the quality of teaching and the enthusiasm within our teachers to do their best for their classes, we don't always get it right. Sometimes things that used to work brilliantly, just stop. Sometimes the things we have done for years suddenly look problematic, sometimes the best of intentions, start to feel forced or contrived. As hard as this might be for us to accept, the demographics of pupils change and with that change comes the need to constantly consider whether we're still relevant. No one wants to feel irrelevant, and of course as individual teachers we are far from it, however collectively, we might be if we don't keep up with our pupils' needs.

When we can identify areas of our provision which no longer appear to be resonating, motivating or engaging groups of our pupils, we have an obligation to at the very least, consider why this is happening and whether there are things we can do to address this. Whilst we can feel the pressure of history, of expectation, of tradition, none of it should overshadow the unavoidable truth that our first and most important priority should always be to the children in our care. When we know something is not providing positive experiences for all of our students, we have to change, we simply must.

> **Reflective Questions - Identifying issues**
>
> - How do you 'know' something might not be right?
> - Where do you look for evidence to support your feelings?
> - Do your department colleagues feel the same?
> - Have they noticed different potential issues and how do you discuss this?

## Recognise - We see something we believe is better

Teachers, by our very nature, are inquisitive and curious beings. I think one of the reasons I resonated so strongly with the idea of retraining as a teacher was an overwhelming desire to learn again and that has never left me. Since qualifying and the pull of learning is as strong in me today at 45 years old as it ever has been. This inbuilt need to grow and develop our skills and knowledge, means we're always exploring our subjects, our pedagogy, our profession. The saying 'every day is a school day' is an apt way of viewing our inherit desire to continuously develop. It's not learning and developing because we are told to, nor is it purely for career progression, but the understanding that our professional capabilities are an ever-evolving entity and the love of learning that we encourage in our pupils, is present within us as well.

With all this knowledge harvesting and processing, it's no real surprise that we regularly uncover practice, ideas, perspectives or research that makes us question our own provision. Indeed, the more I read, whether it be on social media, via printed media or indeed just on the internet, the more I realise just now how diverse the practice is within physical education, not to mention education as a whole. You could spend a lifetime exploring and recording all the different perspectives and approaches to any one subject and never even get close to exposing yourself to every differing version out there.

The practice of PE teaching, and teaching in general, has always been influenced by that which has gone before, and that which is yet to come, in equal measure. There has never been a time quite like the one in which we currently find ourselves within our subject. Technology permeates everything we do. Collaboration takes place at a level we never ever dreamed of. Growth, expansion, and creativity within practical PE is happening at levels we can barely keep pace with and the volume of research, evidence, data and discussion around our subject is at fever pitch. There is no doubt it is a great time to be a PE teacher, looking for opportunities to create meaningful change within their context. This book is really testament to the creative thinking happening globally around physical education, with contributions from practitioners from every corner of the world. The opportunity to discover something that someone else, somewhere else has tried, tested and succeeded with, has never been greater, and the opportunity to then integrate that into your own provision, has never really been easier.

We work in a field that is actively encouraging debate, actively encouraging creativity and actively encouraging change. School leadership teams are looking to their PE teams, no longer through the eyes of traditionalism but through the lens of cutting-edge educational creativity. We're no longer those teachers in shorts who don't have to do marking, more likely we're leading CPD, working with challenging students pastorally, creating new opportunities for our communities and acting as the face of our provision. Certainly, within my own context I've found myself in a position where we're not just treated with equality but actively sought out to drive change and progress within our school. I bet you are too.

And then there's the pupils. Let's not forget them. Where once there was trepidation and nervous uncomfortableness, now there is expectation and enthusiasm. Our pupils have realised we're not just important but influential, they expect more from their PE lessons and they expect us to be right there at the cutting edge, providing new and exciting opportunities for them to engage with physical activity and movement. Once upon a time we related to the 'sporty kids', the ball players, the athletes. Now we must relate not only to them, but also the skateboarders, the dancers, the pupils for whom parkour, climbing, triathlon, open water swimming, hiking, yoga is just as important. We understand that in today's complex and layered societies, PE is no longer just about sport and fitness but so much more, and the pupils know this too. They no longer want to have to shift their perception and thinking to fit into our traditional model, but rather we shift our model to fit the world in which they are growing. Change comes in all sorts of forms, and the shifting perception of what physical activity has become, is a great example of this. As we realise that our provision needs to change, we hunt out those creators and activists within these new, dynamic, exciting new fields and what we discover, uncover, and realise, shifts our provision in ways that are often unexpected, but always positive.

## Reflective Questions:
## How to identify new approaches?

In your next department meeting, share your work-related social media and resources and discuss examples of things you've all seen on your different social media that you've considered implementing.
- Are they the same?
- How do you track/log/save these ideas and share them as a department?
- Have you tried something you've seen on social media and how did it go?
- What other methods do you have for sourcing information/research/ideas and tools?
- How often do you set aside time as a department to share the things you've discovered?
- How much do you use the expertise of individuals within your department and school in your planning?

## Review - Our context changes, so must we

The final, and arguably most important, reason for change, is that of necessity. Our schools are fluid, flexible, evolving and dynamic. No school (even the most traditional, red brick, boater hat wearing institution) stands still, because to stand still, is to die. That's not exaggerated, that's fact. A school that doesn't seek relevance, quickly becomes irrelevant. A school that sits on its laurels, soon withers and for the pupils within schools, irrelevance can come very quickly, be very damaging and take far longer to overcome. It's a far better idea to think quickly and evolve with our changing student population, than attempt to mould them into a form that fits the traditional model.

There are an infinite number of ways, both subtle and explicit, in which schools change. To list them all would be an impossibility, but they can be grouped into three broad categories for the purposes of our discussions here:

- Stakeholder Changes
- Logistical Changes
- Framework Changes

Each of these bring challenge, but also opportunity and each can have significant implications for the way in which our schools evolve and develop. Often the first signs of the needs for review are linked to the idea of redress and recognition. We realise something has changed, and perhaps things that were working, don't seem to be quite so effective as before. When we recognise the need for review, it is likely that the resulting reflections lead us to the realisation that one of the three categories above, is the most likely reason for it. Let us explore each in a little more detail, and the underlying implications for us as the harbingers of change.

### Stakeholder Changes

When we talk about stakeholders, in this context, we mean everyone who has a stake in the effectiveness of our schools. The community that benefits from the school and those linked and implicated by any changes of circumstances surrounding the school's functions. This can mean pupils, colleagues, parents, leadership teams, boards of governors, external agencies or agents and the wider community around the school. Everyone can effect change, and everyone is affected by change to a greater or lesser extent. To understand how change can impact on different stakeholders, let's briefly explore each major group.

### Departmental Colleagues

People come, and people go. Whether you work in international or national education, the likelihood is that regular turnover of staff within your department or area of responsibility is regular. It isn't always consistent, but we all gain and lose colleagues during the course of our teaching careers. In international education this is far more significant, with the two, four or more year turnover a normal part of school dynamics, but even within national public education today the profession is more transient than at any time in the past.

This transience can catalyse change or can stifle it. If a colleague is a major part of a team working on change, then their departure (whether out of the school or into a new role) can slow or even halt the progress of the project in its tracks. Obviously, the opposite can be true as well. The departure of a particularly stubborn opponent of change can loosen the strings holding back the project and allow it to be a springboard for change.

Likewise new colleagues coming into a school can bring enthusiasm and new ideas, galvanising evolution and encouraging new reflection and perspectives on things that have existed previously. Capturing the vibrance of new colleagues and getting them to engage in ongoing change projects can be a really positive experience for everyone involved in the process and whilst not every new member of staff wants to dive straight into project management or even project support, if they do, cease the opportunity to get them involved.

### Pupils

As we've mentioned previously, shifting pupil demographics are some of the most impactful changes that schools go through. When the demographic of even just one year group cohort can have a significant impact on the culture, in a very short period of time, it's reasonable to assume that change in our pupils will impact on the fundamental way we approach our provision.

COVID-19 has shown us, clearly, the impact that changes in our student population can have on the way that our schools' function, feel, look and act. If we ever needed evidence of the impact changes in our pupils can have, it has been highlighted post-pandemic within our schools. Our students have changed, and we've all had to adapt our practice, policies and approaches to compensate. As our students returned to school, after extended periods in a very different life structure, they adopted attitudes and behaviours that whilst unsurprising in hindsight, somewhat blindsided us as teachers. We had to change the way we engaged, communicated, challenged and cared for our students, often looking at the fundamental foundations of our school's approaches to adapt to this 'new normal'. Over time, our pupils will change again, hopefully back to something resembling pre-covid; however, who knows? We could be entering a totally different phase of our provision, and with this could come significant positives and opportunities, or challenges and deficits. Ultimately regardless of what the post-COVID years present us, the inevitable is that change will continue to be ever present in our provision.

The way in which our pupils perceive physical activity and physical education is ever changing. The way in which pupils within schools today perceive physical activity looks nothing like what I experienced in my school environment all those years ago. The activities that our young people relate to, engage in and observe are different, and as such the traditional foundations of our PE curricula are shifting to meet those adaptations. Where once there was Hockey or Athletics there may now be Parkour or Skateboarding. Whilst no one PE curriculum can be said to be right or wrong, as context is everything, what is clear is that we must be considering the desires and wants of the children for whom we serve. This expansion of activity areas is driving change, as PE departments look wider and further afield for inspiration and potential. Arguably, the most exciting way in which we can change things within our curricula is through the opportunity to add, create, design, develop and influence meaningful, positive experiences. By doing so we can shape the perception of pupils in relation to PE and movement exposure within our provision, and throughout their wider school experiences.

**Senior Leaders**
Often change is brought about by a change of culture and often this is instigated by changes to the makeup of our senior leadership teams. Senior Leaders can have a profound impact on a school's vision and approach and this in turn can influence the direction and ethos surrounding our curricular provision. From setting the whole school vision and mission through to strategic planning, our Senior Leaders define what our school looks and feels like. If you have a very 'holistic' set of Senior Leaders, then it is likely that they will look for curricular provision that meets those personal and cultural perceptions of what the school should be. Likewise, if your Senior Leadership team have very traditional backgrounds when it comes to school sport then the likelihood is that they will be aspiring to provide a similar approach within their school sporting programme, which in turn could influence the direction they want you to take your PE provision. Ultimately the lived experiences of our Senior Leaders can and does have a direct impact on the approach that the teams they lead will take when creating and delivering their subject areas.

Our Senior Leadership teams will most likely be aiming to use data to inform decision making. They will be looking at factors beyond impact in the classroom on a day-to-day basis and that the experience of data-driven decision making can have a major influence on how they perceive the quality of provision. This isn't unique to PE but will be happening across all the subject areas within the school. Data-informed decisions may mean they look for you to take your provision in a certain direction and this in turn may mean change is inevitable.

**Parents, Governance, Policy Makers**
Schools do not operate in isolation. Every school has groups or individuals who they are accountable to, whether that be policy makers and regional/local governance or indeed boards of governors and owners, ultimately someone will be overseeing the provision at a strategic level. Whilst these individuals or groups may not direct daily influence over what you offer and how you offer it, the strategic direction and governance of a school will eventually feed down through the management structure to subtly or explicitly influence

the direction that your provision is required to take. Whilst this isn't often a barrier to change at curricular level, the influence of these groups will undoubtedly be something to consider when deciding how to approach your project plans and certainly when deciding how to communicate and advertise your project and its desired/achieved outcomes. Whilst you may never come into direct contact with strategic level decision makers within your school, inevitably someone will report your progress and impact to them at some point, especially if it's going well.

There is another group of stakeholders who you are far more likely to come into direct contact with and who are very likely to have a perception of the direction your curriculum design project is taking. That is your parents. How influential and actively visible your parents are to you and your team, will obviously be determined by your context. Different types of schools will have greater or lesser engagement from their parent community and the nature of the interactions between parents and school will vary hugely, however it is likely that instances where you have to explain, justify and prove the value of the provision you offer or intend to offer, will exist in your school. Parent evenings, school events, the school gates at the start and end of the day are all moments where you might get asked to discuss your provision and it is important to know how to respond. Clarity of message is important here, as you are talking to people for whom PE is not their subject specialism. Likewise, you could be talking to people for whom PE was not a positive experience. We carry our lived experiences with us throughout our lives and inevitably we allow those lived experiences to shape our perception of the things that influence us and our loved ones. For parents, they will have a picture in their minds of what PE is, likely based around the experience they had at school. Unfortunately, these were not always as positive as the ones children of today are receiving and therefore, we must always be sensitive to that potential starting point for those conversations. Parents may think PE is Sport and therefore careful explanation of the difference may be required. Other parents may have issues related to their specific children that aren't directly related to the curriculum but more about the wider, holistic provision or experience they are having. Regardless of the conversations you are having, it is worth remembering that an objective of any curriculum development should be to impart enough positivity into our pupils that the messages going home about PE are reflective of those positive experiences.

### Logistical Changes
Schools are organic environments. They shift and flex, grow and shrink. They evolve and develop. Sometimes they are literally transformed, and every adaptation, from the largest

infrastructure change to the smallest, subtlest change in budgeting can have profound impact on the way we provide our curricular experiences to our pupils.

New facilities, new equipment, new local sporting venues can all change the potential offer that we can consider. Whilst we're rarely afforded the luxury of a new, purpose-built facility, just the creation of a new indoor or outdoor space or the repurposing of a facility can open opportunities that previously were unavailable to us. A great example from my own teaching experience was the development of a purpose-built table tennis centre at the end of our sports block. Whilst this was not directly funded by the school, the access to this facility radically changed the offer we were able to provide to our students. Within a year of the facility being opened we were offering extensive amounts of table tennis whereas before it wasn't an option at all. This radically changed the perception of the PE offering within that school and opened opportunities to provide new experiences within our curriculum.

When you are planning your PE changes it is important to really consider the facilities you have, and how best you can use them. Very few, if any, facilities are single use. Even swimming pools can be used in multiple different ways. A fitness centre can double as a dance studio, a running track can offer multiple opportunities for fundamental movement activities, a football or rugby or hockey pitch is a blank canvas that can be used in more ways than you would ever be able to list. Formulating your provision around the specific facilities you have available, is certainly one approach, but I would argue that being creative with the use of your facilities opens new and creative avenues for provision that could and will enhance your offering way beyond the obvious.

It is also important to look into the future and plan for it. If you know that there is a likelihood of a new development in your facilities or equipment levels, make sure to plan for this. If you know that a new piece of equipment or the repurposing of a facility would allow you to enhance your offering, pitch it. Don't be afraid to work with what you have, whilst thinking about how to develop this for the future. Often a well-designed, clearly planned out proposal that requires investment is far more likely to succeed than a brief request for something without explicit explanation as to the potential benefits and impact of that investment. Building this into your project plan will increase the chances of making it a reality.

**Framework Changes**

Often the most direct, if sometimes least frequent driver for change is the adaption or replacement of part of our direct framework. Whether it be a national curriculum, a trust or school group policy about PE provision or indeed a takeover, when the fundamental requirements within which we must work change, we have no option but to respond to those changes.

The most obvious examples of this are national or regional curriculum changes. In England they have had numerous iterations of the National Curriculum for PE. More recently this has happened in Wales. The United Arab Emirates introduced a new PE curriculum in the last few years, fundamentally shifting the focus of provision and expectation across all their national schools. Across the world there are regular adaptations to the National Curriculum frameworks of nations or states, and with each of these comes the need for PE departments to change and adapt to the new expectations required of them. These shifts in focus can often precede a change in assessment or inspection requirements, meaning departments are left with little choice but to revise their provision to meet the needs of the new approach.

Whenever a framework adaptation takes place, it presents both challenges and opportunities. Often the catalyst for change can be forced as much as it can be desired, but nevertheless this allows stakeholders the chance to thoroughly review and evaluate what they are doing to and assess, against the newly provided frameworks, whether their provision is current, modern and appropriate. In some ways the inevitability of a change review and potential change management process can be a pressure release for those instigating a project as the choice is taken from their hands, releasing them of some of the responsibility. To make sure all students benefit from an updated curriculum; we shouldn't wait for curriculum reviews to be forced upon us. Keeping the status quo may seem like a good idea when there are no external pressures, but it doesn't benefit future students who will miss out on the enhancements. We should take responsibility for instigating change ourselves. This way, all students will have the opportunity to benefit from the updated curriculum, not just the ones immediately before a framework change.

CHANGEMAKERS

> **Reflective Questions: What type of change?**
>
> - What type of change do you think you are engaging with within your curriculum?
> - Who is driving the change within your context? Is it you, or someone else?
> - Who are the key stakeholders involved that will influence your outcomes?
> - How will you ensure positive, collaborative relationships between everyone involved?

## Changemaker Reflection: Kayali
*MYP-DP - Lead Practitioner - DIA Dubai*

**Empowering Educators: Transforming Classroom Environments for Engaging Learning**

So, picture this: I've been in the teaching game for 17 years. But you know what? My journey didn't start in some fancy classroom with all the answers. No, it began with memories of overcrowded classrooms from my own childhood. Almost 50 students crammed into a space, some even standing because there weren't enough seats. Fast forward to my own teaching career, and I was determined to change the game. I didn't think I needed to be an architect, but I sure felt like one as I transformed my classroom into a hub of excitement and learning.

**Approach to Driving Change:**

My story of change? It's all about design and student-centred magic. I wanted my students to own their learning, so I turned my classroom into a vibrant, interactive space. Imagine walls adorned with exceptional student work, QR codes linking to grammar tips, and a roadmap showing the path from struggle to success. But that's not all.

**Collaborative Learning Environments:**
Enter my cluster groups, a mix of talents and abilities. I didn't just throw students together randomly; oh no, I analysed data like a detective. CAT4 scores, class performance, and my own observations guided me. The result? A classroom buzzing with positivity and enthusiasm. Imagine a place where every student is challenged, where learning is a shared adventure, and teachers are guides, not dictators.

**Results and Impact:**
In my classroom, it's not just about academic growth; it's about creating memories. The atmosphere is electric with positivity and respect. Challenges are tackled head-on, transforming into opportunities to shine. My students don't just learn; they thrive. And guess what? The teacher-student relationship isn't a one-way street; it's a partnership where everyone learns and grows.

**Tips and Ideas for Other Educators:**
So, fellow *Changemakers*, here's the deal. Want to transform your classroom? Start with passion, sprinkle in some creativity, and tailor your approach. Use every tool in your arsenal – interactive displays, tech wonders, and thoughtful groupings. But above all, create a home within your classroom. A home where learning is an adventure, where every voice matters, and where students feel safe to explore, question, and learn.

**Conclusion:**
I'm not just shaping minds; I'm creating an experience. My classroom isn't just a place; it's a feeling. It's the laughter, the 'aha' moments, and the unwavering belief that every student can shine. So, fellow educators, let's not just teach; let's inspire. Let's not just talk; let's engage. Together, let's make every classroom a place where dreams take flight.

# Chapter 6 - Process For Progress

## The Process Of Change

**'What's dangerous is not to evolve.'**
*Jeff Bezos*

### Theoretical models of Change

Research into modelling change within educational contexts is limited in its scope. It's just an area that lacks thorough academic exploration at this point. Therefore, much of the theoretical modelling and discussion around change, comes from organisations outside of education. If you look at the theory of change more generally, you will find many different and diverse attempts to model the processes involved in a change management project. Whilst theoretical modelling will have limited usefulness in terms of practical delivery, it is interesting to understand the evolution of thinking in relation to change models and how our current understanding of the process of change has evolved in recent history.

An early pioneer into change theory, Kurt Lewin (1951) developed a model based around three steps that he titled 'unfreezing, moving and refreezing'. Unfreezing describes the loosening or relaxation of the things that keep organisations at a specific level or static in its development, that was required to allow change to begin. Moving was the period in which the organisation would identify and develop a new way of functioning and then freeze described the steps then required to 'codify and calcify' the new approaches into permanence. Whilst respected and praised at the time, there are criticisms of Lewin's change model in that it lacks recognition of

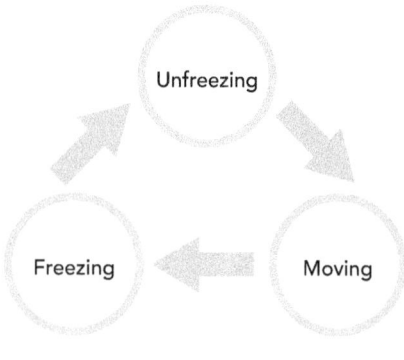

## CHAPTER 6 - PROCESS FOR PROGRESS

individual, group, organisational or societal accountability for the progress of change, and it doesn't reflect the complexities of change.

Utilising the initial work of Lewin, in 1967, Larry Greiner devised a more comprehensive six phase model. Greiner's 'growth' phases form a chart or curve that demonstrates the process through which organisational change would occur. The six phases were:

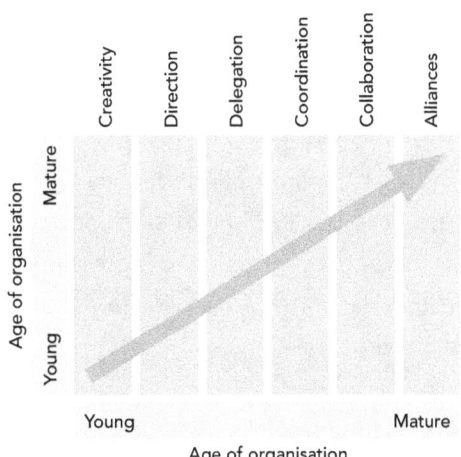

- Growth through Creativity
- Growth Through Direction
- Growth Through Delegation
- Growth Through Coordination and Monitoring
- Growth Through Collaboration
- Growth Through Extra-Organizational Alliances

His model attempts to demonstrate a sense of urgency, initiation, and planning throughout the life cycle of a process of change at its inception whilst the middle phases represent the diagnosis and intervention required to facilitate the change and the conclusion demonstrates the importance of reinforcing the change into an organisation's fabric.

In 1975 Ben Harris at the University of Texas utilised the essential arguments of Lewin and Greiner's pre-existing models to develop a five-phase model which suggested that the process of change was a continuous non-discrete process from Educational Planning, to planning and initiation, through momentum building, onto responding to new problems created, turning point, and finally termination of the project. Harris's model tries to demonstrate the overlapping nature of phases within project lifecycles and the more complex

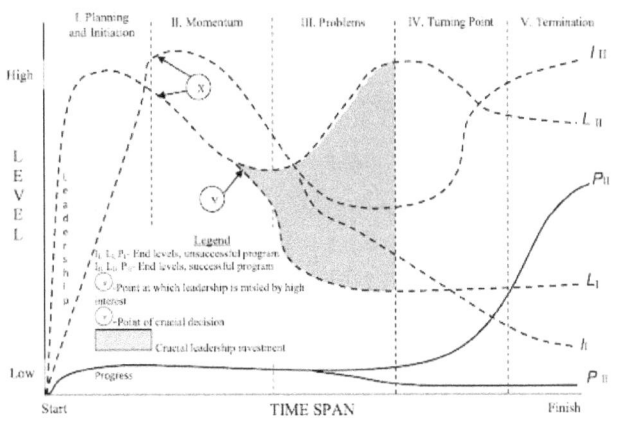

*(Lunenburg, 2010)*

and often chaotic nature of change management.

The last theoretical model we will look at is the 1995 eight step model developed by Kotter and published in the Harvard Business Review that same year.

The elements of Kotter's model are similar to the underlying themes set out by Lewin forty years earlier, in that the development of a climate in which change is encouraged and then establishing a sense of urgency, creating project teams who in turn develop and communicate the vision,

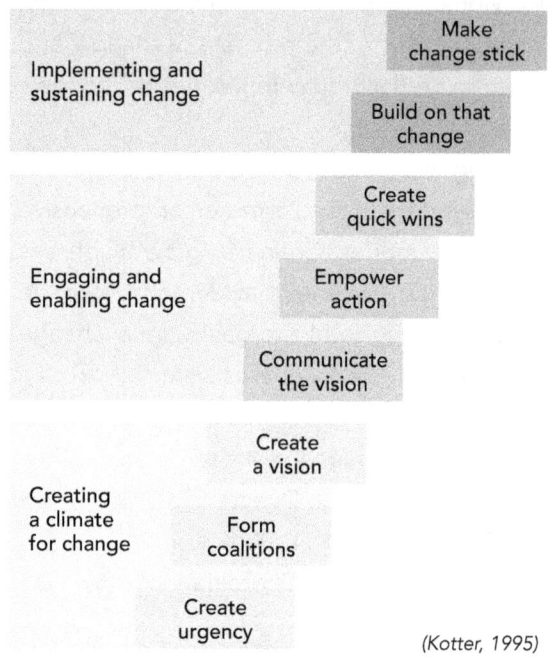

(Kotter, 1995)

delivering the change itself and then embedding it into an organisations frameworks gives the best opportunity for that change to stick. Kotter used aspects from all the previous theoretical models to develop a framework which has gone on to form the basis for many project management approaches, including Six Sigma. (We talk more about Six Sigma later in *Changemakers*.

---

Any PE department embarking on transformative activity, that will directly impact on the provision they offer to their pupils, should adopt a 'plan first, reflect last' approach to their project. It's the structuring of the process that will ensure that the outcomes are appropriate, timely, justified, tested, monitored and proven. Whilst it's really tempting to dive straight into picking apart your curriculum plans and adding in new and exciting ideas, if we are to ensure that we are making effective change, without wasting energy, productivity or good will, and that we are only making meaningful change that will have positive and lasting impact, we should always start with some form of structured plan for our project. Whilst this is initially time-consuming, the benefit in terms of time and resource/energy saved makes it not just worthwhile but an absolute priority. Let's look in more detail at the specific benefits of starting your project with a clear plan:

A well-structured project plan acts as a roadmap, it will provide clarity and direction for everyone involved in the change process and will help to ensure that all stakeholders are working towards a common goal. It will allow you to reflect and agree on the steps, tasks, and responsibilities involved, at least at the initial phases of the project. It will also help you to identify and explain to everyone involved how their individual contributions fit into the larger picture.

Planning will help you allocate resources effectively; avoid duplication of effort and save you wasted time. By carefully considering the steps involved, the potential challenges, and the resource requirements, the change process can be streamlined and executed more efficiently.

Planning is essential to help identify and assess potential risks associated with any change and will give you the opportunity to implement risk management plans and avoid doing anything that will impact on the delivery or experience. Whilst it doesn't necessarily seem like risk is a factor when we're designing or adapting our curriculum, of course we have to think about the impact of our new plans on both pupils and staff alike. Thinking about mitigating any risk will reduce the likelihood of unforeseen obstacles and disruptions that could minimise the overall positivity of your project.

Deciding who is going to be involved in your project as early as possible will allow you to engage with them from the outset, increasing their sense of ownership and commitment to the process. We know that early adoption leads to greater buy-in and helps us avoid tricky situations with stakeholders resisting change because they haven't felt included or valued in the planning stages. When stakeholders understand the rationale behind the change you are proposing, when they understand their roles and the expected outcomes, they are more likely to engage. When we can clearly identify the potential positive impact that the change may have, on them and their teaching, as well as the expectations on them in relation to their time and effort, they are more likely to embrace the change and contribute positively. Put simply, planning helps to facilitate effective, positive communication and coordination between different stakeholders and this collaboration at the start makes it more likely that they will remain positive supporters throughout the process as a whole.

Creating a project plan gives you a framework that supports continuous monitoring, evaluation, and adaptation. By giving yourself a trackable structure with clearly defined goals and objectives, it allows you to be more specific and more targeted in your progress tracking. In turn, your ability to track progress and impact throughout a process, provides you with ongoing data and evidence to support your plans and objectives. It also gives you the ability to recognise where things are not going to plan, where progress is perhaps less effective or timely and where there are areas of the project that need improving, adjusting or refining. The clearer your plan is, the more likely you are to end up in the place you want to be at the end of the project.

When developing your initial project plan, at the very outset of your project it's important that you consider the whole project not just the starting point. Trying to picture, visualise and plan the whole journey will help you maintain focus and progress. When you are having to constantly consider and decide on the next step, it's a far more mentally challenging process. Start early, think long term and make the whole process from start to finish clear to everyone.

Ultimately, planning at the start will allow you to set the groundwork and boundaries for your project that will help you to create lasting, meaningful change, rather than rushed and reactive actions that may or may not positively impact your pupils.

Having been through this process personally on several occasions, with differing approaches and differing levels of success, I have learnt that forward planning and real clarity of vision and scope are absolutely critical if we are to create the successful changes, we are setting out to achieve.

In my experience there are 10 clear project considerations that you need to think about at the very start of your planning. These things will (I hope) help guide you in your thinking and discussion. By working through these factors you can be confident that your plan has considered each stage of the upcoming change process and has considered and reflected on every aspect of the project and any factors that could impact on the effectiveness of our developments.

## 1. Recognise why we want/need change

Before any change can take place, we need to understand the context in which we believe change is necessary. Having evidence to support your belief that change is necessary forms the foundation for the rest of your project plan. When we clearly and concisely identify the things that need addressing, we can make sure that our project focuses on these specific things, does not become unwieldy and does not end up impacting on other areas of our provision that do not need the same change to occur. The identification and recognition of the driving force behind the change is critical, as it provides a clear direction and impetus for the project we are going to undertake.

## 2. Establishing your vision and objectives

Once we know why we want something to change, we need to develop a 'vision' for what we think we would like that changed provision to look like. Picture a normal lesson before and after the change process. What is different? What adaptations have taken place and what positive outcomes have resulted. To make our vision solid and achievable we should try to adhere to the principles of being specific, measurable, attainable, relevant, and time-bound (SMART), thereby creating a roadmap for the project. Furthermore, the use of SMART goals within the overarching vision helps to break down the project into manageable steps and gives us our framework within which we can regularly monitor the progress of our work.

## 3. Evaluating the Impact of Change

Before we embark on any kind of implementation, it's critical to decide how we are going to evaluate any potential changes and the impact they will have on the individuals, classes, year groups and the school as a whole. Without a clear and communicated plan on assessing the progress and impact of your project, you won't have the necessary data and evidence to show you have achieved what you set out to do. This entails identifying potential risks, challenges, and opportunities that may arise as a result of the change and specifically addressing how you will observe, record, evidence and present those outcomes, both positive and negative. By really considering the impact, all the stakeholders involved in the process can be confident our plans are robust, meaningful and will have impact.

## 4. Forming Resilience within your teams

All projects need collaboration. Even the most independent PE teacher will need the support of others to enact meaningful change. There is no situation where a project will be as effective if those around the project are not informed, engaged, recognised, considered and valued. To be truly sure that the support network around your project is both engaged and informed, the planning stage needs to identify, acknowledge, inform and support those for whom the project will have an impact. This could be fellow teachers, other colleagues, senior leaders, governors and the wider support network that helps formulate the provision within your school. If one group or individual is left outside this circle of consideration, we risk developing resistance or apathy towards our project and subsequently opening the door to negativity regarding our goals and desired outcomes. The presence of a committed, proficient and well-informed team to guide and support the implementation will also provide you with access to additional expertise in multiple ways, including communication, project planning and change management.

## 5. Facilitating Effective Communication

Open and regular communication is critical within any change initiative. Without ongoing and open dialogue between stakeholders, things become open to interpretation, and incorrect or inaccurate interpretation can be a significant barrier to our chances of success. When we leave things to individual interpretation we allow bias, life experience or attitude to influence others, potentially damaging the cohesiveness and transparency of our project's goals and outcomes. Do not allow yourself to be tempted to keep things to yourself, to only consider your own perspectives or to assume that you always know best. Challenge to our ideas and plans is positive and if it is conducted in open, transparent and positive ways, then negative feedback can be just as valuable as positive. Regular updates, department and staff meetings, and clearly defined feedback mechanisms need to be established from the outset. Your senior leadership teams and colleagues will want to know they are being kept in the loop, and a clear, consistent and realistic plan for how this will happen will instantly reassure all your stakeholders that you are meaningful in your approach, open in your ambitions and clear and honest in your information provision.

## 6. Empowering and Engaging Stakeholders

This one is really important! As we have already discussed, we cannot enact change on our own. Even those of us trying to work on our own will need the buy-in and support of others to successfully accomplish our goals. Change often results in explicit or subtle power shifts and changes in the working dynamics within teams and the wider school faculties. We may not realise the impact our project is having outside of our direct sphere of influence, but schools can be 'snippy' places where it is easy to feel threatened by something happening outside of our direct control. This is a dangerously negative thing which we need to ensure we avoid from the very outset of our projects. Remember that buy-in is a far more powerful tool than opt-out and by encouraging engagement through positivity and a sense of ownership we can ensure that we are limiting the negativity or sense of threat our project might otherwise instigate within others. Look at it this way. If you're doing something amazing and creative in your PE provision, will the other subject leaders think they're going to be expected to do the same? If that was the other way around, would you feel threatened by it? If we can show, demonstrate and reassure everyone that what we are doing is only going to have a positive impact on their areas of responsibility, (for example sharing resources and strategies to offer pupils more active learning opportunities in their classroom-based subject), are they more likely to get on board with us?

## 7. Provision of Training and Support

We cannot and should not assume that all our colleagues have had the same level or type of training, development and exposure as each other, or ourselves. This is especially true if you are trying to implement change at the start of your career within a school or department. Likewise, we cannot assume we know more than those around us. Even the most researched and read amongst us does not have the right to assume we know everything. Recognising and celebrating the knowledge, experience and skills of others will help develop that collaborative community we are looking for. Where there are gaps in knowledge or experience, help to close them. There is so much in the way of professional development opportunities available now, through our PE networks, online and offline, that we can tap into. The level and quality of PE-specific research have never been greater, and the accessibility of subject matter experts or research-driven PE consultants willing to support and provide knowledge has grown exponentially. Tap into that resource and encourage your colleagues and stakeholders to do the same. It is likely, at the outset of your project, that people will ask for evidence to support your claims or ideas, so make sure you have this in volumes. If you don't have it, perhaps begin with a search and if it's still not available, perhaps reflect on why?

Ultimately the success or failure of your plans could rely heavily on the ability of those around the project adapting and embracing new behaviours and ideas. To support this, we need to make sure that we are offering and providing the right level of training and support to equip them with the right set of skills, at the right time, to really benefit from and navigate through the change process. A change initiative heavily relies on the ability of individuals to adapt and embrace new behaviours. To facilitate this, it is imperative to provide comprehensive training and support to stakeholders, equipping them with the necessary skills and knowledge to effectively navigate the change. Any new resources, technology, platforms, techniques, activities and any other implementations need to be supported with quality training, either inhouse or externally provided. No one should feel they are being asked to engage with something that they are not fully equipped and prepared for. As the 'changemaker' instigating the project, you must remember you have a responsibility to the care and wellbeing of those for whom the project will impact or influence. This will inevitably require you to reflect on the makeup of the teams around the project and ensure they are supported to feel valued, considered and prepared for the inevitable change that is coming.

## 8. Monitoring and Assessing Progress

Change for the sake of change is never a good thing. Uprooting our curriculum and changing it can cause disruption for our pupils and colleagues and without a clear plan for implementation and evaluation the change can look, feel and seem like a 'tick box' exercise. We need to think carefully about how and when we are going to assess the impact of our curriculum developments. This doesn't only mean tracking pupil progress but far more comprehensive and holistic consideration of the value and limitations of our changes.

We will talk in more detail in a later chapter about how we evaluate our changes and some of the ways in which we can do this, but an understanding that evaluation must form an integral part of our change management plan, from the outset is critical. Understanding, planning and communicating how we are going to evaluate and feedback on our changes and their subsequent impact helps stakeholders and other interested parties with their perception of the value of the process. Building this plan from the start of your project will make the evaluation more organised, and less ad hoc and will help those involved in evaluation and monitoring to feel it is less formal and pressurised and more like a normal part of the process of change.

## 9. Formalising and Embedding Change

Once your project has neared completion and the impact has been shown to be positive and meaningful, we are going to want to be sure we have embedded the changes, the culture and the value proposition within our school structure. Knowing and planning for this, from the outset of your project, will make this process seem far easier when the time arrives.

We want to ensure we have created something long-lasting that will become a foundation for ongoing progression rather than something that will be changed again after a short period of time. This is often one of the hardest things to achieve as new staff, new curriculum leaders, new senior leadership like to make changes to show they are immediately adding value. In International PE departments we see this happen all the time. A curriculum change is made, implemented and proven and then a new Head of Department arrives and the whole process begins again. I have been guilty of this myself. Sometimes this curriculum leader driven change is more about showcasing their own capabilities rather than directly for the benefit of the pupils, but often it is more to do with wanting to make an instant, positive, impact and done with the most positive of intentions. Whilst frustrating for those existing staff members being asked to change direction regularly, it is an inevitable part of school evolution and whilst we can mitigate the chances of regular change, it is not something we will always be able to avoid.

The best way to ensure your project becomes embedded in the schools framework is to ensure it is proven, with evidence and data to support its effectiveness and then to ensure this evidence is communicated and shared with all your key decision makers, influencers and stakeholders within your school community. If you can show, without a doubt, that the changes your team have made have had positive and meaningful outcomes for pupils, you are far less at risk of the change being undone or ignored by future changes to staffing or school leadership. You will need to consider updating policies, clarifying procedures and responsibilities, consider updating job descriptions to reflect the new approach you have implemented and ensure you have aligned any external influences such as co-curricular or extracurricular provision. Remember to update your tracking and monitoring spreadsheets and templates and ensure your new approach is embedded into your reporting structures. Check in regularly with local or regional partners to ensure they have clarity of your new approach and seek like-minded departments locally with a similar approach to network with. You could create and deliver professional development to your team and the wider staff within your school, and you must advertise, celebrate, recognise and communicate to pupils and parents on what you are doing and why. The more noise you can make and the greater the exposure you can give your programme, the more likely it is that your change will be embedded into the fabric of your school, supporting its sustainability beyond the initial implementation phase.

## 10. Commemorating, Celebrating, Recognising your Achievements

At every stage of your project, it is important to recognise and celebrate achievements along the way, regardless of their magnitude. Identifying small successes rather than focusing on the final outcomes not only boosts morale but also helps identify and publicise the positive aspects of the changes you are implementing. This in turn should increase the motivation of stakeholders to remain committed to the process. Often change within PE and other curriculum areas can be a long, time-consuming task and when we think about how long it takes to write a single scheme of work, we can see just how important it is that stakeholders feel they are being recognised for their efforts throughout the period of time, not just at the end. Celebrating and recognising the impact and influence of those involved in your project really helps reinforce the positivity around your activity and in turn motivates those colleagues who are working so hard, to persist in their efforts.

Additionally, the recognition of successes helps us manage the emotional impact of any aspects that perhaps are not going so well. It's easier to give critical feedback when you can frame it within all the positive things that have happened. When you have to present your project and findings to senior leadership and admit that something hasn't worked and will need to be reviewed, it's a much more comfortable conversation when you can recognise all the things that have improved and are working.

Ultimately, a well-designed and thought-through project plan will save you time, effort and stress. Whilst the start of a change management process can be a mix of excitement and nervousness, the more formalised and structured our plan is, the more likely we are to manage, cope, follow and accomplish. We are setting out on a journey of change and adaptation for all the right reasons, but the difference between ultimate success or failure and the final benefits for our pupils, could be determined not by what happens at the conclusion, but what we do at the very start.

CHAPTER 6 - PROCESS FOR PROGRESS

## Changemaker Reflection: Jon Campbell & Matthew Trowbridge
*Leading Change in the Curriculum for Wales*

To understand the two change-making stories in this chapter, it's important to give some context to the educational reform that has taken place in Wales (it is enormous - so as briefly as possible!). The introduction of the Curriculum for Wales (C4W) (Welsh Government, 2020a) marked a significant departure from the educational outcomes and approaches of the 2008 National Curriculum. As with the prelude to the Scottish educational reform, Graham Donaldson's 'Successful Futures' (2015) detailed the shortcomings of educational systems in Wales, and how a bespoke approach in each school setting was needed to ensure young people in Wales left school with the requisite skills to thrive in a rapidly evolving social, economic and technological landscape. The C4W represented a comprehensive re-think; a renewed focus on pedagogical approaches and subject content that emphasises and encourages the role students play in their learning processes and outcomes.

The authors of this chapter recognise through their experience that PE teachers in Wales have generally devised curriculums based on the rigid scope of a sports-technique driven model; no different to most countries around the world (Kirk, 2010; Casey & Kirk, 2021). But this approach has been widely debunked in the literature when its efficacy of achieving the outcomes of school PE is considered. The C4W sought to move away from these approaches by seeing teaching and learning approaches through a holistic lens, where the growth of students as good people is as vital as the skills and knowledge gleaned through their subject specific education. This holistic approach is not just unique to PE either - it a central tenet as schools seek to meet the 'Four Purposes' (Welsh Government, 2020b) of the C4W, ensuring that learners become (1) ambitious, capable learners, ready to learn throughout their lives, (2) enterprising, creative contributors, ready to play a full part in life and work, (3) ethical, informed citizens of Wales and the world; and (4) healthy, confident individuals, ready to lead fulfilling lives as valued members of society.

The C4W has found its subjects organised in a different way - 'Areas of Learning Experience' (AOLEs) - with PE falling under 'Health and Wellbeing'. Within the AOLE, a holistic approach to teaching and learning is advocated through the Health and Wellbeing statements of 'What Matters' (Welsh Government 2020c). Through the experiences in Health and Wellbeing, students need to understand that (1) developing physical health and wellbeing has lifelong benefits, (2) how we process and respond to our experiences affects our mental health and emotional wellbeing, (3) our decision-making impacts on the quality of our lives and the lives of others, (4) how we engage with social influences shapes who we are and affects our health and wellbeing, and (5) healthy relationships are fundamental to our wellbeing. Within the PE context of the reflections in this chapter, changes to approaches to curriculum, pedagogy and assessment differ, but fit well with the bespoke nature of curriculum design demanded by the C4W and the journeys of change required to achieve it.

## Jon Campbell experience: Student voice, aligning curriculum decisions and embedding 'pedagogies of affect'.

To effect lasting change, you have to be willing to change yourself in the first instance. You have also got to be willing to fail. I understood that instigating change in a setting with deeply held traditions of what PE is and how it is delivered would be a difficult task, and that challenging the status quo would inevitably meet resistance from stakeholders. It had been apparent to me for a while that the curriculum offered at my school did not connect in a meaningful way with the majority of my students and that, with the C4W demanding a re-think of what experiences we facilitate for students in our subject areas, change was now necessary - in fact, legally mandatory.

Designing meaningful PE experiences requires the input of students themselves. I saw a carefully considered student voice activity as the perfect tool to engage senior leaders and staff within the department in constructive conversation that challenged their thinking about the efficacy of our curriculum. A 'disconnect' between the curriculum choices made by PE teachers and preferences of students is something that Banville et al. (2021) identify and was clearly present in my setting. The student-voice activity simply asked students to rank 10 principles of PE in order of personal relevance. The results are shown in the table opposite.

# CHAPTER 6 - PROCESS FOR PROGRESS

| PE core principles | 1 | 2 | 3 | 4 | 5 | 6 | 7 | 8 | 9 | 10 | Aggregate score | Rank |
|---|---|---|---|---|---|---|---|---|---|---|---|---|
| Happiness and enjoyment | 46 | 26 | 20 | 13 | 9 | 10 | 7 | 5 | 7 | 1 | 1107 | 1 |
| Mental health development | 34 | 27 | 18 | 22 | 5 | 9 | 6 | 9 | 5 | 8 | 1025 | 2 |
| Developing self confidence | 21 | 27 | 31 | 10 | 17 | 12 | 9 | 5 | 6 | 5 | 1001 | 3 |
| Physical development and physical activity | 12 | 14 | 19 | 25 | 14 | 15 | 9 | 15 | 13 | 7 | 846 | 4 |
| Developing leadership skills | 5 | 6 | 11 | 20 | 20 | 23 | 25 | 13 | 11 | 8 | 740 | 5 |
| Social development and collaboration skills | 6 | 12 | 11 | 19 | 25 | 11 | 11 | 17 | 19 | 12 | 739 | 6 |
| Developing personal movement skills | 6 | 6 | 10 | 11 | 18 | 21 | 21 | 19 | 17 | 15 | 674 | 7 |
| Sport tactics and techniques development | 5 | 12 | 10 | 8 | 12 | 15 | 29 | 21 | 21 | 11 | 673 | 8 |
| Sport rules and regulations | 4 | 5 | 5 | 10 | 12 | 16 | 14 | 26 | 22 | 30 | 555 | 9 |
| Competitive sport provision | 5 | 9 | 9 | 6 | 12 | 11 | 11 | 13 | 22 | 46 | 545 | 10 |

Aligning curriculum designs with the needs of students is a little like inserting a battery into a child's toy; the intention to make the toy light up (learning in a meaningful and personally relevant way) is there because you've inserted the battery (your decisions and energy). But if the battery is inserted the wrong way around (not aligning curriculum with student needs and motivations) so that it's not connected properly - the toy won't light up at all. The student voice results showed to my department that the curriculum which centred on our own deeply held traditions of competitive sport, rules and regulations of sport and sports techniques, did not connect with the priorities of students. Evidently, students cared about these principles the least. And there it was - our problem. It was time to take the batteries out.

Connecting students to the 'right' kind of PE would be essential if we were to contribute towards realising the four purposes of the C4W, but also the wider statements of 'what matters' in the Health and Wellbeing AOLE. Understanding that significant change to current practices was required was not an evaluation that those practices were bad, but it identified, through lesson observations and critical reflection of my own practice, that the dominant teaching approach used within the department was demonstrably direct instruction; a teacher-led approach that perhaps didn't engage learning across the domains as well as it did in the physical. Although there is nothing inherently wrong with this approach, it did not provide holistic learning opportunities that might allow experiences across the Health and Wellbeing 'What Matters' statements and the learning themes within them when used exclusively. In addressing this issue, it was important to belay the trepidation of 'starting from scratch' by pushing the message that we were looking to add to or enhance our teaching - not reinvent it. Staff were therefore provided information on models-based practice (Casey & Kirk, 2021) and the concept curriculum (Sullivan, 2021) and given the agency and autonomy to choose and trial elements of it throughout units of work.

Within the options of models-based practice, I chose to focus specifically on, what Kirk (2021) described as, 'pedagogies of affect'; pedagogies that focus explicitly on learning in the affective domain. Through this, outcomes detailed in the C4W 'Four Purposes' and 'What Matters' could be impacted through teaching approaches that developed motivation, confidence and self-esteem, determination and resilience, responsibility and leadership, respect and tolerance, and communication (Lamb et al., 2021). These skills, when analysing the learning themes in the Health and Wellbeing 'What Matters' statements in the image below, could be easily interpreted as the desired outcomes of themes within the AOLE.

### Health and wellbeing AOLE learning themes

| WM1 | WM2 | WM3 | WM4 | WM5 |
|---|---|---|---|---|
| Physical health and activity | Mental health and emotional wellbeing | Decision making | Social influence | Relationships |
| Physical literacy | Emotional regulation | Choices, decision and goals | Social awareness and interaction | Types of relationships |
| | | | | Communicating feelings |
| Impact of nutrition | Communication and seeking help | | | |
| | | Impact of decisions | Identity | Friendships and conflict |
| Emotional and physical connection | Reflection | | | |
| | | | | Safety in relationships |
| Physical health and safety | Empathy | Managing risks | Attitudes and values | Rights and respect |

# CHAPTER 6 - PROCESS FOR PROGRESS

When leading change, resistance is certain. However, resistance can be eased, and momentum can be gained by giving staff ownership of their own learning journey; agency and autonomy without the fear of failure is key to ensure other teachers are willing to try something that is new to them. Providing justification for change and the evidence of its successes should inform your approach, but the willingness of each person in a team to embrace challenges will be tested. Learning from the successes and the failures are key to finding and adopting strategies that work. But ultimately, in a subject like PE where relationships and role-modelling are essential components of the learning process, how can we expect students to embrace new challenges if we can't demonstrate it ourselves?

# Chapter 7 - Research And Reflection

**'There is nothing permanent except change.'**
*Heraclitus*

So, you've decided the time is right for a review of your curricular provision. For any of the reasons we've already talked about, you have committed to a process and developed your project plan. You won't yet know where the project will go, or how it will ultimately conclude and you may not yet know exactly what you want the final curriculum to look like, but you're setting out on a pathway and you're feeling good about the journey you are about to take.

## Research

So, your first step, once you've finished your plan, is to really (and I mean really), research the current evidence and information that is out there, to form a clear picture of what opportunities and options there are for you to consider. We're lucky that we are living and working in a world in which there is more research into curricular PE provision than there has ever been before but, as with any project, being informed rather than just opinionated, is critical, so knowing what research and literature you are going to explore is important.

The great thing about teachers is that we know how to research. Whether its skills learnt at university or from reading generally around our subject area, we know how to go and find information to better educate ourselves. All this

| Academic books | Blogs | Scholarly journal articles |
|---|---|---|
| Video | Reports | Professional journal articles |
| Internet | Social media | Conferences |
| School networks | CPD sessions | News and current affairs |

information is at our fingertips and with tools such as Google Scholar we have access to more research than we could ever hope to actually read!

Think about how you are going to structure your search. This book is not the place to go into the details around literature search methodologies or literature reviews but suffice to say knowing roughly what you are looking for is key to helping you avoid diversions and distractions and slipping down many internet 'rabbit-holes'.

Think about your key terms, think about the broad outline of the type of curriculum you think you want to explore. Consider the key names you've heard who are involved in curriculum development and CPD around curricular provision and look for articles and online posts from them. Build up evidence to support the development of your thinking. When you try to sell your plans to your stakeholders, having evidence to back up your thinking is a very powerful tool.

## Student Voice

One of the most powerful tools you have at your disposal when formulating your plans for your revised curriculum is the pupils for whom it will have an impact. Regardless of your individual context your pupils will have their own perspectives and opinions of what PE means to them, what it should/could look like, the bits they like and the bits they don't, the meaning of PE for them as individuals and the experiences they want from their PE journeys. This is important and useful information so taking the time to canvas those opinions and listen to those voices is a worthwhile activity.

Student voices come to us in a wide variety of ways. In the following section we predominantly focus on formal questionnaire or survey type activities, because this will provide us with good qualitative and quantitative data, but it's important to recognise that this is only one way we can listen to the opinions and ideas of our pupils. We can use a wide variety of different situations and contexts to gather the thoughts and ideas of our pupils to help inform our departmental discussions around what they want to see, feel and learn within their PE programme. The key to this is knowing how to record and reflect on this information without being overwhelmed by it. Often, for this very reason, we adopt a formal approach to gathering student voice, through some form of questionnaire or survey.

There are many easily accessible examples of student voice surveys and questionnaires. If you need a starting point, then go back to your research and explore your options online. If you have links to local universities or other educational partners, reach out to them to see what they have to support you and talk to other PE departments in your local area or even globally over social media to see if anyone can share their experiences and resources around their student voice activity. There should be no need to start from scratch with this, as many departments and schools have already undertaken this type of activity. Finding a starting point and adapting it to suit your own context is a valid and perfectly reasonable approach to take but remember the adaptation to suit your needs is important, as no-one else's pupil demographic is going to be the same as yours. Whilst beginning with someone else's resources will save you time, just using it verbatim is probably not going to give you the realistic, contextual picture you are looking for.

A critical consideration when developing your student voice activity is to think about the way in which you are collecting the information. There are a myriad of ways in which you could collect your data and inform your decision-making but each will provide you with a slightly different perspective. Are you going to send out a survey to all your pupils via a tool such as Google Forms or Survey Monkey? If so, you must consider how and where you are going to save the data afterwards and how are you going to analyse it to really find the evidence you are looking for? Are you going to conduct some form of interview and if so, what additional pressure are you putting on your pupils in this environment and how will you overcome that? If you are selecting your subjects for the study, are your outcomes unconsciously biased to suit the vision and plans already in your head? If you just interview GCSE PE students for example, are you really getting the full picture? Are these interviews going to be one to one or focus group style? Will your pupils share their honest opinions in front of each other, or indeed will they be honest with you? Really thinking through the process will ultimately provide you with better evidence, your pupils with a better experience and in all likelihood a better response in general.

Consider how you formulate your questions. This will, in part at least, depend on your pupils' age and demographics. If you are asking primary-age pupils, then your questions will need to consider the language and age appropriateness, whilst still gathering the level of response you need to accurately analyse the data. If you are questioning older pupils, are you giving them the right type and style of question to explore beyond simple yes or no responses? How many questions are appropriate for your subject group? Too short and you won't really scratch the surface but too long and they may switch off. Considering the style and make-up of your questioning is going to help you gather more meaningful data. Again, if you need some inspiration then you can look at what others have done already.

What is the longitudinally of your study? In other words, are you looking for a snapshot in time or a more developmental exploration of changing perception? Perhaps to start with we want to know where our students are with their thinking and feelings, but as we progress, we want to explore their changing value set and opinions. Giving them the same questions at relatively regular intervals might help to build a picture over time of the direction your project is going and the evolution of your offering from their perspectives. Knowing what is happening on the ground now is good, knowing what's always happening on the ground is better. Think about the intervals, think about how you will analyse and explore the changing perception and ultimately think about how that longer term evidence trail will influence and impact on your project.

As you start accumulating data and evidence to support your project, how are you going to disseminate this across the various stakeholders and interested parties within your community? Whilst having the data is great, keeping it to yourself will not realise its full impact. The opposite can also be true though, whereby spreading the findings too wide could lead to comment, criticism, influence or interference. Telling your pupils the outcomes of your survey could be positive, in that they will see that you are taking their feelings and thoughts into account, however it could also lead to disengagement if the general findings don't link to the individually held perspectives of particular pupils or groups. How we use the evidence we gather is important and we need to think carefully in our project planning about how, when and where we will share our findings. Obviously if you are collecting personal information (which I would personally avoid whenever possible - anonymisation of data will support a more honest reflection of pupil voice) then this should only be shared in line with your school data protection policies as well as adhering to any regulatory requirements or rules around this. Do not, ever, share individual responses with other pupils unless completely anonymised, otherwise you will lose the trust and confidence of the pupils for whom you require support.

Whenever we ask others to reflect and comment on our performance, we risk criticism in return. We have to accept that not every response will be positive and if it is, then perhaps we need to relook at the questions we are asking. In fact, we need that criticism, as difficult as it can be to receive, as this is evidence to support our belief that change is needed. Without the feedback about things that pupils don't feel as positive about, can we be sure we are adapting and redesigning the right aspects of our curriculum?

Thinking about how you are going to review and reflect on the more negative responses we receive, will help us manage the potential emotional responses we feel when going through this process. Often, reviewing or reflecting in groups, with colleagues, is a good way of managing this process, as we can provide support and share the criticism more widely rather than potentially taking it very personally. Obviously, we want to avoid any questions that lead to direct critical responses of colleagues, but we also need to ensure that we can accept more general departmental criticism for what it is, honest feedback.

Negative or positive, the voice of our student body will help guide us throughout our project. If we are open and listening, they will tell us a huge amount about the way forward. Listening to our students isn't just about making them feel like they are valued and respected as humans, but gives us evidence, data, perspective and so much more. Whenever you make a change that impacts on a student, a group of students or a whole cohort, it is critical that you observe and understand the change through the most important eyes involved, those of the children in your care.

CHAPTER 7 - RESEARCH AND REFLECTION

## Changemaker Reflection: Aaron Davey
*Head of PE, Kent, UK*

### How student voice supports change in curriculum planning

While implementing a PE concept curriculum and restructuring the timetable to provide more continuity across year groups, I used student voice to explore how to group students. Student agency is a broad topic and there is plenty of research to explore, I found a short collection of research within a publication by Toshalis and Nakkula (2012) ('Motivation, Engagement and Student Voice'). In this Mitra (2009) is paraphrased by the authors, 'we use the term student voice activities to refer to those pedagogies in which youth have the opportunity to influence decisions that will shape their lives and those of their peers either in or outside of school settings'. As a new Head of Department, it was so important to me that students felt valued in the changes that I wanted to implement.

Combining research from Sport England 'Under the Skin' and PE Scholar I adapted a range of questions that would elicit students' understanding of values within PE, the strengths within their own personality and what PE, Sport and Physical Activity meant to them. The evidence collected from student responses highlights their understanding of the values of physical education, the strongest value students selected was Happiness and Fun. The personality section responses resulted in two clear groups, those who wanted to work with similar ability peers (an emphasis placed on PE and sport) and those who wanted to work with peers who shared attitudes (an emphasis placed on socialising & enjoyment).

For our 4 classes (half year group blocks) we have used the results and the personality studies from Sport England 'Under the Skin' (Sport England, 2020) to form our groupings. Highly confident and able pupils (mixed ability), two single groups based on mindset (easy going, less enthusiastic) and a thoughtful improver group (mixed ability).

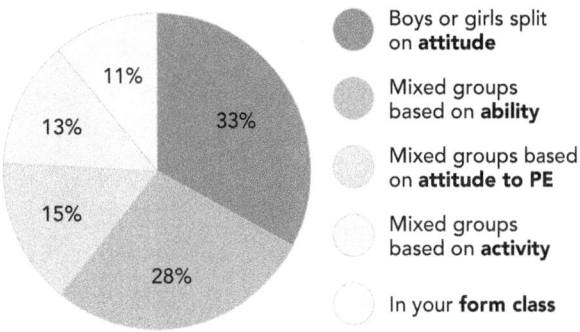

Student preference for choice of groupings

- Boys or girls split on **attitude**
- Mixed groups based on **ability**
- Mixed groups based on **attitude to PE**
- Mixed groups based on **activity**
- In your **form class**

## Stakeholder Voice

Embarking on an exciting and inspirational project, aiming to make real change, that you believe is meaningful and positive, only to be told it doesn't fit with the direction the school is taking, the budgetary realities of the school, the regulatory framework in which your school operates or the ethos and vision of the school, can be devastating. Depending on how far through the process you have got, weeks or months of work could be wasted and the emotional impact of the withdrawal of support or block on progression can be significant and long lasting. In the worst-case scenario, the impact of such an event could ruin the working relationship you have with those decision makers irreparably. A much better approach would be to gather those perspectives, opinions, suggestions and concerns before embarking on any project steps. By engaging with the adult stakeholders within your school community you can begin your planning in full possession of the facts and with clearly defined boundaries for your project's scope and reach. It may well become apparent that not everything you would like to do is possible or realistic at that point in time, which may be frustrating, but knowing this up front and considering this at the start, will allow you to adapt and create something worthwhile and effective within the parameters you have been given.

## Perspective Gathering

Teachers, by our nature, training and skill set, are generally collaborative in our approach. We share ideas and plan together as departments, groups or the whole school. Collaboration is a skill we should intentionally develop in our pupils and is a recognised and effective method of teaching within our classrooms. When considering the planning of a new project or programme, the idea of collaborating with those around us, is as important as it is in any other educational context. Your team will have good, manageable and impactful suggestions and it's important you take the time you need to share and discuss those ideas. You could structure these idea and perspective-gathering sessions around a strategy such as De Bono's Six Hats technique (De Bon, 1985), where you consider a problem or idea in six different ways, to try and take your discussion beyond your initial positions and explore a range of different perspectives. By carefully considering each 'hat' you are less likely to make hasty or 'snap' decisions about the rights or wrongs of an idea or suggestion.

We have already said that the best way to gather buy-in from colleagues is to make them feel valued and respected as professionals, and the quality and value of the ideas they have are equally as important as their engagement. In many ways, the differing ideas of your colleagues are the most valuable resource you have. Unless you have all worked together in the same office since you all qualified from teacher training then the likelihood is that you will collectively have vast and varied experiences. Someone in your team may have already seen what you are envisioning in practice, or at least something like it. They may have read something or heard someone talk about exactly the idea that is floating around in your head. Their perspective of a potential problem may provide the breakthrough you are looking for, or the alternative option that was alluding you. Without doubt your project will benefit from the collaboration that comes with working alongside your team rather than without them.

**Six Thinking Hats** *(Edward De Bono, 1985)*

**Creativity**
Be creative in our planning, develop associative thinking and look for new ideas, brainstorming, think out-of-the-box

**Process**
Structuring your thinking, developing a high-level overview of the situation and looking at things from the big picture.

**Feelings**
Opinions, thoughts and feelings. How our emotions and personal experiences can shape our understanding of the world.

**Facts**
It's important to think in a logical and practical way, based on reliable information and what's possible to achieve.

**Benefits**
Thinking in an optimistic way, being speculative and identifying opportunities. Looking at the best-case scenarios.

**Cautions**
Critical, sceptical thinking that focuses on the risks, involved in our project and identifying any problems that could occur.

When we sit down with our department to brainstorm at the beginning of a project, we may not really know what we're planning on deciding or discovering. The conversations are likely to be quite broad and unstructured and that's okay. If we over plan those first brainstorming sessions, we might end up hampering the creative process. Obviously, some broad initial discussion points or questions will help to keep the conversation on track, but we don't want to guide the direction of the exchanges too much. What will certainly help the cohesiveness of your collaboration is the distribution of actions as outcomes of each meeting. Allocating individual tasks both lightens the workload on any one individual and encourages a positive buy-in culture within the department. As our plans begin to formulate, we can become more structured in our meeting plans and agendas to ensure we are focusing on the key aspects or decisions that need to be covered. There will be an increasing number of actions as the project progresses and we will want to become more formal in our meeting minutes and next steps to keep things moving forward. It is, however, always good to schedule some time during department meetings for a broader, more unstructured discussion on thoughts, reflections and findings.

## Changemaker Reflection: Charlotte Roxburgh
*2nd i/c PE, UAE*

### How to Manage Effective Meetings

Charlotte, like many of us have sat in countless departmental, phase, pastoral or whole school meetings. In her time in middle leadership roles, she has developed a framework and strategy for ensuring the meetings that she is running or involved in, are as effective as possible. For *Changemakers*, we asked Charlotte to summarise the main points that she believes help formulate effective and meaningful meetings:

**Before meetings**
- **Agenda:** These should be sent or shared beforehand and they should allow people the opportunity to plan/contribute if they have ideas.
- **Time:** Try to arrange your meetings so they are not seen as a chore or additional burden. It is often a luxury not to have to run meetings outside core working hours so try and ensure you are giving enough time, in as manageable chunk, as possible. The best solution is to secure an off-timetable slot each week to ensure everyone is available together.
- **Share Resources:** send any presentation slides beforehand, staff can note down any questions, rather than it be presented as new information during the meeting.

**During meetings**
- **Credit:** Always try and start meetings by giving credit and thanks to those who have contributed or if it is their idea. Also recognise the impact and effort that individuals have contributed since the last meeting. This is a great way to create positivity early.
- **Presenters:** Try to encourage different people to talk, not always the HoD or DoS, it should be those with knowledge/strengths on the topic.
- **Groups:** Find opportunities to break into sub-groups, allocate a spokesperson and contribute ideas to a shared document that everyone has access to.
- **Coffee/snacks:** Seems like a small thing, but little tokens of appreciation for using people's time/effort can go a long way to making individuals feel valued and respected.

**After meetings**
- **Actions:** Send out minutes and any notes, including using SMART targets and agreed actions/outcomes by specific people for a specific time. Get everyone to agree to them and commit to timeframes where possible.
- **Working groups:** Don't be afraid to create working groups for a specific area after the planning meeting, as most people leave a meeting feeling that most things won't be actioned and really are only 'blue sky' thinking.

Generally, we should try to keep meetings sharp and focused wherever possible. Whilst there is always a benefit to 'blue-sky thinking' type meetings, most of them should be concise/explicit and staff should know what is coming to the table before they arrive at the meeting. Combining prior and post meeting review/minute sharing will help keep your department on track, focused and working to your agreed timescales.

## Observing others

There are so many iterations of PE being delivered all over the world. Even within your local area there will be variations of every type on display. One of the best ways to experience the differing approaches to delivery and provide inspiration for your own project planning is to get out amongst your peers and observe. Obviously, you will need good connections to do this but most PE departments, and schools as a whole, are delighted to showcase their provision to interested parties. Often it can take as little as an email, social network connection or a phone call to organise an opportunity for you, or one of your team (or indeed more) to get in and spend some time in another department. Observe and reflect on what you see, discuss it with the department leaders and teachers and if you can, make some notes to take back and share with your team. Seeing things that could work within your context really helps establish your understanding and perception of your plans and there is a positive sense of comfort when you see something similar to what you do, or are planning to do, really working elsewhere. Remember though, context is key, and you cannot assume that replicating what you observe will work with your own school dynamic. Like every resource or piece of data, it's a starting point not a perfect fit.

You can also spread your observations wider than just schools like yours. Going to watch a different phase, a different type of school, a university ITE programme, a community physical activity provider, leisure centre, college or sports club can all offer the opportunity to discover little nuggets of ideas to take back and consider within your planning. Universities are a particularly important resource as they will usually be running community outreach programmes with local schools, many will have PE teachers within their ITE and Sport Science faculties and they are always, without fail, keen to work with practitioners who are trying to develop their offering. They may even have a project already in progress that would link well with your own one. It's certainly always worth a conversation with the lead lecturers or staff within the education departments of universities in your area.

Whilst time is always a precious commodity within departments, and the pressure to deliver your lessons and stay on top of all the other tasks that are required daily, the value of taking some time out to visit and observe others cannot be understated. If you have evolved a collaborative and supportive environment within your department and you have a team around you, pulling in the same direction, then it is always worth a bit of internal cover to allow members of your teams to get out into the wider community and gather some evidence and ideas to percolate into your own project plans.

## Networking and Collaborating

Just as with getting out and observing others, taking the opportunity to interact and engage with the huge volume of subject specific networking and development activity currently being offered, is a great way to develop your team's wider knowledge. Teams of PE specialists from schools, universities and private organisations are increasingly offering affordable and accessible CPD and conferences, often with practical and theoretical sessions, both online and face to face. It's a great chance to make connections, discuss your plans with others, seek advice from those who have already been through a curricular development project and obtain specialist knowledge from subject experts. Just remember that whenever you send a colleague on a CPD opportunity, or you go yourself, bring the knowledge and learning back to the department and share it with everyone. Often conferences and workshops will provide slides and handouts that will allow you to summarise and share your findings, spreading the impact wider and giving you ever more discussion points and potential aspects of provision to consider within your own project.

This is all before we investigate the huge volume of support and knowledge being shared across social media platforms. X formerly Twitter and LinkedIn are great starting points, as are subject specific Facebook groups, but there are also blogs and websites, podcasts and YouTube videos covering pretty much every variation of PE provision to tap into. Focused time spent online is not wasted in this context. Just remember to be specific in your searching and try to keep a track of your findings and where they came from so you can always refer to them. Making a resource/reference matrix tracking websites or social media posts, key words, brief overview and author is a relatively straightforward task that will really help you manage all your information as it builds up.

Wherever you go for external engagement, the positivity between the PE community is always exceptional. There will certainly be people willing to take time to discuss things. PE teachers love talking about PE and sharing their practice and ideas with others and if you can tap into that community, you can not only feed off the knowledge of others, but you can begin to support others going through similar change projects as well. It's always good to find someone or a few people in a similar position to your own department, who you can develop a professional relationship with, to obtain and provide some trusted support.

### Changemaker Reflection: Shrehan Lynch
*Senior Lecturer in Initial Teacher Education, University of East London & founder of Socially Just physical education & Youth Sport*

Change is something that is easily resisted. I am lucky that when I joined UEL, I was in a team of one, so I was able to create my own vision for the programme I wanted to run. I was heavily informed by my recently completed PhD and armed with academic reading to create the most research-informed PE PGCE programme I could imagine.

My focus was explicit and intentional, I wanted to help teachers understand the complexity of schools and that have an awareness of contemporary sociocultural issues. I want trainees to understand the hidden curriculum and how it being perpetuated in research-informed PE was essential. The programme had to have ample space for reflection to provide trainees with the tools and courage to carve their own philosophies toward education. It has always been a battle each year to challenge dated notions from trainees around traditional practices they have seen in school (continued recycling of sports or warm up, drill, game, lesson setups for example), but I have often found that when you present ample research that supports your ideas there are more open-minded responses. I aim to provide a consistent message; my philosophy, pedagogy, and practice aims to be aligned.

I practise what I preach, which is why I founded the Socially Just PE and Youth Sport project, a space that amplifies social justice work within the sector. The change work can be very easy when you believe in your own ideas.

My biggest tip for anyone starting out in making change is to be bold! Have your own departmental vision and ideas for your PE department, get your team on board by doing it together. Then, amplify your vision across the school: in school hallway displays, whole school meetings, infographics in the staff room, at parent/carer evenings and by your presence – think about what you wear and how you could have a logo on your PE kit that represents your vision. Live, breathe and represent the change you want to see. On the back of our t'shirts at UEL, I had 'Be the Change' imprinted onto our kit. This is a personal but also outside reminder of the aims of my PE programme at UEL.

Also, try to align yourself as a school with a university so you can share ideas and build a research-informed programme. You might also get some free CPD, which is always useful for tight school budgets! It is completely okay to push against the grain if you believe you are creating a better movement space for young people to flourish in PE!

# Chapter 8 - Let's Go!

## Getting Started With Project Implementation

*'Today was good. Today was fun. Tomorrow is another one.'*
*Dr. Suess*

It is possible that the process of getting to this stage has already taken significant time and energy, and you haven't even started the process of designing and developing your curriculum and certainly haven't got to the implementation stages yet. This next bit is the exciting stuff though, where all the hard work you've done to get here, starts to pay off in your provision. How you progress through the design and development phase and onwards to implementation, can be critical, if you are to achieve the goals you set out in your planning phase, so don't rush (however tempted you are) to embed things into lessons and get a half-finished curriculum plan up and running. Patience is your best friend now, and taking a bit longer to implement is not a negative, if the outcomes are all the better for it.

### Timescales

It is probably at this stage, if you haven't already done it, where timescales for implementation start to be discussed. Are you planning on getting going quickly at the start of a new term, or perhaps at the start of a new academic year? Knowing the timescales you are working to, will define the volume of work each team member will need to undertake and how much pressure you are willing to put on yourselves. There is no right or wrong timescale here, as you will select a timeframe that fits with your own context. Some of this will also depend on when you are starting this project. If you're well into the current academic year it might make good sense to plan for the start of the next academic year, using your remaining time to test and practise aspects of your new curriculum in isolation.

## CHANGEMAKERS

**Target market**

You will also need to decide who you are going to implement your new curriculum with. Are you going for all out total change or are you going to focus on a particular key stage or even with one year group. Do you have a plan to run some form of pilot or trial project so that you can get colleagues to experiment and then feedback their findings, to allow tweaks to be made before you go for a wider implementation? Are you going to start afresh with Year 7 or Year 1 (or your contextual equivalent) and let it flow through with those students, or are you aiming for a total overhaul, all in one go?

It's important to remember that curricula inevitably look different within different key stages or phases. To implement a cross-phase curriculum is a real challenge, as you are effectively having to design numerous programmes all at once. What will work in Key Stage 3 may not be applicable for Key Stage 4 or 5. Likewise your Key Stage 1 curriculum will be fundamentally different to your Key Stage 2 one. Whilst it can be very tempting to go all out at this, it is important to consider the volume of work involved and be sure that you can manage that process on such a large scale all at once.

(If you work in a region where Key Stages don't exist then please accept my apologies for my UK centric terminology. Obviously, you can translate this into your own context, but the principle remains the same. Trying to change everything all at once is obviously going to be a significantly larger and more challenging job than implementing piecemeal at a pace that works for you)

So, once you've made some decisions over who you are targeting and when you want to implement, you are ready to start with your curriculum development. This is, without doubt, my favourite part of the change process, as it allows your creativity to really come out. This is where all those ideas you've gathered and discussed are formalised into long term curriculum maps. Your new or improved schemes or units of work, activity plans, facility schedules, assessment processes, reporting structures and resource creation all happen at this stage. This is the time where you think of memorable acronyms or clear and impactful diagrams and logos, colour schemes and flow charts. This is where you test your ideas and see whether you can influence a change in your pupils and most importantly, this is where you can start to prove your plans are going to really benefit your classes. Remember, at every stage, you need to be thinking about things through the perspective of those pupils. Ultimately everything you are doing is supposed to benefit them, so as fun as it is to be creative, don't spend time doing things that are not going to directly impact the teaching, learning and engagement of your classes.

A major factor that will shape your project's progress will be the identification of exactly what type of evolutionary programme you are embarking on. There are many variations of a change management process within education, and knowing exactly what it is you are entering into will be influential to the approach you will take towards the project and its individual progress steps. In the next chapter we will explore, in more detail, the types of change management programmes that we may be considering and see if we can decide which one is most like your project plan.

### Reflective Questions - What are you doing?

- How would you explain your plans to a departmental colleague?
- How would you explain those plans to your Senior Leaders?
- How would you explain those plans to your pupils?

It can be a reflective exercise to either speak and record you answering these three questions or writing brief journal entries answering them. Taking the time to voice your thoughts and ambitions can really help you formulate a solid purpose that you can then 'sell' to your stakeholders.

**Remember:**
If you don't know your why and what, how will you explain it to anyone else?

## Changemaker Reflection: Louis Fearn
*Head of PE, NCBIS, Egypt*

Unexpectedly inheriting a PE and sport department in a post Covid slump with no fixtures or sporting competition for 2 years and a staff body that were enthusiastic and largely supportive, yet lacking direction presented both a challenge and an opportunity. Faced with a relatively clean slate to build upon but a lack of time in which to demonstrate impact, establishing clear aims for the department seemed the most pressing need. Being a firm believer in the power of people and knowing that an effective curriculum underpins all areas of an effective PE and sport department, I proposed the 3 pillars of focus of Participation, Performance and Student Leadership.

Having established the focus, it was important to gain staff 'buy in' and establish the 'how' elements for achieving the aims. Following some thought and consideration, the 2 elements ended up being solved in the same way. Collaboration.

Having shared the development aims, it seemed natural to involve the department in establishing the 'how'. As previously mentioned, I believe that curriculum is king and that an effective curriculum delivered by subject experts has an impact beyond pupil progress and development of skills and knowledge. Initially we looked at the curriculum and how we could tailor it around the 3 pillars identified above. It was decided as a team that whilst we would allow opportunities for 'Performance' within lessons, this would primarily be developed within our after-school provision.

This left a clear goal of developing 'Participation' and 'Student Leadership' within our curriculum provision. In addressing these goals, from a Primary Curriculum perspective, the decisions were taken to move away from a sport-based curriculum and focus on 'themes'. Within Secondary, a broad and balanced curriculum was developed allowing time for traditional sports but also 'alternative' activities with the hope that all students will find their element. The whole curriculum provision was underpinned by the Head, Heart, Hands (Frapwell, 2014) assessment model. Using Sports Leaders UK allowed us to offer accredited Sports Leadership awards across Primary and Secondary through the Playmaker Award and the Sports Leaders Level 1 and 2 awards.

Finally, the idea of expert delivery was one that stuck with me and with time at a premium, the problem of upskilling my team was once again solved through the idea of collaboration. Finding time for a weekly department meeting was vital and not wanting to waste this, I established a T&L10 programme aimed at developing teaching and learning based around Quality Assurance identified needs. The first 10 minutes of every meeting was set aside for the development of teaching and learning within the department. The focus ranged from Sport Specific aspects e.g. health and safety in gymnastics to pedagogical principles such as differentiation in PE. Involving the team in the delivery of these areas allowed for a sense of safety and collaborative development that has had a meaningful and noticeable impact on curriculum delivery.

Measuring impact is always challenging but in the past 12 months, the department has seen its highest ever IB Sport Science results and a GCSE uptake increase of 3 times the previous year. Whilst these are only indicators, they are signposts that the department is heading in the right direction.

# Chapter 9 - What Are You Doing?

## Implementation, Reform Or Transformation

**'If you don't like something, change it. If you can't change it, change your attitude.'**
*Maya Angelou*

'Any proposed change initiative must have a purpose: a 'why'. This purpose is typically a problem of practice, a challenging area of learning or need to change something that is interfering with progress toward a goal' (Meyer-Looze et al, 2019.). Regardless of the nature of the context in which change is being proposed, there are underlying observations or considerations that have led to the point at which change within our curriculum has been decided upon. It is likely that, in most cases, this is with the objective of developing more meaningful and beneficial opportunities for the pupils within our programme. It is critical that throughout the project ahead, we retain that sense of 'why' we are doing this. Ultimately every action or initiative should be conducted with the perspective of developing or enhancing opportunities for the pupils in our lessons and cohorts to flourish

Whilst there are immeasurable adaptations that occur on a constant basis within educational structures, be these pedagogical, logistical or organisational, there are, essentially, three types of change management projects within education. Implementation, reform or transformation. To keep things simple, we are going to focus specifically on the generic elements of these three approaches rather than delve into the theoretical intricacies of each variation.

## Types of change

|  | Implement | Reform | Transform |
|---|---|---|---|
| **Core Question** | Who does things better than us that we could adopt? | What can we improve within our provision? | How can we fix the things that don't work well? |
| **Purpose** | New approach | Change things for the better | Make existing things different |
| **Key driver** | Change to strategic approach | The need to transform the way we do things | Expanding on our existing provision |
| **Core actions** | Find something than works better than our existing provision | Create something that would change what we already do | Make improvements in our existing provision |
| **Approach** | Negotiation - what can we do differently? | Envisioning - how could we do it differently? | Mediation - what works and what doesn't? |

*Adapted from 'Achieving transformational change', Steve Waddell, 2019; www.i2insights.org*

## Implementation

Implementation is the adoption and embedding of a curriculum into our provision. Normally this curriculum structure is already designed, either internally created or externally acquired. When you purchase a curriculum framework or package from a provider and introduce it into your programme it's an example of implementation in practice. Bringing a pre-existing curriculum from a previous school or adopting the practice of a newly recruited member of the department is another example of implementation taking place. Implementing something that already exists can provide significant savings in terms of time and budgets and often is far less consuming than creating something from scratch. Often these 'off the shelf' packages will be evidence or research driven and offered by experienced practitioners or academics with proven track records of exploration and research into the specific approaches then delivered by their offerings.

This all sounds great in principle. Pay online, download the curriculum, distribute it out and off you go. However, as we have already discussed, the danger of implementing someone else's systems or strategies is that it could lead to the adoption of a generic approach that may not suit your pupil demographics. Often these packages are designed to cater for mass audiences and whilst they will work to an extent, the amount of work involved in adapting provision for each specific context, can be as much as designing your own bespoke programme from scratch.

## Changemaker Reflection: Anna Power
*Principal, BISR DQ, Saudi Arabia*

When opening a new school, there are many things to consider, especially when everything is new and in the early stages of development.

From the very beginning of our school's development, we understood the importance of creating a curriculum that would fit our unique context. We made sure to put our school and our future students at the centre of everything we discussed, created, and implemented. This was particularly important when it came to planning our curriculum.

The curriculum is at the heart of everything the school does. Learning experiences are essential in shaping the individuals in our care into the people we envision them becoming.

In an international school, teachers come with various skill sets and experiences from around the world, so it is important to be clear about the culture we want for our school. We need to focus on why, what, and how.

Knowing the culture, we want to create from the start and keeping the end goal in mind is crucial. Having resources and ideas that align closely with the long-term model we want to implement ensures that our efforts are not in direct contrast to what has already been established. Teachers work hard to create schemes of work, and having to change these can create frustration and unnecessary angst when significant effort has been put into establishing them initially.

We chose a planning template (Understanding by Design) that we knew we wanted to use in the long term. We trained teachers on how to use the template and understood that the more complicated elements would develop over time. We then developed certain areas over time.

Establishing a common language and systems is essential to ensure clarity for both teachers and learners. By establishing consistent terminology and processes, we can enhance communication and understanding within educational settings. This approach fosters a supportive and cohesive environment, ultimately benefiting our entire learning community.

We supported our teachers by providing significant time for planning and coaching them, so they felt supported in the curriculum design projects by the leadership teams.

Throughout the initial phases of our school's curriculum development, we made sure we always had a model of what we believed 'good' should look like. We worked with teachers using models that had elements that had been proven to be effective in the classroom. To do this, we had to first find the research that underpinned the value of these models we were potentially adopting, and as such, had to spend significant time researching them ourselves.

When we knew what we believed 'good' would look like within our context, we used these models to provide clear examples of best practices and guided teachers to develop appropriate instructional approaches through these models. By having these tangible examples to reference, our educators were better able to understand and implement the strategies and techniques that we believed would lead to positive outcomes for our students.

Finally, but no less importantly, was the critical consideration of 'the bigger picture'. We had to remember that while working on details and minor elements, we needed to retain our vision of what the whole school would look and feel like. We wanted to create a curriculum that didn't just contain a disparate set of subjects, but was joined up, thought through, and linked across every aspect.

## Reform

Throwing everything you have away and starting again is probably the most daunting thing a department could consider doing. The idea of a blank sheet of paper can seem exciting, but the practicalities of creating, from scratch, a new programme of study, whilst maintaining provision in the process, is something that most departments will not have the time, resources, budget or capacity to manage effectively. Even if you do manage to establish a plan to make this a reality the time involved in creation of a completely bespoke offering is often an unrealistic objective. The likelihood of you needing to completely replace everything you currently do is very low, and whilst it might seem like an opportunity to reinvigorate your provision, the complexity of doing so means that in almost all contexts it's both unnecessary and unproductive to do so.

Where this has been attempted, it often involves bringing external expertise or consultancy into the department to work with the team to shape and formulate the change. Whilst this will inevitably ease the pressure on the workload of individual teachers, the cost implications and the loss of ownership of the project means this is rarely adopted as an approach. Generally, with something as significant as a complete reform of your existing provision, the sense of ownership and control over the project objectives and progress is not something many of us would want to give away.

The most commonplace and likely scenario where this type of radical creative activity would take place, is within new or start up schools. When formulating the approach of a completely new department then you have no choice but to start with a blank sheet of paper. Whilst you will be guided by leadership over frameworks and curriculum structures, this is the one time when you can genuinely forget about what has gone before and focus solely on what you collaboratively believe your provision could look and feel like. New schools rarely open to full capacity and so the likelihood is that you will begin by designing the curriculum purely focused on the phases or year groups that you are going to have initially, with the intention to expand outwards as the school grows. Whilst this makes the process far more focused and manageable you are still going to need to consider the future growth and the transition points between sections of the school, at this point, rather than leaving it until you're just about to open a new section or year group up.

## Changemaker Reflection: Helen Battelley
*www.musicandmovement.org.uk, UK*

### Chase me, Chase me! Daily Mile in the Early Years
Jogging, running, or travelling fast on two legs…whatever you want to call it…the daily mile is a great way to increase the heart rate, invigorate mind and body and regulate the amygdala for focus and concentration. During my time as an Early Years PE teacher, I have seen The Daily Mile being delivered in unfavourable and unsustainable ways, resulting in low buy in and causing future negativity towards PE practice and physical activity engagement.

Young children love to run, their bodies are designed for such exertion. But many young children in schools are not engaging with such pursuits due to poor practice and delivery. The daily mile requires very little planning and research suggests, when delivered in a developmentally appropriate way, can be a great motivator for future efficacy in physical activity (Booth et al, 2022).

How can we engage nursery and reception children to run for 10-15 minutes every day?

When I walked into a school recently, the teacher and TA were 'telling' the children to run around the playground while they held their thermos flasks of tea – occasionally spouting out commands such as 'keep going', and 'you're nearly there'! The school had made the decision for The Daily Mile to add towards PE/Gross Motor PD time. I would argue this should be in addition to fun and engaging movement play supporting fundamental movement skills.

After a period of reflection, I delved into my tool bag of useful equipment and selected a lion's tail (the staple item for any early year's educator!)…I attached it around my waist and headed off in pursuit of the children…With a gigantic roar, I sped ahead of the group bellowing 'I am a lion, catch my tail, pull it off and I will wail'…immediately the children started running faster and giggling as they ran in an attempt to catch my tail! They were hot on my 'tail' for the last few minutes until finally we returned to the playground to line up. The children were still giggling and asking to play the Lion Game again!

When it comes to assessment in early years, we align to the Early Learning Goals of Physical Development, but it is also useful to be mindful of the national curriculum guidance for KS1 PE. Observing the children within the activity, I could identify the whole class were happy and engaged. Some of the children who initially may have been less inclined to participate were showing increasing levels of self-determination and intrinsic motivation. The efficacy of the activity was present in the resounding 'again, again' from the children. They demonstrated a competent use of space in avoiding each other, coordination in manipulating uneven terrain, teamwork in collectively working together to capture my tail! Further development of the activity may include selecting two or three children to be the lions, whether at the front to not be caught or at the back to chase their prey!

### Transformation

Far more likely than change or implementation, is the idea of transformation. Taking a reflective approach to your current provision and adapting it to enhance the experience and outcomes of your students, is almost always the approach that departments take when it comes to curriculum development. This approach is very broad however, almost like looking at it on a scale, where a significant volume of content is being replaced or renewed at one extreme, or very small, subtle changes are being made at the other. Your project will sit someone on this scale, if you already have something in place, and are not planning a complete curriculum replacement. A good way to look at the transformation approach is that it is a refresh of an existing curriculum, considering the evolving nature of your school and pupil demographics, and adopting the latest approaches and forming a research-led evolution of your curricular offering.

Transforming your existing curriculum is often the approach that requires the most early-stage planning, as you will need to explore what works and what doesn't before you identify the objectives of your project. You will need to do a significant amount of evidence gathering and research within your context to establish these parameters and whilst this exercise is a hugely beneficial one, the additional time will need to be considered when deciding when and how you will adopt your newly revised approach.

## Reflective Questions:
## Implementation, Reform or Transformation?

- What do you really like about your existing PE provision?
- What doesn't feel right to you?
- Are these things the same as the rest of your department feel - Do you all like different bits or are there some consistent themes about the aspects you dislike?
- Do you know what aspects your pupils like, and do these correlate with your own thinking?
- What approach do you think you need to take?

## Changemaker Reflection: Christopher Jackson
*Whole School PE Teacher, British International School Riyadh*

During my time leading a PE department, in Moscow Russia, it became completely clear that my PE curriculum was solely based on the sheer number of sports that I was able to offer. I was even commended during the ISI inspection for being able to offer 26 different sports across the whole school. While this inevitably produced good sports teams it was tunnel visioned with only one successful outcome - victory in external competitions. Students came and went as expatriate life happens and I was left with a dilemma - Am I truly helping the students in my care?

This led to some soul searching toward my 'Why'. Why did I become a PE teacher? Was it to win sports competitions, build up a catalogue of medals and trophies to show around or was it to be around a special group of children for which I can help form positive relationships and experiences for everyone?

Fast forward to my current school - British International School Riyadh where students are immersed into a Physical Literacy model. Pupils can develop skills that can help all of them become more physically active and be able to access fundamental movement skills.

While this approach has seen all students, not just sporty ones, excel I still have the same dilemma. What is my Why? My answer has come from experience of both curriculums and wishing to blend the ideas - Context plays a vital part into planning curriculums. Allowing for adaptive teaching models and the needs of all individuals has led me to firmly believe in providing a well-being first model that also develops and pushes contextual skills at the stage accessible to any student.

In short, context towards individual learning is key. How can I get pupils engaged with a love of movement while challenging and aiding them at any stage of their journey. This leads me towards the power of relationships in your classroom. PE teachers have long been hailed with a 'superhero' like ability to engage with students on their level. The reality is much simpler - opportunities, kindness and a willingness to engage provide a toolbox or your way in. It has long been stated by Ignacio Estrada 'if a child can't learn the way we teach, maybe we should teach the way they learn' (Gutierrez, 2014) while this remains ever clear I would argue a precursor to this statement to include planning the way they learn, avoiding a one-size-fits-all model at all costs.

Remember, teachers can change lives but also the ability to negatively affect them - take care with the students in your care and always fight for their best interests wherever your individual context leads you.

# Chapter 10 - Nuts And Bolts

## Curriculum Review - Turning Your Vision Into Reality

**'Great things are done by a series of small things brought together.'**
*Vincent Van Gogh*

This chapter is really the core of *Changemakers* and the key to formulating and delivering effective and meaningful change. In this section we will look at all the elements that you may need to consider when adapting, changing or reshaping your provision. Not every department or team will have, or need, every one of these elements, but they are all important to consider.

What follows will cover:

- Mission and Vision Statements
- Departmental Handbooks
- Curriculum Overviews
- Schemes or Units of Work
- Lesson Frameworks
- Lesson Plans
- Resources
- Risk Assessments
- Assessment Policies
- Assessment Trackers
- Feedback Policies
- Reporting Structures

It's a long chapter coming up, and obviously every version of a PE department's approach to each of these things will be unique to your school, but considering what you need and ensuring you have these things in place, will give your newly developed curricular provision substance, structure and hopefully long-term viability.

CHANGEMAKERS

## Changemaker Reflection: Phil Mathe
*Director of Sport, UAE*

I remember vividly, sitting at my desk in our department office, on Sunday at 7.30am. We'd just returned from our winter holiday and getting out of bed that morning had been a struggle due to the time difference between the UK and the UAE.

This precise moment had been a long time coming and now it had, I felt slightly overwhelmed by it. My team and I had spent a significant amount of time last term, planning and discussing how we were going to move our PE curriculum forward in the coming years, but now all the discussion and reflection had finished, the task of turning this into something concrete that we could use, really hit home.

Where to even begin? There seemed so much to do, all at once. Should we start by revising our mission and vision documents, our department handbook, our curriculum overview? Would the scheme of work for Term 1 be the right place to begin or should we look at assessment and how we were going to track exactly what we were going to achieve?

I knew that in a few moments, the team would begin coming in through the door and we would need to get ready for the teaching day ahead, but in this brief, quiet moment, I reflected on just how much work I had committed us to, on top of all the hard work they were already putting in. I knew they were as motivated by the project as I was, but even so, I felt the burden of pressure to make sure that we accomplished something meaningful and purposeful whilst maintaining our high standards of delivery in the meantime.

Whilst I had delivered projects within PE departments before, it never got any easier. I knew in my head where we wanted to get to, and what we would need to do to get there, but delivering on this vision was a whole different ball game. I think it was at this moment that I realised just how important planning out the project in front of us would be. If I was having these thoughts then the chances are the rest of the team would be feeling the same and if I was to maintain our focus and motivation, I would need to make sure that I was in control of the process, to allow them to focus on their areas of expertise. If I could demonstrate that I had things in hand, I knew they would pull it all together.

So, with a deep breath, I took out my pen, got a blank sheet of paper, and wrote my first PE project plan. I still have it today, as a reminder, of what can be accomplished, with a little bit of bravery, and a whole lot of organisation. I now look at it and think how simplistic and disorganised it appears, but at the time it was just the right first step, with its colour-coding and highlighted scribbles. I don't know if the people I worked with are aware that I kept it, but whenever I've had to think about a project since, I've looked back at where I started and smiled! A lovely reminder of how positive my experiences of project planning and delivery have been, and how much it's helped me grow.

---

Once you get into the actual change process itself you soon realise just how much there is to do. Even small or subtle changes have an impact and an effect on numerous different areas across our curricular provision and each of these aspects need to be considered carefully.

A well-crafted, well-integrated curriculum should look and feel cohesive and synergised and whilst the surface level consistency, colours, terminology and the like, can be relatively easy to accomplish, the deeper integration of different pieces can be harder to fit together.

So, let's look at each of those aspects in more detail. There's no way this can be a comprehensive list as each curriculum model will be contextual and unique, but we can use broad strokes to consider the key and commonplace components of a well-coordinated curriculum. Throughout this section I have included some examples from my own experience, to try and show what these might look like, but of course, there are a multitude of variations out there and I am sure you can find a variety of examples to help your own creation. It's also important to point out here that whilst you can see what we offered, in each of these contexts, it's not suggesting that your programme would or should look the same!

## Your Mission and Vision Statements

The first thing any department should do is discuss, reflect and generate a mission and vision statement that summarises what they offer, why they offer it and how they implement this in their activity. Often this sits at the front of a departmental handbook and on a school website's PE section, but it is much more than just words. It needs to reflect the attitude and approach that your department is going to shape all of its provision around. Everyone in your department needs to be involved in the creation of this in order to ensure complete buy-in from all your team and it needs to be present in every discussion that takes place around curriculum or students. A good way to keep this at the forefront of everyone's thinking is to create a tag or strap line or simple overarching statement sentence that you can display within your PE office or on the walls of your facilities. Refer to it regularly, check everyone's understanding and make sure that any new additions to your team are provided with it as soon as they are recruited. A well-written and clear mission and set of values can shape the entire atmosphere and attitude of not just a department but the whole school's approach towards physical education and movement.

The formation of this critical document can be done in many ways, but a good starting point is a discussion around your why? Why are you all there, doing what you are doing? What perspectives do different members of your department have when they are thinking about what they do as PE teachers and what values are most important to them? It is likely

# CHAPTER 10 - NUTS AND BOLTS

that whilst there will inevitably be subtle differences of opinion, on the whole you will have more similarities than differences and pulling everyone's values and perspectives together into a brief, succinct and powerful statement of intention will really help to focus your department's minds on why you are doing what you are doing, as well as supporting the consistency of approach and focus on the really important things within your curriculum. Ultimately there should be explicit recognition of the desired benefits for our pupils at the very heart of any vision, mission or value set we formulate as our foundational documentation.

**Junior School Physical Education – Delivery in Practice**

Junior School are provided with 2 Physical Education Lessons per week. The calendar for PE is:

| Half Term 1 | Physical Education | Swimming |
|---|---|---|
| Half Term 2 | Physical Education | Physical Education |
| Half Term 3 | Physical Education | Physical Education |
| Half Term 4 | Physical Education | Physical Education |
| Half Term 5 | Physical Education | Swimming |
| Half Term 6 | Physical Education | Swimming |

(Swimming will continue into Half Term 2 until it is too cold – normally around Mid/Late Oct)

The Junior School Physical Education programme combines a Games and Phys Ed focus together to form units of work with the titles:

"Movement, Problem Solving, Health and Fitness, Creativity, Leadership and Challenge"

There are a wide variety of ways in which each of these units of work can be delivered and will change depending on year group, class size and demographic of pupils. The schemes of work reflect this freedom to deliver and individual JS PE teachers will have the ability to adapt the programme of study to suit the needs of individual groups of pupils. The main objective of the JS PE curriculum is to develop a well-rounded and established set of fundamental movement skills and abilities and a deep routed enjoyment of physical activity and movement.

**Senior School Physical Education – Delivery in Practice**

The Senior School Physical Education year is split into 6 "phases of study" which generally match the schools calendared half terms. These 6 phases are broken down into 12 distinct "units of study". 6 of these are "PhysEd" and 6 are "Games". In practice this means that one lesson per week is "PhysEd" and one lesson per week is "Games".

The Categories of "Games Activities" are: **Field, Court, Net/Wall, Pool, Striking** and **Alternative**. Whilst there is a direct attempt to avoid using the word "Sport" when describing our curriculum, it is fair to surmise that these categories are linked to specific sporting activities:

| Field | Court | Net/Wall | Pool | Striking | Alternative |
|---|---|---|---|---|---|
| Football | Netball | Badminton | Swimming | Cricket | Dodgeball |
| Rugby (touch) | Basketball | Tennis | Lifesaving | Rounders | Orienteering |
| Gaelic Football | Handball | Table Tennis | Water Polo | Softball | Leadership |
| US Football | Benchball | Volleyball | Swim Fitness | Baseball | Other Activities |

The Categories of "PhysEd Activities" are: **"Movement, Problem Solving, Health and Fitness, Creativity, Leadership and Challenge"** These are specifically alighted with the 12 KI's that Physical Education teachers are looking to identify in pupils through their work.

These 6 activity areas are not linked to specific sports and can be delivered in any way that individual PE teachers wish.

There are 2 variations possible:

**Variation 1** – Keeping the **PhysEd and Games** lessons separate and delivering different activities/focuses in each. i.e. In lesson 1 (games) you could deliver Football and lesson 2 (PhysEd) you could deliver Problem Solving. This allows pupils to get 12 distinct units of study throughout the academic year

**Variation 2** – Combine the **PhysEd and Games** lessons into one unit of study but focus on different aspects in each of the two lessons. I.e. In lesson 1 (Games) you could deliver Football and lesson 2 (PhysEd) you would deliver Problem Solving through football. Whilst the activity is the same, the focus of the lesson and the assessment focus is different.

Individual teachers can choose the structure that works best for them, in any given phase of study. The Director of Sport will work with each teacher to understand how the 12 units of study are being covered and ensure full coverage across the year.

## Department Handbooks - 'Go-To' Or Gathering Dust?

The department handbook is a second critical document that needs to be formulated before any specific units or schemes of work are generated. Your handbook is your go to resource to constantly refer back to reflect on and update as you progress with your curriculum implementation. At its heart your handbook should form a clear and easy to follow guide to the approaches you take to everything that happens within your departmental spaces. Everything that happens during your practice should appear in your handbook and there should never (rarely) be a situation that arises that isn't considered in your handbook. Often, formulating one can require a significant time commitment, but the benefit of a comprehensive overview of all your policies and procedures cannot be underestimated. A great approach to your handbook is to design it so a non-specialist coming to work within or supporting your department could pick it up and understand it. Try to avoid too much subject-specific jargon and acronyms and avoid anything that could appear contradictory or confusing.

# CHANGEMAKERS

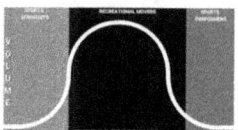

Distribution of workload can really speed up the process of putting your department handbook together and like most things in education a quick search of the internet or a reach out to your networks will probably find someone with a template or example to share. As with everything that you use from somewhere else though, it's a starting point and not an off the shelf solution but it can speed up the timescales significantly if you have a starting point to edit.

## Curriculum Overviews - Selling your vision

The first step of any curriculum remodel is the top-level overview of what you are going to offer, when you are going to offer it and to who. There are many different ways of creating curriculum overviews, some with more creativity and design than others. Essentially what you are creating is an easy to follow and simple guide to how your curriculum is going to flow during any given academic year. This could be through some form of roadmap or flow chart but equally could be a simple spreadsheet. The best approach is to think about how it would read to a pupil taking part in your provision or a parent trying to understand what their child may experience during the course of the year.

To create this important document however, you are first going to need to make some decisions on the approach you are going to take towards your provision. Will it be sport-

# CHAPTER 10 - NUTS AND BOLTS

driven with each half term or unit of work focusing on an individual activity or group of activities? Will it be concept-based with units of work focusing on more holistic aspects or another form of model? To make this important decision, you are first going to need to really take your time and explore the different options out there. It is likely that alongside this you are going to be considering how you are planning to assess your pupils' progress and it would make good sense to consider appropriate types and approaches to assessment at this stage, even if you aren't going to design your actual assessment documents and procedures at this stage.

There are many good examples of curriculum overview designs available with a quick internet search, however you will need to carefully consider many of the factors you discussed previously with your department during your brainstorming sessions to be sure that you are creating a cohesive programme that all your department buy into and feel equipped and motivated to follow. It is very likely that this process will take several reiterations and

**Lesson Structure**

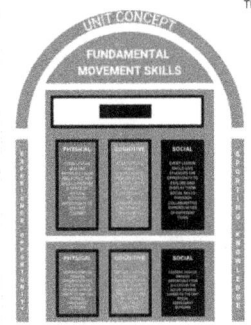

The lesson planning model for The School's PE is designed to be as flexible as possible to allow individual PE teachers to creatively develop lesson plans and schemes of work that focus specifically on individual students and individual teaching classes. Rather than utilising a prescriptive lesson planning template the image to the left attempts to show how the lesson should be structured and what constituent parts should make up a typical School PE lesson. This is a framework rather than a descriptive structural requirement and as such individual teachers are free to develop lessons in their own way.

The key elements expected in a typical School PE lesson are:

Clear and concise reference to the overall unit of enquiry or topic. This can be in the form of a learning objective or 'big question' and could be present on a display to lead learning during the lesson

Clear link to a Fundamental Movement skill or set of skills underpinning the entire lesson or series of lessons. This should come from the 12 FMS guides as set out in the curriculum overviews for phases and linked to the success criteria for the lesson and for the wider unit of enquiry. Consideration should be given to how this FMS frames the entire lesson and critically every lesson should beactive by designwith the majorityof the lesson set aside for movement based activity.

There should be regular reference back to the Schools motto and pillars ensuring students are regularly reminded of the importance of the wider holistic frameworks operating within the school

A typical lesson will have aspects of active learning that support the development of the three assessment strands, Physical, Cognitive and Social. Lessons should attempt to impact development in all three of these areas and utilise specific terminology to underpin the development in all three areas. It is okay if lessons only provide learning opportunities in two of these areas however thePhysicaldomain should always be present.

The lessons can be framed by two alternative development mechanisms to suit the individual teacher or unit being taught. Lessons can either be structured to provide sporting knowledge or through opportunities for physical experiences. It is not a requirement of The School's PE curriculum framework for 'Sport' to be delivered although it is deemed to be an appropriate vehicle for delivery in some circumstances. Units of work should not focus solely on the development of sport specific skills and should not be delivered entirely through one activity or sport.

**Assessment in Core PE**

**Junior School**

Assessment in junior school PE is based around two strands, Physical and Conceptual.

Physical links to the fundamental movement skills associated with each unit of work. These can be seen on the diagram on the right. When assessing pupils these should form the primary indicator of level and progress.

Physical  Conceptual

Conceptual assessment links to the overall unit outcomes as provided for each year group. These are Personal, Social, Cognitive, Creative, Applying Physical Skills and Health and Fitness. Each unit of study should link to one of these areas and formative assessment of pupils should relate to these individual concepts. For greater detail on the assessment criteria for each unit, please refer to the unit planners on the website.

**Data Tracking**

Half termly data tracking should be undertaken for each year group, on the departmental data tracker:

https://docs.google.com/spreadsheets/d/1POGVNpLRHt0gaYhQmGKme3zW0IHWkpTx81mDz3Dmo/edit#gid=0

allowing individual pupil progress to be tracked during the course of a year. The departmental tracker for junior school will provide evidence of pupil progress and should be used to form the basis for reporting cycles.

Data should be entered against the whole junior school criteria of:

**Working Towards**

**Expected Level**

**Greater Depth**

However the RealPE assessment criteria areEmerging, Expected and Exceeding

Therefore, for the purposes of reporting the following should be used when translating the terminology to be used:

Working Towards = Emerging, Expected level = Expected, Greater Depth = Exceeding

# CHANGEMAKERS

redesigns whilst you tinker with the makeup of your curriculum plan. Facility availability, staffing levels and other commitments of staff, timetabling restrictions and equipment are just some of the things that are going to influence your planning at this stage, as will the volume and makeup of your pupil cohorts. Whilst it's a great ambition to deliver whole-year group units standardised across your timetable, large schools or schools with limited facilities may not be able to achieve this, and this will mean you will need to think about how you structure your curriculum to ensure equity and balance of provision for all.

**Middle School (IMYC)**

Assessment at Middle School (IMYC) level should follow the structure as set out by the IMYC curriculum across the wider senior school.

The PE curriculum provides assessment opportunities across Physical, Cognitive and Social domains within the framework provided by the individual unit of enquiry. There is also an opportunity to assess on the affective domain through reflection related to the framework across the wider school.

Each year there are 5 units of enquiry delivered to specific year groups. These can be viewed to the left. Each unit has been allocated an activity thread to provide structure and balance to the physical activity offered during the course of each year, however this is to be used as guidance only and individual teachers are encouraged to plan activities that provide the most meaningful experience for each class.

These units will remain static for the coming academic years allowing for structured planning and schemes of work to be created.

Individual lesson planning should use the lesson structure set out above, in order to ensure consistency across different year groups.

The assessment grades for IMYC are:

| YEAR 7 | | YEAR 8 | | YEAR 9 | |
|---|---|---|---|---|---|
| DISCOVERY | ATHLETICS | CURIOSITY | GAMES | IDENTIFY | ATHLETICS |
| ADAPTABILITY | GAMES | COURAGE | ADVENTURE | CHALLENGE | ADVENTURE |
| CREATIVITY | MOVEMENT | COMMUNICATION | ATHLETICS | DEVELOPMENT | CHALLENGE |
| CONSEQUENCES | HEALTHY LIFESTYLES | RELATIONSHIPS | MOVEMENT | INTERPRETATION | HEALTHY LIFESTYLES |
| BALANCE | ADVENTURE | TRADITIONS | HEALTHY LIFESTYLES | ENTREPRENEURSHIP | CREATIVITY |

| Beginning | Developing | Mastering | Innovating |
|---|---|---|---|

(We do not use innovating unless in specific circumstances within discussion with the HOD)

Which are reflected on all reporting systems and reporting cycles throughout KS3.

| Name | Form | Gender | SEND | UNIT 1 | | | UNIT 2 | | | UNIT 3 | | | UNIT 4 | | | UNIT 5 | | | UNIT 6 | | |
|---|---|---|---|---|---|---|---|---|---|---|---|---|---|---|---|---|---|---|---|---|---|
| | | | | P | C | S | P | C | S | P | C | S | P | C | S | P | C | S | P | C | S |
| Example | 7Y | M | None | D | D | M | D | M | M | D | M | D | M | D | M | M | M | D | M | M |

The data tracker from IMYC provides the opportunity to enter grades across three strands of PE at the end of each unit of work (usually half terms) using the assessment grades. The three compulsory assessment strands for IMYC are Physical, Cognitive and Social. Descriptions for each of these can be found at the end of this document.

Teachers are encouraged to enter grades at the end of each unit of work in order to track progress across each of the three assessment domains. Moderation between teachers in individual year groups will be undertaken wherever possible to ensure consistency and robustness in assessment and grading.

It is also at this stage that you will need to make decisions about things such as gender balance, appropriateness of activities and your general approach to fair and inclusive provision for every pupil. Anyone who has read other work I have done will know that I genuinely believe that inclusive and equitable provision for all is a must for PE departments in today's modern educational systems. It's so important to ensure that every pupil, regardless of gender, learning need, physical ability or any other individual need or consideration is offered the most appropriate and equitable access to meaningful, high-quality provision. What this actually looks like in practice will be up to your individual department to decide but you are going to have to make some important decisions about how important equity of provision, gender neutrality and inclusiveness is within the context of your curriculum offer. Often this is an ever-moving goal and it's okay if you make this an ongoing project to consistently review and improve but from the outset you must be considering the needs and requirements of every individual pupil with your strategic-level planning.

Finally, at this point you are going to want to consider whether every pupil within a PE class or cohort receives the same experience within your PE provision, or whether you are going to look to individualise your provision to meet the needs of differing groups of pupils. There is a growing volume of PE departments using pathway-style models to offer different experiences based on the type of experience you think they need, or your pupils ask for. Pathways offer a great opportunity to provide more meaning for pupils within their PE lessons but do require significant planning and thinking to ensure each group is experiencing not just quality provision but the most appropriate and effective provision. It's no longer acceptable to give the 'sporty kids' a more effective experience and let the 'less sporty' kids just coast through PE without challenge or positivity. If you do decide to explore the use of pathways there are excellent examples of it in practice as well as models you could consider adopting, some of which have utilised significant general educational and PE specific pedagogical research to formulate their structure. Yet again though, I must remind you of the running theme here that these are starting points, and you will still need to adapt anything you use, to suit the specific needs of your pupils.

## Schemes or Units of Work - What We Do

Once you have your curriculum map in place and you know what, how and to whom you are delivering across your academic year, you can start working on your individual units or schemes of work. Again, there is a vast array of approaches to this in place around schools globally and you will need to find one that works for you. Once upon a time, these mid-tier documents would set out lesson by lesson what should be delivered, in an attempt to replace the need for individual lesson plans, however in many examples today these unit plans have evolved into more holistic overviews, identifying the broad scope and breadth of a unit of work, and clarifying the learning objectives, outcomes and approach but leaving individual delivery pathways to teachers, encouraging creativity in approach to teaching. What is important in your unit plans is the explicit inclusion of information that a teacher would need to effectively deliver the unit for the first time.

**CURRICULUM 22/23**

- Field Games
- Court Games
- Athletics
- Swimming
- Striking and Fielding
- Net/Wall Games

CHANGEMAKERS

Developing a strong work plan is key for effective teaching and learning and will really support curricular alignment by making sure your unit plan addresses all pertinent curricular goals, objectives, and learning outcomes that you set out in your more strategic documents.

Your schemes or units of work will recognise the specific location of the learning within the wider curriculum plan. It will help teachers understand what prior knowledge has been accomplished by pupils and good unit planning will help to prevent knowledge/understanding gaps and will help develop flow within your curriculum rather than providing stand alone or siloed learning.

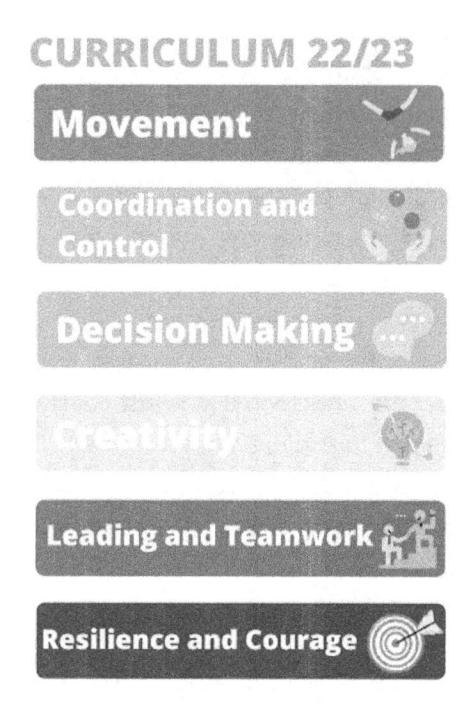

You want to ensure that your scheme/unit of work contains the following as a bare minimum:

- A clear summary of the topics that will be covered and how these link to prior learning, subsequent learning and the wider syllabus
- Allusions to the concepts or activities to be delivered during that unit of work
- Identification of equipment/facilities/resources required to effectively deliver this unit of work
- Suggestions or guidance of potentially effective ways to teach the unit of work and the key teaching/learning points.
- Clear identification of how inclusiveness and support has been considered to ensure all learners make progress and gain meaning from the unit
- A guide to how success will be identified during the delivery of the unit of work
- Alternative activities in case of disruption to unit progress (weather, absence etc)
- You will also want to include a brief explanation of how you plan to evaluate the success of your instruction. You will need to plan for efficient evaluation techniques to track development and pinpoint areas in need of improvement to link the unit to subsequent ones.

Whilst not necessarily required and it will extend the amount of time it will take to make your unit plans, there are some other things you might want to include within a good unit plan:

- Where are the opportunities for departmental cooperation and collaboration? How will your department work together to exchange knowledge and create a curriculum that flows. Do you need to build in collaborative planning guidance/requirements into your planning here?
- Clarity on how you will regularly evaluate the scheme's efficacy and provide guidance as to how you will make any necessary adjustments to improve its suitability and effectiveness as well as how you will consider any evolving requirements within your classes, cohorts or school.
- Any important professional development ideas or suggestions to support the delivery of this unit. Signposting to good online resources to help support the delivery and develop your teachers make for a useful additional inclusion. It is always good to explicitly identify how you are going to help your colleagues advance their teaching, as well as your own, and as a team you should always be looking for possibilities to encourage professional growth. Anyone looking at your schemes of work externally will be impressed by the inclusion of this for certain!
- Space for comments and feedback to allow for improvement. Ultimately the effectiveness of a unit of work is only proven once it is delivered to a few different cohorts or groups and consistent feedback opportunities will help identify possible areas for improvement. Encouraging this critical feedback will also help your department colleagues feel they have an ongoing voice in the development of your provision.

But beyond this these plans can be designed to fit in with the wider school approach to unit/topic planning and your school will have its own policies, procedures and documents to guide you through this stage.

**Lesson Structure Framework**
Creativity in teaching is critical if we are going to develop and redevelop learning opportunities that are effective, meaningful, inclusive and positive. Allowing teachers to be creative with their lesson planning is crucial and will have benefits for both pupils and teachers alike. Teacher autonomy will support increased engagement and motivation as

creatively designed lessons are more engaging and motivating for our pupils, which in turn may support deeper learning and improved retention.

While encouraging teacher creativity is essential, having some form of lesson structures within PE departments is important if we are to drive consistency and quality of provision at all stages. This is particularly important for departmental leaders who are accountable for evidencing quality of teaching and learning.

Whilst this does not need to be a significantly time-consuming task, it is important to do this before starting the lesson planning process. Often this will form part of your department handbook so any newly arriving member of the team can easily refer to the structures in which they are being expected to function. Within your lesson framework should be the following considerations:

Justification: A structured approach helps ensure all teachers are working towards a shared vision for the physical education program and they understand the framework in which PE is delivered within that context. This can be as little as an extension of the departmental vision statement but should allude to what the 'look and feel' of any PE lesson should be. Are they all very movement heavy or should there be structured 'down' time where discussion/reflection takes place? Do all lessons start the same way, so any PE teacher could take any group and the pupils would know what the structure of the lesson would be like?

How do individual lessons align with the wider curriculum? Are there specific requirements in terms of recap or recall of prior learning. Do we use written tasks within PE or is everything physical? Structured frameworks will help to ensure every lesson is aligned with the wider teaching expectations and learning outcomes.

From a curriculum leader perspective, it is important we have a framework in which teaching takes place, for quality control purposes. It is difficult to judge the effectiveness of teaching and learning if there is not some form of consistency across different lessons. This could be at year group, or phase level or could be standardised across a whole school. Whilst we do not want to stifle individual creativity, if there are consistencies in delivery it makes the quality assurance process a much easier and more meaningful task.

From a teacher's perspective, a framework within which we all operate helps build a sense of fairness and equity within our teams. If we are all working in similar ways then the difference between lessons and groups should be less, leading in turn to a more balanced timetable and teaching schedule for all. Structure also helps us to ensure all our pupils have generally equitable access to high-quality physical education experiences. It reduces the likelihood of individual teachers diverting wildly away from the standardised approach, increasing the likelihood of consistency between groups and helping the formation of a sense of balance and equity for all.

A teaching and learning framework also promotes collaborative planning. When we are all working in roughly the same way it becomes easier to share best practice, enhancing the learning experiences for all our pupils. When one teacher has established something that really works within a particular class, it is much more likely to work in another, when the framework of teaching and learning is consistent across all groups. It also means we can provide professional development that is more tailored and meaningful to all our departmental members, when we know they are normally teaching in the same way and using the same pedagogical framework within their lessons.

A teaching and learning framework can lead to huge time saving when considering the creation and distribution of resources and materials. Even if individual lessons are not identical, if we know there are standard practices running throughout our provision, we are far more likely to be able to share resources or teaching/learning tools across different classes. The same can be said for assessment. When we know that certain frameworks and approaches are being consistently adopted, we can be assured that any assessment structures are likely to be effective across the board.

Working within a standardised framework makes the management of time and teaching resources much easier. We can swap teachers, cover each other, peer mentor, team teach and more, in the knowledge that generally the approaches we are taking within our lessons are aligned. It reduces the likelihood of 'wasted' learning, when a teacher is absent and someone else covers them, when we know what the lesson should look and feel like. Picking up a lesson plan from an absent teacher becomes a far less confusing and frustrating experience when we already know what that lesson will look and feel like.

Structured frameworks will help us all as teachers to use our time effectively and efficiently. We can use templates and pre-existing examples without having to re-create everything to suit the structure in which we teach. It also helps us manage our facilities and resources more effectively, provide structure for team meetings, professional development events and line management activities. It gives us a clear guide on how we are approaching teaching and learning that we can pass on up the chain of command and it means the teachers within our departments can be sure that those accountable for ensuring our leadership teams are well informed, are passing on the right information and representing our department in accurate and consistent ways. It also means when staff change or departments evolve, a standardised structure remains, making the task of inducting new members of the department much easier and more effective.

When we consider our pupils different learning needs and the importance of inclusive approaches, the consistent application of lesson frameworks is critical. Pupils respond better to structure within their learning, especially so for certain groups of learners with particular needs. The implementation of a standard framework helps provide structure and understanding to our lessons that in turn helps many of our pupils understand and manage their expectations. Do you have certain rules that apply across every learning situation, regardless of environment or topic? Do we have assurance that all our teachers approach their lessons in similar ways, allowing our pupils the emotional security of knowing they will be viewed, treated, assessed and recognised in similar ways, by any teacher within our department? Structured plans can be adapted to accommodate different learning styles and abilities, structure can help facilitate the provision of targeted instruction, to meet the individual needs of all students and structures can help to track our pupils progress and ensure that they are meeting their full potential.

There is nothing worse for a pupil than arriving at a lesson not knowing what to expect from the teacher in charge. Consistency brings a sense of comfort and belonging that is critical if we are genuinely attempting to create safe, inclusive, personally welcoming spaces for our pupils in which they all believe they can flourish. Can you build this into your framework to better ensure this is consistent across your whole provision?

Finally, when we look at data collection and analysis, of which there are increasing volumes and requirements, the consistent approach to delivery and assessment means the data we collect is more valid, more consistent and more meaningful. When we analyse class or group progress, we are doing so within a structure that helps support the assurance that all our pupils are being given the same learning experiences and assessment opportunities across our whole cohorts.

# CHAPTER 10 - NUTS AND BOLTS

Whilst learning frameworks are important, (and increasingly so, as we aim to provide more individualised learning experiences within our lessons), it is critical to remember that these structures should not be overly rigid or inflexible. We need to develop the frameworks in which we are asking our teachers to operate, in such a way as to promote creativity within them. We are not looking to create rote teaching or teaching to a standard set of lesson plans but supporting creativity by developing a shared set of guidelines within which teaching takes place. It might be that in your department there are only a few loose guides, or maybe you set out with a much more rigid set of procedures, as your team adapts to a new curriculum or school. Teachers should, however, still have the freedom to adapt and modify plans to meet the specific needs of their students and context. Ultimately, by providing an agreed teaching and learning framework it should become a 'go to' for all colleagues giving valuable support and guidance. Done well, it can ensure consistency and accuracy of approach, support pupil and staff wellbeing and provide a clear sense of inclusivity, comfort, safety and cohesiveness. So, 'how will I know it's working?' you may say…by seeing improvements in your students' motivation, engagement and outcomes.

### Lesson plans?

In 2021, Stephen Singer said 'Lesson Plans Are a Complete Waste of Time'. He went on to say that whilst personal, idiosyncratic and informal planning is important and effective, formal lesson planning is simply 'busy work' that often has nothing to do with what actually happens within our classrooms and sports halls.

Whether you adopt this viewpoint or not, it is arguable that time consuming and well-designed lesson plans are rarely followed. (Iqbal, et al. 2021) This is particularly clear in the case of physical education where, in my 20 or so years of PE teaching, I can probably count on one hand the number of lessons outside of NQT practice or observations, that I've seen a teacher with a lesson plan in their hand.

The reality is that lesson planning is a contentious area and one that you will need to reflect on and come to some agreements of thinking about, as a department. It may be the case that you work within a context where formal lesson planning is still a requirement of all teachers, but increasingly I think this is an outdated practice not adopted by many leadership teams.

It is critical however, that personal planning still takes place. There can be no argument that planning your lessons and the flow of lessons within a unit is critical if we are to ensure the consistency, accuracy and effectiveness across our provision. How you go about this though, is really up to you as a department to decide.

It could be the case that with a strong and clearly defined curriculum plan and an effective and consistent lesson framework, individual lesson plans simply aren't needed, although the process behind lesson planning will always have an important place in our lesson preparation. There are not enough words left in this book to go through all the different approaches to lesson planning that exist. Every school has its own approach, and many have templates and terminology that teachers are required to adhere to, so it would be fruitless to try to cover all of them. There are, however, some key reflection points that we should go through when considering the planning of our lessons. As always, this is better done in collaborative, cohesive ways and I am a strong advocate for team level planning wherever possible. Whilst not always viable, collaborating in planning with the other teachers, makes for a more effective and enjoyable experience than planning a unit of work all on your own.

If you have gone through the previous steps, creating a shared vision, a curriculum map, a framework for teaching and learning and unit overviews or schemes of work, planning individual lessons should not be the most time-consuming task in your project. It's also something that does not necessarily have to happen before commencement of a new curriculum offering. The most effective curriculum implementation I have been involved in, was a project that took a whole academic year to embed, and we created the lesson plans and schemes of work a term ahead of delivery. This allowed us the time we needed as a department to reflect on what we were offering at that stage, what lessons we were learning and how we could implement those ideas and improvements into the next unit that we were in the process of creating. By the end of the year, we had built a completely bespoke curriculum ready to be rolled out all over again.

The biggest thing about lesson planning is to discuss it with your teams. Whatever your approach and structure, you need to ensure everyone is clear and collaborative towards their lesson planning. If it's formal and documented then it is important that everyone is complying, to create a supportive and equitable working environment. There is nothing worse for the cohesiveness of a department than a sense that not everyone is doing the same thing or to the same level of detail. Whilst it may be the case that some teachers, especially well-established and experienced ones, do not need the formal process of writing down their lesson plans, the sense that everyone is undertaking the same tasks and committing the same amount of time and energy to something, is important if you are to really build a collaborative atmosphere within your team.

Your lesson planning should be viewed as a positive process, within which you are able to really explore and reflect on the creative potential of teaching. When we consider collaborative lesson planning it should be an opportunity to explore different perspectives and approaches and share good ideas and great practice. What have you seen work really well within a particular unit or topic? Can you create new ways of delivering things that consider not just the specific requirements or opportunities within a group of pupils, but the shared experience of a group of professional teachers with diverse backgrounds and knowledge? If you can enter into the process of lesson planning with this goal and attitude, then the process becomes a much more reflective and enjoyable one. Actively encourage your teams to do this together during their allocated planning time, with the support of departmental leaders, rather than as individuals sat alone in the evenings, feeling more pressured.

### Resources

Once we know what we are delivering and how we are going to deliver it, the collaborative process of creating resources becomes a relatively straightforward one. With the vast range of creative tools available to teachers today, creating high quality, relevant and professional looking resources is no longer the significant time-consuming task it once was. Add into this the fast-paced development of AI tools, and creating resources can now prove a relatively easy task. It is important however, that the resources are, at their heart, supporting and developing the learning of pupils, otherwise we could argue they are simply another time consumer.

Ask yourself what resources or additional prompts your pupils really need to get the maximum learning opportunities from lessons and start with those. Whilst colourful posters and wall displays are nice and often enhance the sense of positivity within your teaching environment, the creation of those should never detract from the time available to enhance teaching and learning.

If you are creating resources for use in your department's teaching and learning, make sure they adhere to your mission and vision. Think about the approach you are taking to PE within your context and make sure your terminology and message is emphasised and communicated effectively throughout. For example, I once saw a department that emphasised inclusivity and equity for all, but then displayed posters of famous sporting icons, with only male performers on them. Is this really in line with the message they were trying to communicate to their pupils?

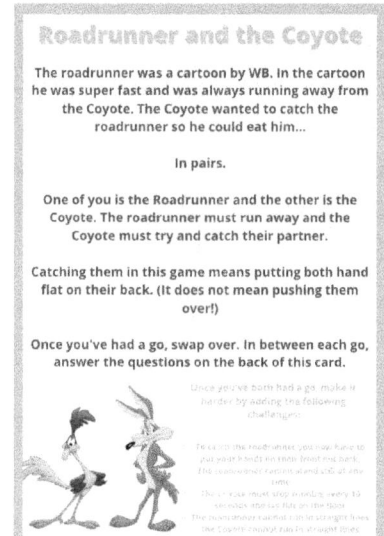

Consistency is key here, as coordinated use of language and imagery can really support the sense of inclusion within your teaching. For example, if you are using the dual coding approach, try and remain consistent with your imagery to reinforce certain aspects of your messaging. If you have an image or design that represents communication, then make sure all your resources consistently use the same image, to really reinforce the message that communication is something you are looking for within your lesson structure. The purpose of dual coding is to help with the information retention within your pupils and by using differing images to represent something, you are confusing the message. As with everything, collaboration within departments is key here, helping to coordinate and create consistency in approach.

Another great tip is to think about the relevance of imagery in your resource creation. If you are displaying a group working together on a task or activity, can you use an image of pupils from within your school doing this, rather than an abstract one from the internet? The relevance of pupils similar to those observing the resource, cannot be underestimated. Think about getting your own image bank to use in resources and really reinforce the message that this is something you want pupils to do, and show them examples of their peers actually doing it. Again, you need to think about the inclusive nature of imagery here as well and make sure that all your pupils, regardless of who they are as individuals, can feel a connection and  identification with the images they are viewing. Always consider the diversity of all the children you teach and therefore any imagery or displays you create will need to recognise this. When done well, displays can really enhance the inclusive message you are trying to present, but when done without care and thought, they can potentially put-up barriers to receiving the positive messages you intend to communicate to your pupils.

Delivering PE within the connect, IT-driven world our pupils exist in, means we must consider our electronic resources as much as our hard copy ones these days. We have a host of useful technological tools available to us to enhance and extend our teaching, but as with all resources, we need to consider how and why these are being introduced into our lessons and the positive impact they are having on our pupils' learning experiences.

As a rule, if the technology provides a positive cost-to-impact balance in your opinion, then it is worth pursuing as a potential tool. Be aware though, that many digital resources can seem beneficial on the surface, only to end up obsolete due to subscription cost, the steep learning curve and time taken to teach to pupils and the impact it can have on movement time within lessons. A great example of this is the use of fitness trackers which on the surface can provide an interesting and positive dynamic and yet when you actually try to implement them into your lessons can actually present more challenges

# GAMIFICATION IN PHYSICAL EDUCATION

GAMIFICATION IS THE APPLICATION OF GAME-LIKE ELEMENTS TO NON-GAME CONTEXTS. IN PHYSICAL EDUCATION, GAMIFICATION CAN BE USED TO INCREASE MOTIVATION, ENGAGEMENT, AND LEARNING.

MOTIVATION IS A KEY POINT TO ACHIEVE SUCCESSFUL LEARNING (RYAN & DECI, 2017)

WHEN REWARD IS INTRINSIC TO THE GAME IT HAS A GREATER IMPACT ON INTRINSIC MOTIVATION, WHILE REGARDLESS OF WHETHER IT IS MORE TANGIBLE OR EXTERNAL, IT AFFECTS EXTRINSIC MOTIVATION (RYAN & DECI, 2000, HANUS & FOX, 2015)

GAME BASED LEARNING AND GAMIFICATION IS SIGNIFICANT AS A LEARNING METHODS DUE TO ITS IMPACT ON STUDENT MOTIVATION, ACADEMIC PERFORMANCE, AND COMMITMENT TO IMPROVING HEALTH AND PHYSICAL PERFORMANCE (CAMACHO-SÁNCHEZ ET AL, 2023)

A SYSTEMATIC REVIEW OF 11 STUDIES FOUND THAT GAMIFICATION WAS ASSOCIATED WITH IMPROVEMENTS IN MOTIVATION, COMMITMENT, AND ACADEMIC PERFORMANCE IN PHYSICAL EDUCATION.

GAMIFICATION IS CHARACTERISED BY APPLYING SOME GAME ELEMENTS IN NON GAMING CONTEXTS (DETERDING, 2011)

## ISN'T PE ALREADY GAMIFIED?

GAMIFICATION IS ABOUT APPLYING GAME MECHANICS IN A NON-GAME SPECIFIC ENVIRONMENT.

WHILST ASPECTS OF VIDEO GAME DESIGN/STRUCTURE/LAYOUT CAN BE USED TO 'GAMIFY' AN ACTIVITY OR LESSON, GAMIFICATION IS OFTEN CONFUSED WITH UTILISING 'GAMING TECHNOLOGY' IN PE. THIS IS DIFFERENT. AS PERFECTLY POINTED OUT BY @MRANDERSENPE 'A QUICK GOOGLE OF "GAMIFICATION IN PE" WILL LEAD YOU TO VARIOUS ARTICLES AND BLOGS TALKING ABOUT APPS, THE NINTENDO WII AND SUCH INNOVATIONS'

## 5 POSSIBLE STARTING POINTS

1. SET UP A POINT SYSTEM AND START ASSIGNING POINTS FOR COMPLETING TASKS. THIS WILL GIVE STUDENTS SOMETHING TO WORK TOWARDS AND TRACK THEIR PROGRESS. YOU CAN USE A SIMPLE POINT SYSTEM, OR YOU CAN GET MORE CREATIVE WITH IT BY CREATING DIFFERENT LEVELS OR CHALLENGES THAT STUDENTS CAN WORK THROUGH.

2. PROMOTE HEALTHY COMPETITION WITH LEADERBOARDS. THIS IS A GREAT WAY TO MOTIVATE STUDENTS TO WORK HARDER AND IMPROVE THEIR SKILLS. YOU CAN CREATE A LEADERBOARD FOR THE ENTIRE CLASS, OR YOU CAN CREATE SEPARATE LEADERBOARDS FOR DIFFERENT ACTIVITIES OR GROUPS OF STUDENTS.

3. ASSIGN BADGES & AWARDS. THIS IS A GREAT WAY TO RECOGNISE STUDENTS FOR THEIR ACHIEVEMENTS. YOU CAN CREATE YOUR OWN BADGES OR AWARDS, OR YOU CAN USE A PRE-MADE SYSTEM LIKE CLASS CRAFT.

4. CREATE A MISSION WITH AN OBJECTIVE. THIS WILL GIVE STUDENTS A SENSE OF PURPOSE AND DIRECTION IN THEIR PE ACTIVITIES. YOU CAN CREATE A SIMPLE MISSION, OR YOU CAN GET MORE CREATIVE BY CREATING A STORY OR ADVENTURE THAT STUDENTS CAN WORK THROUGH.

5. GO FULL BOSS MODE. THIS MEANS GIVING STUDENTS MORE CONTROL OVER THEIR LEARNING AND PROGRESS. YOU CAN DO THIS BY LETTING THEM CHOOSE THEIR OWN ACTIVITIES, SET THEIR OWN GOALS, OR TRACK THEIR OWN PROGRESS.

### READ MORE →

GAMIFICATION IN PHYSICAL EDUCATION: A SYSTEMATIC REVIEW
ARUFE-GIRÁLDEZ ET AL, 2022

GAME-BASED LEARNING AND GAMIFICATION IN PHYSICAL EDUCATION: A SYSTEMATIC REVIEW
CAMACHO-SÁNCHEZ ET AL, 2023

GAMIFICATION IN PHYSICAL EDUCATION: EVALUATION OF IMPACT ON MOTIVATION AND ACADEMIC PERFORMANCE
FERRIZ-VALERO ET AL, 2020

GAMIFICATION AND FLIPPED LEARNING AND THEIR INFLUENCE ON ASPECTS RELATED TO THE TEACHING-LEARNING PROCESS
PARRA-GONZÁLEZ ET AL, 2021

than a simple stop watch and finger/thumb heart rate count. That's not to say things such as heart rate monitors don't have their place in our lesson, of course they do, but only in specific lessons covering specific topics. Whilst there is the temptation to make our lessons technologically cutting edge, we must balance this against reducing impactful movement-based activities.

Videos are a great way to provide relatable and easy to absorb resources and learning tools for your pupils, however they are also a very grey area when it comes to usability and appropriateness. We must be very careful when using pre-recorded examples from the internet, especially if we are considering a genuinely inclusive approach to our provision. Whilst sites like YouTube have seemingly unlimited volumes of useful resources, how relevant they are to you and your context is only really for you to judge. Often, we need to consider videos based on the positive vs. negative impact they can have. A simple example of this is showing your class some examples of high-level training drills from professional players and then expecting them to replicate within your lesson. This is never a good idea, unless we have really reflected on the expectations, we are placing on our pupils using such examples, and whether our pupils can directly relate the video they are watching to their own life experience or perceived capabilities. If we just show videos without considering the lens in which they are being viewed, all we are really doing is showing our pupils examples of what someone else can do.

Videos have a place in our lesson/unit creation, as well as a powerful professional development tool, however we must be careful when using them as a primary resource for our pupils. That's not to say you shouldn't use them, only you should reflect carefully on the message, both explicit and subtle, that you are sending out when using them.

Depending on the age groups you are working with, the style and themes for your resources can make the difference between getting great engagement or a lack of motivation. If you are considering themes that run through your units of work, such as 'Superheroes' or the Olympics , can you make sure that theme also runs through all of your resources. Even better, can you think of themes that really resonate with the pupils within your cohorts. If you are thinking, for example, of running a unit of work that is 'gamified' in some way, can you make the resources represent this through the use of imagery from currently popular computer games? This meaningful connection with the world in which our students operate, can really enhance the relativity of our subject to their actual lived experiences.

Some of the best lesson resources (both electronic and hard copy) that I have seen work within lessons are pupil-created and shared down through subsequent cohorts of pupils. The level of relatability and relevance is turbo-charged when you take the language, terminology, ideas, creativity, and relative understanding from pupils and feed it back to other pupils. They know how to talk to each other, without jargon or acronyms. They know current, relevant examples that we aren't aware of as adult teachers, and they can inform and encourage in a way that speaks far more to the pupils than we can. We might like to think we're 'cool' PE teachers, but usually we're not! Let your pupils do the talking. Save those resources from lessons, engage with your pupils to help you make videos, encourage them to generate ideas and opportunities and save it all. Then embed this into the resource bank you use for years to come.

Whatever your resource creation process looks like, it is much more time-effective to do this in bulk and share the workload. Rather than three members of your team all creating resources for their own lessons within a shared unit of work, it makes far more sense to share the workload and create consistent resources that all the teachers working on a unit or topic can use. Think carefully about how to distribute this workload out so resources can be made ahead of time and proofed, checked and distributed in a timely fashion, giving each teacher time to digest and process the information contained within, before the lesson takes place. Then make sure the resources are filed in both hard and soft copy versions, so they can be used repeatedly.

**Risk Assessments**
No one likes talking about Risk Assessments, but we must have them, they have to be kept up to date and more importantly they must be usable and used.

Risk assessments are like your protective shield, keeping everyone involved in the provision of physical education from any form of harm, by exploring, reflecting, anticipating and then mitigating any danger before they may occur. As much as they sometimes feel like it, they are not just about ticking boxes and keeping senior leadership or governors happy, they're part of the process we use to create a sense of awareness and a culture of safety and security. Ultimately risk assessments help us in the process of really looking at and understanding our facilities, our activities and our provision. Often it is the process of creating or updating risk assessments that spark conversations about how we utilise our facilities and can increase the chances of finding new and interesting ways to deliver activities or opportunities for our pupils. As with everything in this book, it's about understanding our own context and viewing it in positive ways. Risk Assessments are just another opportunity for discussion, collaboration, reflection and positive engagement with our subject matter and our pupils.

Chances are you already have risk assessments. I don't imagine there are many schools that don't have them these days, even if they are filed in a box or drive and rarely looked at. This means in all likelihood you are updating and revising them rather than starting from scratch. If you are starting with nothing, there are some excellent templates and ready-made ones to use as the foundation for yours, via a number of membership organisations or PE websites. Whilst saving you time initially, remember that these are a starting point, not an off-the-shelf option that doesn't require any input from your team. If you are revising your already existing risk assessments, then you just need to check and reflect on whether they have all the aspects of your provision covered and that anything new has been considered. The key elements you need to check over are:

**Safety and well-being of students:** Whilst we are primarily thinking about physical safety when revising our risk assessments, it is worth using this opportunity to consider the wider implications of PE on our students, and our potential impact on their social and psychological safety and security as well.

Well-maintained sports facilities with appropriate equipment, clear safety procedures, and qualified supervision are essential for fostering a physically secure environment. Our pupils need to know they won't be hurt by faulty equipment, the actions of others or by their over enthusiasm or through activities that potentially exceed their limits. This, however, is just the starting point for our discussion around pupil safety within our provision.

We also need to consider our pupils' emotional safety, their sense and perception of being able to perform, free of ridicule, exclusion, or pressure to perform beyond their current capabilities. Our fully inclusive PE environments should be designed both physically and emotionally, to celebrate diverse body types and differing skill levels all with the aim of fostering a genuine sense of belonging within which all our pupils can participate, as themselves, without fear of judgement. It is amazing how important our physical spaces are to this sense of belonging, and how much impact warm, welcoming spaces can have on our pupils' sense of belonging.

Psychological safety also plays a vital role. Students need to feel comfortable taking risks, trying new things, and even making mistakes without feeling like their self-worth is on the line. PE teachers who create a space where vulnerability is met with encouragement and support, not criticism, nurture this crucial sense of security.

Finally, social safety ties it all together. Feeling like they have a voice and agency in their PE experiences matters to students. Having opportunities to provide engagement with each other in a variety of different ways, whilst always feeling secure, safe and valued. Being given the opportunity for positive feedback, having the option to choose activities, and even collaborate in designing PE lessons, fosters a sense of ownership and control, further solidifying their secure place in this sometimes-dreaded subject.

**Identifying potential hazards:** Risk assessments will help you recognise, identify and remedy any potential hazards that exist, that could present a barrier or challenge, not just to pupil safety but also to the effective delivery of your new curriculum units and activities. Your PE spaces may not have been developed specifically to provide the activities you are now planning to deliver and therefore we need to consider the physical spaces we have available and their suitability for the potential alternative use. A good example of this is the traditional sports hall. Certainly, in most of the sports halls I have worked in, they are designed to provide a large number of different activity opportunities, often with dedicated pieces of equipment. If, however, you are doing an alternative activity that is not originally planned for within the space, the pre-existing equipment, wall fixtures, cupboards, goal posts, basketball hoops, may impact on the safe delivery of this new activity. Whilst this isn't necessarily a barrier to delivery, it is an important identification we need to make when planning the logistics for our provision.

Once we know what we want to deliver and in which spaces, and we have then identified potential risks within those spaces, we can start to think about implementing control measures. By going through the process of identifying the hazards, we can then build remedial plans to avoid any unnecessary risk to our pupils. For example, if you are now delivering a unit of Parkour which involves significant bits of large equipment for pupils to move over, across and under, then the storage of this equipment needs to be considered, so that it does not impact on the level of risk in the next lesson, which may involve less structure and move high-paced movement, for example futsal. You can see how easily this could be overlooked; we've all seen sports halls with piles of matts stacked up in the

# CHAPTER 10 - NUTS AND BOLTS

corner of the room. As well as spoiling a clean, empty, well-prepared space, it can have an impact (albeit in this example relatively low) to the wellbeing and safety of our pupils.

Equally as important as promoting safe spaces, is the promotion of safe practice. Again, the risk assessments most of us have used will focus on the physical practices but the risk assessment process is a good opportunity to consider and collaborate on potential psychological, behavioural and social risks to our pupils too. Developing a culture of awareness and a consistent approach that reduces or removes the risk of 'trauma' within our PE, will in turn support our development of safe, inclusive, equitable spaces where pupils can come to feel comfortable, supported and safe at all times.

'Do no harm' in physical education

## Changemaker Reflection: Neil Moggan
*Founder of Future Action Limited & Creator of the '9 Step RISE Up Roadmap'*

**Trauma Informed PE: Relationships at the heart of physical education**
I started road testing a 'Trauma Informed PE' approach at an inner-city secondary school in Norwich, UK from September 2022 and was blown away by the outcomes it created for my young people and myself. I will outline my why, intent and impact and how I have used that programme to create change in schools across the country.

**My 'WHY?'**
I wanted to deepen my knowledge of trauma-informed practice to help young people to recover from trauma and particularly the impact of Covid for the children I taught.

As we returned to education in a post-lockdown world, like many schools across the country, the pandemic had taken a significant toll on staff, the children we serve, our local community, and there was considerable political instability and disruption.

I had never been more committed to improving outcomes for the young people I served, but for the first time in my teaching career I was struggling to build the quality of the relationships I wanted with my young people, particularly with my most challenging children. I had to find a solution as my current strategies just weren't working in my setting anymore, so I enrolled onto the Diploma in Trauma and Mental Health-Informed Schools through Trauma Informed Schools UK.

**Finding a solution in psychological safety**
I had to find a way of getting my most challenging children on side by rebuilding our relationship, developing trust, getting them to feel psychologically safe and enjoying school, and engaging them in their learning.

Firstly, I started by helping my young people feel psychologically safe through an ultra-positive meet and greet and by using my body language to increase safety cues. Our face, voice and body are crucial to this. When it is successfully actioned, we trigger their social engagement system rather than their social defence system. The additional strategies I looked at were:

- Creating a sense of belonging
- Using physical activity to widen our children's window of tolerance
- Introducing 'Play wrapped in Care' and Biophilia
- Creating a non-judgemental environment
- Managing behaviours that challenge adults in a way that maintains high standards without re-traumatising young people.
- Impact

Through the implementation of trauma-informed practices, I saw a drastic reduction in send-outs by 95% in just one term.

This shift created a safe and supportive environment where all students felt understood and valued, leading to increased engagement and a significant boost in progress and attendance.

My most challenging students in my exam PE groups, experienced a remarkable increase in their predicted grades by 1.5 grades. Their attendance also improved by 5%. This demonstrated the power of trauma-informed practices in positively impacting academic outcomes.

Not only did my young people benefit, but I experienced a renewed sense of joy and fulfilment in my teaching. By creating an environment that prioritised wellbeing and connection, teaching became enjoyable again, leading to an improvement in my own wellbeing.

### Creating change on a wider scale

From road testing various techniques and approaches in my school, I created the 'Recover Roadmap', a 7-step process to guide colleagues in implementing trauma-informed practice in their PE department to transform relationships, wellbeing, engagement, behaviour and progress in the short term, and children's life chances in the long term.

Through online courses, writing, presenting, and talking about Trauma Informed PE, I have continued to strive to improve outcomes for young people and their teachers. I've always believed that whatever this looks like, it must fundamentally meet the needs of individual pupils, within their unique contexts.

(If you want to know more about Neil's work, you can find much more at www.futureaction.net)

**3 Top tips for undertaking your own change management process:**

1. Outline your intent - what do you want to achieve?
   Why is that important to you and your young people?

2. 'Who?' not 'How?'. Your time is precious, who has already solved this problem? How can they save you time? Research and reach out to them for support.

3. Bring your colleagues with you - ask for their input to give them ownership and present solutions in a way that meets their needs.

Obviously, the ultimate objective of our risk assessments is to ensure we meet all our legal and legislative legal requirements, which will vary depending on your context. Taking the time to really understand the wider picture when it comes to risk assessments and risk mitigation is time well spent and should not be seen as a chore or tick box exercise. Your school will undoubtedly have templates and formats you are required to use which may feel fit for purpose, or not. Discussion with line management and H&S teams will help ensure that the pre-existing documentation supports your development process and does not hinder them; there are numerous examples and variations available online for you to use as reference and guidance should you want to explore alternative approaches.

As with everything we do in the journey of curriculum development, we are aiming to create environments that promote effective teaching and learning at all times. Everything we do should feed into the enhancement of the learning experience of the pupils in our classes. Do not see risk assessment as an activity that is wasting your time or perceive it as something you are required to do for others. Well-considered and reflective risk assessment development can extend the planning and development phases of your project but can also enhance it significantly, giving you the opportunity to get away from your planning documents and PE office and consider your curriculum delivery in the reality of the spaces within which it will be delivered. You can use this opportunity to 'see' the delivery and reflect on what it might look and feel like to the pupils receiving the provision. Will your plans on paper translate into meaningful, effective, safe and supportive PE in real life? Enter into the risk assessment process with this objective in mind, and you will soon see the benefit of it.

### Assessment policies and processes

A major part of any redesign process is the development of methods, procedures and justifications for checking the progress of our pupils, and in turn the effectiveness of our programmes. In every single PE context, some form of assessment will play a critical role in the wider acknowledgement of the impact of our provision.

This section is not going to explore different types of assessment you could adopt, as that is a huge topic and covered extensively elsewhere. This section is really going to look at the process you will have to go through to establish what your assessment framework looks, feels and works like within your context.

CHAPTER 10 - NUTS AND BOLTS

Assessment generally has two key strands within PE, with a third strand, often less focused on but generally present in some form, even if subconsciously. These are not always explicit but when you are planning your assessment approach, you do need to spend time with your department considering how you will ensure all of these elements are built into your assessment processes.

- **Formative Assessment**
- **Summative Assessment**
- **Norm-Referenced Assessment**

It is really important here, for me to make clear, that this is not going to be a discussion as to the relative benefits/negatives on each type of assessment, nor to make judgement as to which is better or which you should use. Ideally (and more than likely) you will be using all of them, in the most effective way possible, to create a comprehensive assessment process, that gathers as much evidence and data as possible to really understand your pupils at every stage. The ability to gather and analyse data at individual, class, cohort and whole school level, will undoubtedly provide you with the best chance to really understand where your pupils have been on their PE journey, over differing periods of time, but how you choose to do that in practice, as always, will totally depend on your own departmental values and vision, as well as your own context.

Let's look at each individual, against the same four evaluation criteria to see how we can make these as effective as possible. We will consider each through the lens of:

- Promotion of Effective Teaching and Learning
- The Measurement Of Effective Learning
- The Enhancement Of Wellbeing And Motivation
- Ensuring Equity and Inclusion

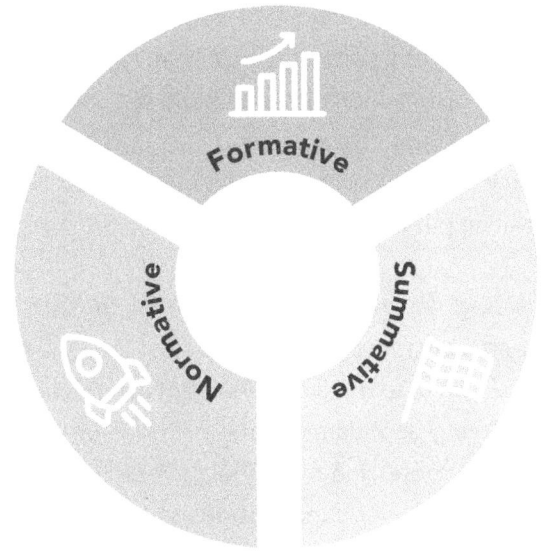

### Formative Assessment

Formative assessment is the ongoing, continuous process of collecting evidence and reviewing outcomes related to our pupils' learning throughout the entire teaching and learning process. It's like taking the pulse of each pupil at regular intervals, to identify and understand their individual areas of strength and development needs as well as taking a gauge on their engagement and motivation, their sense of wellbeing, safety and inclusion and anything else that sits within your assessment criteria. It's not about just finding a grade for a pupil, but it is more about informing and supporting the provision your teachers are giving to that pupil during their learning journey.

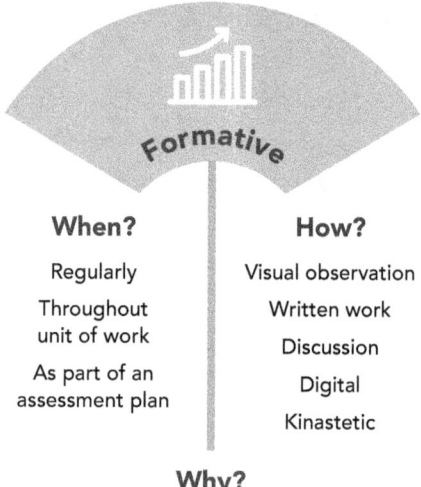

**When?**
Regularly
Throughout unit of work
As part of an assessment plan

**How?**
Visual observation
Written work
Discussion
Digital
Kinastetic

**Why?**
To identify knowledge gaps
To improve teaching and learning
To problem solve specific learning issues

It can be done through a number of different assessment processes. Most often in PE, which by its nature is a less paper-driven subject, it is done by teachers through observation of pupils within their PE lessons. Subjective observation is always going to be a challenge, especially in relation to standardisation and moderation, however the reality is that your teachers' observations of engagements from individual pupils are always going to form a significant part of your formative assessment practice. Alternatives could be through peer observation or assessment, the use of technology or written tasks. When it comes to written formative assessment, a good rule of thumb is 'less is more' as any time taken away from activity and movement will potentially limit the effectiveness of our physical activity within our lessons.

### Using formative assessment to aid the promotion of effective Teaching and Learning

The use of formative assessment can provide us with a powerful tool to promote effective teaching and learning as it provides us with continuous evidence and understanding of pupil progression throughout a lesson, a series of lessons or a unit of work. It allows us to adapt and alter our provision 'on the fly' to enhance the effectiveness of our teaching and in turn its impact on our pupils' learning and development. Formative assessment allows us as educators to gather valuable insights that will help inform instructional decisions 'in the moment' and, through effective and timely feedback, can empower our pupils to take more ownership of their own learning journey. The dynamic cycle of formative assessment and real-time feedback and reflection can foster a sense of deeper understanding of subject knowledge, can promote more meaningful engagement and support the inclusivity and individuality of our provision for every pupil, fostering that all important sense of belonging with their PE lessons.

**Using formative assessment to support our measurement of effective learning**

Waiting until the end of a unit of work, or term, to do our assessment means we potentially miss opportunities to intervene with pupils learning journeys at just the time they might need it most. Formative assessment allows us to monitor, at an individual level, the impact we are having on our pupils in a myriad of ways and adapt our processes accordingly. To do this

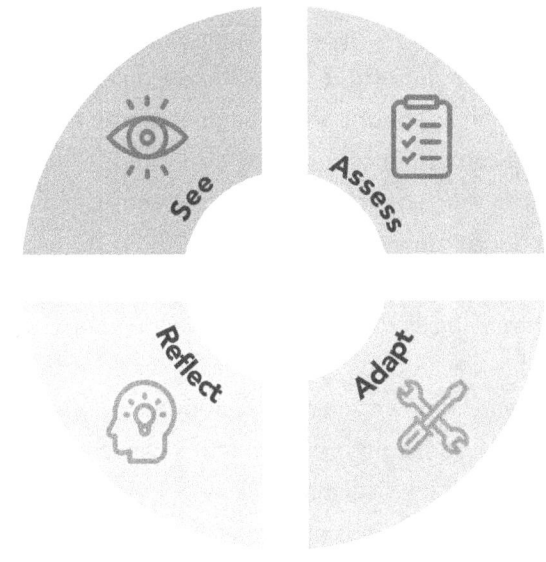

effectively we have to have some key criteria we are assessing our provision against; this can take significant time to really develop and hone. Once in place, though, formative assessment against a set of criteria can indicate immediate adaptations we can make to enhance the opportunities for learning within our lesson structure. Using a process such as **See-Reflect-Adapt-Assess** is a good structure to base this process around. We see what our pupils are doing within their lessons, and we feed back to them in the moment as necessary. We then reflect on what we have seen, either within the lesson or afterwards and we adapt our future provision accordingly. Once any adaptation or change is made, we need to assess it to see if it has a positive, beneficial impact and then start the process again. Teaching and Learning should never be static, and we already know we should be adapting our provision to suit the immediate learning needs of our pupils, but formalising this into our assessment framework means it is more measurable and more likely to happen within the busy world of PE delivery.

### Using formative assessment to enhance wellbeing and motivation

We all understand the basic principle that engagement and motivation lead to generally higher outcomes. This is not new or unproven. What is most important is that we learn to recognise what good, meaningful engagement looks like, at both class and individual pupil level. We need to be willing and able to adjust our teaching and planning to ensure we are getting maximum, sustained engagement from as many pupils as possible. When we are formatively assessing our pupils within and immediately following lesson delivery, we can identify aspects of lessons where motivation or engagement was reduced or lacking, at an individual pupil level, and adapt our plans accordingly. It could be as simple as thinking about the language or lesson focus, or as complex as group demographics or core curriculum engagement; without the formative observation and reflection we cannot accurately assess which aspect of our provision is most likely to increase engagement and motivation.

The same can be said for pupil wellbeing and sense of safety and belonging. When we set out to develop teaching spaces that are inclusive and equitable and have a sense of safety within them, we must think about how we can observe the effectiveness of this within each lesson, from the perspective of each pupil. Indicators such as disengagement, group dynamics, physical mannerisms or behaviour could all be indicators that something needs adapting. Recognising this within the lesson is far more effective in terms of enhancing wellbeing than it is recognising it after provision is complete. We need to be good at spotting the indicators and understanding the tools and approaches we have at our disposal to resolve any potential issues before they become ingrained or permanent. Our primary objective within every PE lesson should be 'to do no harm' and by recognising the indications that trauma, discomfort or instability could be occurring we become far more equipped to manage these situations positively. A lot of this comes down to our individual approaches as teachers, how aware and observant we are of these indicators, and how confident we are to address and challenge things when they arise. By having a clear and collaborative approach to this, it will certainly support any less confident members of our department to intervene should the need arise.

### Using Formative Assessment To Ensure Equity and Inclusion

Effective use of formative assessment through a variety of means, provides us as teachers with a powerful tool to ensure our lessons are founded on equity and inclusion. Offering our students a wide variety of opportunities, suited to their individual needs and desires and encouraging them to feel safe and valued when engaging and interacting with their learning, will support that overall sense of inclusion and personal meaning. As with wellbeing and motivation, we can learn to spot the indicators of inclusion or lack thereof, and adapt our teaching to develop this further, be it at classroom or individual pupil level. There is never a situation where PE should be provided at the expense of individual equity and whilst this can be driven by the curriculum we develop and deliver; we cannot be sure we are achieving this without formatively assessing these factors within lessons. It is not about levelling the playing field here, it is about recognising individual needs and characteristics and adopting practice that recognises, supports and celebrates individuality within physical education. Starting with a standpoint that

### Equity
Aspiring to a curriculum that provides the **right** access and opportunity for everyone, regardless of individual differences.

Providing the **most appropriate** programme to everyone throughout the curriculum.

Regardless of need or any other individual difference.

### Equality
Aspiring to a curriculum that provides the **same** access and opportunity for everyone, without consideration of individual differences.

Providing a **balanced** programme to everyone throughout the curriculum.

Everyone is provided with what they need to succeed.

*Angus Maguire, 2016. Adapted from PE Scholar*

every pupil, regardless of who they are, deserves an equitable and meaningful experience with physical education, means we can look for formative ways to assess this and adapt as we go, to further achieve our objectives here.

## Summative Assessment

Summative assessments are generally used within PE to create a final appraisal of our pupils learning at the conclusion of a learning period. Whether this is a unit of work, half or full term or at the end an academic year, we see summative assessment as the final piece of the assessment process and usually (although not always) it is used to create some form of summative grade or report that we then provide to pupils, parents and colleagues to conclude our process and establish the relative effectiveness of our delivery against predetermined criteria.

**When?**
Consistently
At the end of a unit of work or activity
Usually linked to a reporting cycle

**How?**
Visual observation
Written work
Discussion
Digital
Kinastetic

**Why?**
To collect evidence
To benchmark progress and attainment
To assess quality of teaching

When done well, it allows us to offer any interested parties a quick and clear overview of the general knowledge, skills and capabilities that pupils have learnt and developed during a certain period of learning, and it is often the assessment that forms most of our reporting structure.

Approaches to summative assessment within physical education can include physical, cognitive, social or emotional development. Indeed 'what' is being assessed can be as unique to your context as anything else in PE. Whatever you are assessing, whether practical 'skill' or something else, it can be done formally through end of unit assessment of performance, either through explicit observed assessment such as in competitive situations or isolated performance against a reestablished set of ability levels. Sometimes this can be taken from internally created criteria but can also be standardised against more regional or national statistics related to a particular activity or activity group. Either way, rubrics are the most common way of establishing these assessment criteria or key indicators and if this is the approach you are planning on taking, then the creation of rubrics alongside the scheme or unit of work is the most effective way of producing these documents.

In some instances, the use of written assessments may be used. These could come in the form of workbooks or ongoing portfolios of work and reflection, or through one-off written tasks. As we have said previously, whilst there is certainly a place for these within some PE provision, any written activity should not impact or reduce the volume or quality of active movement time within our lessons. Do not sacrifice physical movement for static activity.

Summative evaluations can support the development of insightful information about our pupils learning journeys and can help us identify gaps in knowledge and areas of particular success, however in order to effectively summarise an individual pupils progress upon completion of a unit or topic, we should have built this picture using regular formative assessment opportunities rather than waiting until the end and trying to recall all the successes and challenges an individual pupil has experienced during a long period of work.

**Using Summative Assessment to aid the Promotion of effective Teaching and Learning**

Summative assessments are traditionally viewed as the end of a learning journey, but they can also be effective in continuous development of teaching and learning. By analysing student performance data through summative means, such as standardised tests, performance tasks, or written projects, we can identify general or specific areas where students excel and areas requiring further instruction. We can then use this data to inform wider curricular adjustments, adapt departmental teaching methods, adapt our learning materials and resources or source new and more effective ones, and we can look to summative assessment to actually review whether our assessment approach is effective against our objectives and whether there are any adaptations we can make to better address student needs, outcomes and learning gaps.

Summative assessment can also be an effective way of evidencing the impact of any adaptive teaching approaches we may have built into our provision. We can look for evidence of the impact of targeted support and/or enrichment activity that were designed to cater for individual pupil learning needs and whether these have had an impact in relation to previously gathered data. Often, we need to see patterns in our data over time to really be able to judge the impact of these specific teaching and learning initiatives as at a formative level it is far harder to identify trends on a lesson-by-lesson basis.

Summative assessment can help with the formation of the next set of learning goals. Often summative assessment provides us with 'big data' that means we can review at class or cohort level the general pattern and trends in outcomes against objectives. This can then be used to form our approaches to those groups of pupils for upcoming units of work. It is only really by looking at groups as a whole that we can see whether interventions or approaches have had the impact on teaching and learning as a whole.

At an individual pupil level, summative assessment provides us with the opportunity to 'fact check' our formative assessment and check for consistency. This is particularly useful when classes are taught by different teachers across a period of time, as we can create more generalised evidence of the impact of certain aspects of our provision against each other, at an individual pupil level. Summative assessment also allows us to identify pupils who may need additional support in relation to their peers, either in general or in specific types of activity.

Finally, and no less importantly, summative assessment gives us the ability to celebrate individual success in as many ways as we have data points. Anyone who has read my previous work will know that I place great importance on the process of recognising and celebrating success in as many ways as possible, be it practical, social, cognitive or emotional in nature. Assessment in PE should be something that is done 'with pupils' rather than 'to pupils' and consistency, clarity and purpose need to be explicit and clearly communicated. A well-designed and comprehensive summative assessment process will give you that opportunity in great volume.

**Using Summative Assessment To Support Our Measurement Of Effective Learning**

When used effectively, summative assessment will provide us with a valuable snapshot of our pupils learning at key points in their journey. As we said, these are generally at the end of a section of work or activity to summarise the overall outcomes of that period of study. The ability to then analyse pupil performance during these assessment windows through standardised or moderated assessment, through performance or observative evaluation or through less common means such as projects, presentations, written tasks or verbal engagement, we can gauge how well our pupils have grasped the key concepts and overall learning objectives of a whole unit of work. We can reflect on how well they can apply those concepts, skills or that synthesised knowledge in a variety of different contexts, and we can measure their progress against previous performance and outcomes. This all, in turn, allows us to establish how effective the learning process has been for that individual pupil and for the wider group within which learning took place. If we are so inclined, we can gauge performance against the performance of a wider group, comparing outcomes and achieved levels across classes, year groups, school-wide cohorts and indeed against historical data. Whether this is an approach you want to take is, as usual, contextual, however I would urge caution when publicising such comparative data to pupils, parents or generally in public.

We can use this data internally within our departments to identify areas where the curriculum might need adjustment or adaptation, possibly due to a lower-than-expected level of outcome but also possibly because we have identified an area where more extension could be offered. We can also identify areas for improvement at individual or cohort level in regard to particular activities or skills that have been a struggle to develop. We can use this data to provide us with the opportunity to implement targeted interventions at individual or group level or justify engagement with learning support colleagues in particular instances.

The data will allow us to evaluate critically the effectiveness of our instructional methods and teaching approaches. It will allow us to have evidence-backed, positive conversations within departments about how we can ensure our teaching approaches are leading towards our desired departmental outcomes and how we can refine our provision to increase this effectiveness in the upcoming period.

Ultimately, using summative assessment data effectively gives us the opportunity to measure the impact we are having on the learning journeys of our pupils. Whilst formative assessment is an important part of this, the value of standardised and moderated summative assessment cannot be underestimated and must be considered when building our assessment strategies. Apart from everything else, it is very likely you will have to provide data back into the wider school data collection processes to allow reporting and analysis to happen at school-wide, multi-subject level. If you know you have to do something anyway, just do it really, really well!

### Using Summative Assessment To Enhance Wellbeing And Motivation

It is a generally held belief that 'high stakes' summative assessment leads to higher levels of pupils' stress, anxiety and pressure. I am not going to argue with that here, because whilst I am not looking to tell you how to formulate your assessment strategies, I have significant years of experience of seeing pupils struggle under the pressure of 'end of term' examinations, across all subjects, and whilst some pupils thrive in this pressure driven environment, some, is not all.

Summative assessments do, however, in the right circumstances, and with the right approach, have positive benefits to certain pupils. Some pupils thrive in the knowledge that their physical or cognitive abilities are being assessed more formally and as such can 'rise to the occasion' and strive for the sense of accomplishment that a good assessment can provide. For these pupils, we should not discount the value of summative 'high stakes' assessment, but we cannot offer it at the jeopardy of the other types of pupils we have within our schools. A more appropriate approach would be to find the best model to fit individual pupils or groups of pupils, where summative assessment in the form of end of unit tests make up one part of a bigger framework. How can you offer the opportunity for summative assessment without risking the wellbeing of the group as a whole, is a conversation every department should have regularly. Whilst there is no reason to remove the summative assessment process, it needs to be carefully crafted in such a way as to benefit the wellbeing and sense of belonging and value that we want every pupil to achieve.

Often, this is a case of linguistics and nuance. The words 'test' or 'assessment' can play a significant part in the increased stress we put on pupils. PE should be seen as the place where pupils come to release pressure and experience joy, not the opposite. Can we use better, more inclusive and more meaningful terminology when we are describing and explaining the ways in which we ensure pupils are making progress?

As with everything we are discussing, the importance of a range of approaches and processes is key to a well-rounded 'holistic' approach to assessment. Together with summative findings, prompt, well-targeted and meaningful feedback helps students identify and accept their strengths and limitations and allows us to work with them to chart a course for ongoing development. An essential component of wellbeing and long-term success, intrinsic motivation is fostered in this empowered learning environment and the right approach to summative assessment, and assessment in general can do wonders for this aspect of pupils' PE journey.

## Using Summative Assessment to Ensure Equity And Inclusion

As with everything we must consider, when designing new approaches to our subjects' delivery, how summative assessment can support the culture of equity and inclusion within our lessons and our environment. At first it would be fairly reasonable to assume that a summative assessment process would not be an aspect that lends itself to an inclusive environment, but the reality is the opposite. When we carefully consider our assessment frameworks from the perspective of individual student needs and outcomes, we can see that appropriate and considered assessment can indeed support a sense of equity for all. In other words we should be assessing at an individual level, based on our pre-existing knowledge of each individual pupil's circumstances. If we can avoid situations where we are directly comparing and especially publicly comparing pupils with each other, instead providing well-defined, reflective, supportive feedback with evidence, to individual pupils, then what we are doing can have real power to shape their progress, value, meaning and personal sense of worth. Helping each pupil understand that we consider and observe them as an individual, on their own merits and not comparing them to others, means they will see the value and importance we place on their personal journey. In turn, hopefully, they will see the positives in that relational activity, leading to individual motivation to better themselves as performers. If done right, this is incredibly powerful.

### Norm-Referenced Assessment

Whilst far less regularly identified as an explicit strategy and usually embedded within summative assessment, it is still worthwhile considering the reality that norm-referenced assessment, also known as benchmarking and diagnostic assessment in physical education, still happens and, in some circumstances, adds value to our assessment strategy.

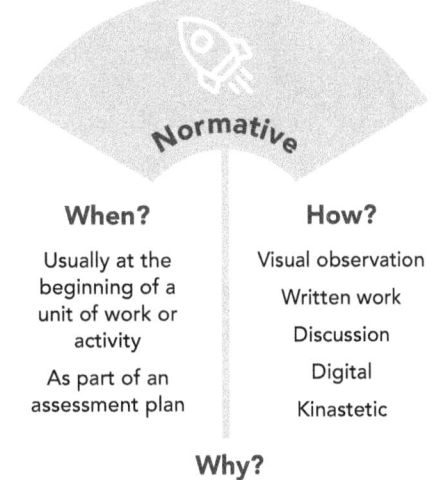

**When?**
Usually at the beginning of a unit of work or activity
As part of an assessment plan

**How?**
Visual observation
Written work
Discussion
Digital
Kinastetic

**Why?**
To establish benchmarks
Understand prior knowledge or ability
To establish appropriate teaching approach

Norm-referenced assessment essentially compares students' performance to a group standard, usually other students of the same age or grade level, within our own school or wider afield. When done at the start of a unit of work, we would see this as diagnostic assessment, establishing a starting place for each of our pupils, however it still falls into the category of normative assessment as we are benchmarking against others.

Imagine a bell curve, where the majority falls around the average score, and fewer students score higher or lower. What we are aiming to achieve here is a form of ranking, of our pupils with a determination of who is 'above average,' 'average,' or 'below average' in a particular skill, concept or activity. Whenever a reporting process within a school uses terms like these to assess and report on pupils, then they are essentially using a norm-referenced approach to their reporting structure.

While norm-referenced assessment can potentially offer us a quick snapshot of student performance relative to peers or national averages, it has significant limitations. Critics will argue that it creates unhealthy competition and discourages students who fall below the average. As well as this, focusing solely on relative performance can seriously overlook individual progress and potential, making for a potentially damaging and certainly less

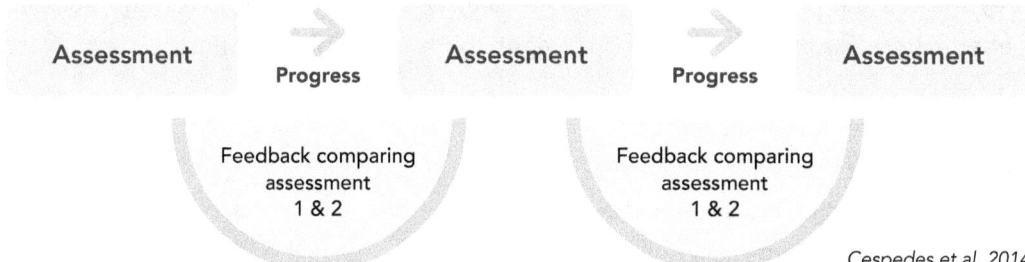

*Cespedes et al, 2014*

inclusive environment in which PE is delivered. For a more holistic picture of student development, educators could combine norm-referenced assessment with other methods like criterion-referenced and ipsative assessments but even this is fraught with potential pitfalls and risks to our pupils' motivations and progress. There are parts of the world however, where this Norm-Referenced approach is still the dominant form of assessment, and within those contexts is recognised as both effective and accurate. Where a country or region has a particular emphasis on school age specialism, in sport in particular, often linked to a sense of political or nationalist identity, this approach identifies at an early age potential elite performers, allowing them to be streamed or developed at a much more aggressive rate. Whether you believe this is appropriate or not for school PE curriculums I will leave you to reflect on, but in the spirit of balance, it is important to recognise this approach and its potential benefits to our assessment strategies.

## Using Norm-Referenced Assessment To Aid The Promotion Of Effective Teaching And Learning

Even though they are predominantly used for ranking and comparison type activity, norm-referenced assessments can be useful in fostering efficient teaching and learning. Through comparing student performance to that of their peers, teachers can evaluate a pupil's relative strengths and areas for development and can determine where pupils are doing well and where they might benefit from further support or intervention. This is also the case when individuals are compared to wider normative data.

Norm-referenced assessment will allow us to make determinations about how well the curriculum is meeting learning objectives at any specific time. Teachers can determine where the curriculum needs to be strengthened or modified by looking at the areas where pupils consistently perform well or poorly.

## Using Norm-Referenced Assessment To Support Our Measurement Of Effective Learning

Access to standardised results can help guide future teaching and serve as a benchmark for tracking progress and effectiveness of teaching approaches. Essentially evaluating the progress of groups against each other allows us the opportunity to identify particular approaches or practices that have seen better outcomes in general.

Standardised or Norm-Referenced assessment does provide an opportunity for data-driven decision-making. It allows teachers to make well-informed decisions about curriculum modifications, resource allocation, and interventions, ensuring that they are optimising learning opportunities for every student. This is much more effective when we are combining norm-referenced data with other forms of assessment rather than using it as our sole method of assessment.

One thing that Norm-Referenced assessment does well, is allow us to measure pupil or cohort progress over time: Teachers can monitor pupil and group progress by giving the same standardised assessments on a regular basis. This longitudinal data will provide us with potentially insightful information about whether pupils are performing above expectations, working within the norm, or needing more assistance.

## Using Norm-Referenced Assessment To Enhance Wellbeing And Motivation, Equity And Inclusion

Although norm-referenced assessments (NRAs) are generally criticised for promoting inequality, when applied carefully and strategically, they can be used within an environment that still prioritises equity and inclusion and does not damage pupil motivation or wider wellbeing. This is a grey area as far as research is concerned and does come with many pitfalls, we need to be aware of within our provision.

For some pupils, norm-referenced assessment can help pupils develop a feeling of purpose and progress by giving them personalised feedback along with well-defined benchmarks. Pupils who are intrinsically motivated in particular can be inspired to create goals, work toward improvement, and recognise their accomplishments when they see how they stack up against their peers. This is, however, never used to the detriment of those pupils for whom this public recognition of their performance against their peers would be a demotivating or damaging experience. When feedback using norm-referenced data is used, it should be done with this danger firmly in mind and often the only appropriate way for this to be done is through direct, personal and one to one feedback opportunities. Recognising personal best performances is a commonplace process in activities such as swimming, but even in this example, public comparison should be limited to competitive or competition environments, in my opinion anyway.

**When To Design Assessment Plans**
So now we've considered what our assessment strategy might look like, and what types of assessments we might include in our programme to ensure accurate, meaningful and diverse assessment opportunities are built into our provision. Let's think briefly about when this specific aspect of our design process should occur. Obviously, this is not a definitive absolute and you can do it whenever it feels most appropriate, but a general rule would be to think about it early and build it in at the very beginning of your planning, expanding and specifying the details as you go.

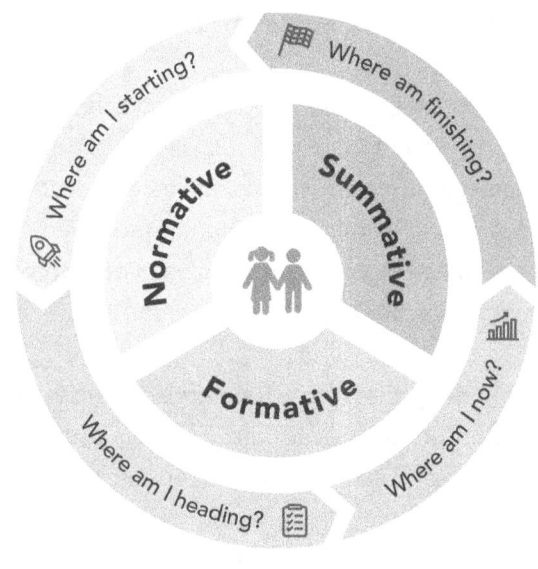

Indeed, it is certainly the case that, instead of being created at the end of the process, as the final piece of the puzzle, assessment plans should be created as an ongoing element of the whole creative process. By doing this it is much more likely that you will develop an embedded assessment programme that seamlessly fits rather than trying to crowbar in an assessment process designed in isolation that doesn't exactly fit the model you are aiming for.

There are some critical aspects to the assessment implementation process that must be considered throughout the process.

When you first establish your curricular learning objectives and goals, you need to consider how you will evaluate your pupils progress toward these goals as you identify and determine exactly what you want the pupils to know and do. This provides a stronger chance that your methods of assessment and your learning objectives will be in sync.

Incorporating discussion about assessment into the planning of your teaching frameworks will enable you to embed assessment, in a variety of forms, into the structure of your lessons, to avoid those terrible end of unit 'assessment lessons' that just increase pressure and vulnerability within our students. In a practical subject like PE, there really are very few situations where a high-stakes, end-of-topic assessment (with the stress and public embarrassment that could cause ) should be necessary. Including assessment in your regular learning activities will provide a far more inclusive, supportive and positive assessment experience, in the vast majority of cases.

As you build your curriculum units or schemes of work, consider where the most appropriate places are for your assessment, and what the least pressurised approaches could be to get this data collected. Things such as peer or self-evaluation can significantly reduce the sense of pressure or visibility around assessment, even when the assessment itself is more 'high-stakes' in nature. Pupils working and observing their friends are more likely to feel comfortable than performing the same skills or activities in front of larger groups or teachers. Building in the opportunity to reflect on practice and performance is another key aspect to assessment that can help to reduce the sense of impact of an assessment.

If we are doing any form of pilot programme, then we need to ensure that part of this pilot considers the assessment piece as well. Piloting a curriculum without an assessment renders it meaningless and you will need the data from the assessments to help formulate your evaluations over the effectiveness of your piloted work.

As we implement elements of our curriculum, we need to ensure we are always considering the assessment aspects of it. We need to make time and schedule collaborative meetings to work without teams to collect feedback and analyse data. Without this important phase then we risk assessment for the sake of assessment creeping into our curriculum.

This process of assessment reflection never really ends and should form a critical aspect of your regular curriculum review strategy. Whenever you reflect or evaluate anything, and within any subsequent change process, the assessment linked to that aspect must also be examined. We want to develop a culture where assessment is not seen as separate but fundamentally embedded as part of our curriculum framework. Indeed, any revisions to our curriculum should be informed by the analysis of the data we have gathered through the assessment process. Without developing a data-driven approach to our reviews, we risk removing or changing the things that are actually giving our pupils the most positive outcomes. Monitoring the development of your pupils over time, tracking the evolution of pupils will help you ascertain the effect of the curriculum and pinpoint any specific areas that might require extra work.

Ultimately PE assessment should not be a separate project that happens exclusively from the curriculum development project. Try to embed every assessment approach into the foundations of your PE curriculum. Guarantee that your assessments are meaningful, positive and effective and use the data that you gather. Use the assessment to drive the positive feedback that pupils receive that really closes the learning loop, and always reflect on the suitability and perception of your assessment from every stakeholder's perspective.

**Assessment Trackers**
Everyone loves a good spreadsheet, or at least, everyone understands the importance of a good spreadsheet, even if the idea of creating or working with one may give you cold shivers. Within your own context, there will have to be a process for collating and recording the data that you are gathering through your assessment practice. You may be lucky and work in a school where a 'data leader' or previous curriculum lead has created something that just works, or you may work in a school who uses their whole school data management system to track data across every subject, but the likelihood is that you will still end up having to create or adapt something specifically aimed at keeping accurate and clear data to inform teaching practice, learning progress and provide relevant, up to date data during reporting cycles and for feedback to school leadership.

Creating an effective assessment tracking tool for PE requires careful planning and consideration and there are some steps that you will inevitably have to go through to establish an effective, fit for purpose tracking system within your department. There are no shortcuts here, because using an off the shelf product or previously created tracker is not going to track the specific and unique data set you are going to want to collect within your unique context.

Before you can put your tracking system together you need to be sure you know what the key skills, attitudes, objectives, concepts or anything else you want to assess actually are. This will determine the design and flow of your tracker, so putting it together before this point is probably wasting time. Clearly defined objectives and data points, ideally with dates and staff responsibilities identified will make the tracking of the completion a bit easier in the long run too.

Deciding on your format is probably the most important decision you will make related to assessment tracking. Are you going to use a spreadsheet and if so, which one? Are you going to find a digital tracking app or website and if so, how are you going to train up your staff to use it and ensure the security and availability of the data when you need it?

The actual fields you have on your tracker is totally up to you and your department but keeping useful pupil data such as date of birth, SEND details, intervention needs, email address etc can really speed up communication about and analysis of pupils when undertaking moderation. Often this information can be bulk uploaded into a spreadsheet but even manually it will ultimately save you time in the long run.

However you decide to use data, it's critical that you adhere to any Data Protection policies or rules within your school or organisation. Sharing, publicising, distributing and even just collecting data can all be part of a wider school approach that you must consider when deciding how to proceed.

Ultimately your tracker will only be as good as the way in which it's used. If you can develop a culture where it is regularly used, kept as simple as possible to administer and input into, if it features in every conversation about curriculum or pupil progress and shared widely and celebrated, it's much more likely to provide positive benefits to those stakeholders engaging with it. A half-filled, overly complicated assessment tracker, that is regarded as time consuming and of little contextual value to teaching and learning, is likely to sit on a drive or in a folder, unused and will just represent significant wasted time and energy.

## Feedback Policies

Assuming you have a well-designed and effective assessment and evaluation system in place, you are going to want to ensure that the evidence of high-quality provision you are generating is utilised to its maximum through a rigorous and meaningful feedback process. There are several different approaches to feedback we can provide to the different stakeholders within our schools, each with important differences. Throughout the design and implementation process it is important to consider how feedback is provided and recorded where necessary to ensure we can track the effectiveness of it and its impact on the learning and progression of our pupils. For the purposes of this section, we are going to look at three specific types of feedback that we should actively and explicitly plan for within our curriculum frameworks. This is not a comprehensive overview of every aspect of feedback, as that is a whole book in its own right, but rather this next section should help guide your conversations as you decide how best to approach this important aspect of your provision.

### Feedback To Pupils

We all understand that effective, meaningful and personally focused feedback is critical for the development of our pupils' knowledge and understanding as well as their physical and skills development. Within the context of PE, this feedback is more often than not provided through verbal means, related to the physical movement or performance being observed by another individual (usually the teacher but not always) and ideally focused on the positives that have been identified from any individual activity or engagement.

There are several subtly different types of feedback we can offer to our pupils when engaging in feedback, each with a slightly different impact and desired outcome. Generally, these fall into three categories, verbal, non-verbal and physical feedback.

Verbal feedback can be descriptive, where we are recognising and commenting on the behaviour or skill that has been observed. For example, 'Your take off was strong and powerful but your landing was off balance' which is giving the pupil detailed and focused feedback on what was observed and should generally be followed by some form of prescriptive guidance as to how this could be corrected or improved, for example 'Bend your knees more when you take off to generate more power'. Almost always, these two aspects should be combined to ensure our pupils understand that we have identified their positives and recognised how they can improve further through technical or tactical alterations. This approach ensures the pupil knows we are considering them as an individual performer and specifically addressing their needs and outcomes and is far more effective than generalised group feedback in developing positive relationships and motivation to try again.

Regardless of the type of descriptive feedback and prescriptive guidance the positivity of our feedback is critical. If we don't identify the successes within our feedback then the general perception on behalf of our pupils is that we are not valuing or recognising the things they have done well,

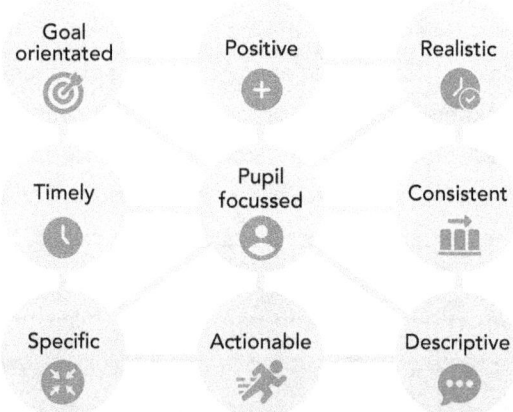

or the effort they are applying to the situation. Without the positivity, the prescriptive guidance could feel like criticism or critique, potentially leading to disengagement and disenchantment with the activity or lesson.

Non-verbal is an important facet of our feedback approach. The use of facial expression, hand signals, such as thumbs up, clapping or specific activity related gestures can all provide a quick and easy alternative to verbal engagement. If you see a pupil do something well, that doesn't appear to need detailed, prescriptive guidance, then a quick high five or thumbs up can have just as much impact on the positivity of that pupil, in a fraction of the time.

There are other varieties of non-verbal feedback, such as encouraging pupils to demonstrate, either in group or pair situations, video recording evidence of performance or even just moving around the activity to a different position to observe, which can all be effective in recognising positive performance or engagement.

The third method of feedback is more formal, physical feedback. This can be done in the form of written commentary, stickers, ticks on a chart or other display or any other means to physically identify and record performance, progress, attainment or engagement. The important factor here is to ensure that this does not become a form of standardised assessment or comparative activity which pitches pupils directly against each other, unwittingly. There may be some situations where you actively want this to happen, but in most cases, we want to avoid anything that may single out individual pupils who haven't achieved a performance level that others may have. Be very careful when considering how you use physical feedback, it can be a tokenistic strategy where pupils are extrinsically motivated to obtain something in return for their performance, can quickly alienate the rest of the class.

There are a few ways we can deliver feedback, regardless of the type we are using. The most impactful in the majority of situations will be individual, one to one feedback that directly addresses the needs of the specific pupil we are identifying. This should form a significant proportion of the feedback we provide within our lessons, as it undoubtedly has the most impact on learning development and motivation. Group feedback can be effective, generally when a small group of pupils are working together on a task or are roughly at the same level of ability or performance. In these situations, it is commonplace that a piece of feedback will be applicable to all pupils within the group and is therefore appropriate. We still need to be very aware of the dynamics involved in this feedback process to ensure that all the pupils are getting the most value from the situation and are not alienated or made to feel less successful than the others. Bringing a group together and singling out one pupil at the expense of the others is never going to be as impactful as speaking to each individual, but there are certainly times when this approach is appropriate and effective.

Peer assessment and peer feedback is an effective way of generating lots of opportunity for praise and recognition within our lessons. You are essentially sharing out the feedback process amongst the pupils and giving them the opportunity to support the process, meaning more pupils get feedback, more often.

The important thing to remember here, is that providing feedback in the correct, positive manner, is a learnt skill and you will need to spend time ensuring the pupils know the approach, structure, manner and positivity within which feedback is given, to then ensure that it is having the positive effect you are looking for. Just assuming pupils are going to be able to provide descriptive and prescriptive feedback in positive, appropriate ways, without being guided, is ultimately likely to lead to disaster. Certainly, it is something that needs to be developed rather than left to individuals to work out for themselves.

Finally, we can provide opportunities for self-assessment and reflection, allowing the pupils the opportunity to give feedback to themselves on a performance or action. Often this is done using rubrics or task sheets, but you can equally use video or other recordings to stimulate reflection and generate ideas on individual improvement. When done well and when supported by the teacher to develop this skill (because, like peer feedback, this is certainly a skill) self-reflection can be a very positive tool in our feedback toolkit.

In PE classes, different types of feedback can be given continuously and not just saved until the conclusion of a lesson. For those of us who have taught feedback at GCSE or A-Level we know that delayed feedback can allow for deeper analysis and goal setting but in the relatively simplistic environment of PE lessons, we are probably not looking for the depth of analysis required at this higher level of performance and in all likelihood in these busy learning environments, delayed feedback quite often becomes forgotten feedback and the chance to build positivity with that pupil or group of pupils can be lost. Even if we remember to provide this delayed feedback, the reality in most contexts is that the next time the pupils will get to perform that action or skill, will be their next lesson, meaning there will be an extended period of delay before implementing any guidance or advice in meaningful ways.

Immediate feedback is far more effective within our PE lessons, as it allows us to develop 'in-time' engagement with our pupils, provide prescriptive guidance or support during skill acquisition or development activity and gives our pupils the opportunity to make real time adjustments to their performance or actions, leading to higher success rates. Ideally, we will create a teaching and learning environment where a combination of the two methods, with immediate feedback supported by more general delayed feedback at group or class level, can increase the general effectiveness of our feedback

There are several other aspects to feedback that we should be considering when we are developing and adopting a department-wide pupil feedback policy. These include focusing on effort and improvement rather than just success or failure, using specific, age appropriate and actionable language so that our pupils can understand and act on the feedback they are being given. Be positive in your feedback, rather than focusing on negatives, to encourage our pupils to develop confidence in themselves and us as supporting adults and help develop motivation to want to continue to try hard on a particular skill or action. Often asking questions of pupils is a great way to help them develop reflective skills and if we can encourage a culture where pupils are willing and able to take ownership of their learning and progress and can identify in themselves the areas they can work on, it will make for far more impactful feedback engagements. Finally, don't be afraid to experiment with different types and methods of feedback within your curriculum. Often varying your feedback approaches will lead to engagement, motivation and interest. Technology can play a significant role here, as we develop new ways to use video, and other recorded evidence, to formulate feedback.

By focusing some time on deciding on the approaches your team will take in relation to feedback will help develop consistency and equity across your classes. Whilst feedback is an individual thing which teachers will do in a variety of ways, identifying the most impactful methods and focusing your plans to ensure this happens, will make your overall provision more effective in the long run. As always though, remember to review and reflect on feedback as you progress through your delivery process, to make adjustments or alterations as you need. Whatever type of feedback policy you develop for your PE curriculum, remember feedback is always more beneficial when it is grounded in positivity, so start with that!

### Feedback To Line Managers And Senior Leaders

It goes without saying that there will always be an expectation on PE departments, as with any other curriculum area, to give feedback regularly and accurately to colleagues, line managers and senior school management. Often these feedback cycles fall in line with reporting timetables however regular and meaningful sharing of data, reflections, and engagements with pupils can support the wider academic and pastoral provision across the school. It's always worth remembering the unique and varied environments in which we see pupils and the information that we gather within our PE spaces can help shape, confirm or challenge the interpretations that we make about pupils in other aspects of their schooling. From learning support, to safeguarding we can provide information and evidence that allow pupils to get the help they need, the teaching provision they require and the interactions they deserve, not just in PE, but across the school.

Regular, concise progress reports to leadership highlighting key metrics like student participation, skill development, and positive changes in physical activity levels can be of huge benefit and from a departmental perception perspective, the volume and quality of information that you can provide to develop wider decision making can really showcase your PE programme and the effectiveness and quality of your delivery. Not all feedback needs to be in the form of spreadsheets or data tables. Regular updates through success stories, newsletter articles, a dedicated PE department website or internal communication tool can be just as effective, as can talking directly to line managers and higher leadership colleagues on a regular basis. When something is identified, sharing that information in a timely and useful fashion can be more impactful and beneficial than adding it onto a spreadsheet that won't be looked at until the end of term. Within all your communication with the wider school, it is important to emphasise how your PE programmes are contributing to the broader school objective and goals beyond just academic performance. Wellbeing, Healthy School Cultures, Movement opportunities, Extra-Curricular engagement and CPD are all examples of areas where PE departments can engage and showcase their outstanding practice. A great example of this, from my own experience, was a project we undertook across the whole school, led and managed by the PE department, to track and increase the number of 'school steps' that took place daily. This encouraged pupils to move more during break times and teachers to find ways to 'activate' their lessons. We saw lessons that normally would be via desk and chair, delivered to groups walking around the campus! This transparency, timely access to evidence and data-driven approach will demonstrate the value of PE programs and hopefully encourage more engagement and support from leadership as well as build the perception of value across the wider school.

## Feedback To Parents

PE departments can effectively communicate student progress to parents through clear and consistent reporting. These reports should include specific examples of strengths and areas for improvement, using a positive and encouraging tone. We will discuss reporting structures and procedures in more detail in the next section.

We can also provide less formal feedback in a wide variety of ways. Phone calls home (positive not always negative!), through websites and newsletters, through online information sites or departmental noticeboards. Whatever ways you decide to engage and inform parents, outside of reporting systems, you should always consider the balance between focus on sport and PE, and the language and terminology you use. Positive is always best and avoiding direct recognition of personal performance or comparison is a good rule of thumb.

## Reporting Structures

In almost all contexts, the way in which information is reported formally, is through a standardised reporting structure and rarely will PE departments get the opportunity to create or utilise a bespoke reporting structure within their programme.

There is almost always likely to be guidance to follow when it comes to report writing as well, and teachers will be encouraged to use a combination of their own writing style with the format required by the wider school. Increasingly written reports are being replaced with data-rich numeric reports; however, many schools do still require at least one written comment a year as a minimum.

There isn't really a lot we can do within the context of our PE curriculum development to develop a bespoke reporting structure, unless you are working with a wider reporting/assessment development programme, which is unlikely in the majority of cases.

You can, however, ensure that when writing reports, we use that same positive, engagement and success focused terminology and language that we have used throughout our curriculum materials. Linking every aspect, including the final reporting or progress, together through the use of language will help with clarity of message and coherence and understanding, from both our pupils and parent perspectives.

The same can be said of verbal feedback at events such as parent consultation sessions. The positive, success-led focus of these conversations should be no different to the feedback approach we give to the pupils in lessons. Start and end with positives and try to reinforce any developmental recommendations with positive messaging. These face-to-face opportunities are rare and are a great opportunity for us as PE teachers to develop positive relationships with parents who in turn can act as additional motivational support for our pupils. Getting adults on side by being positive about their children, cannot fail to help develop the chances of having positive relationships with the pupils themselves.

## Communication And Publicity Plans

Having got to the point at which your curriculum processes and procedures, your maps, schemes, plans, resources, assessment and everything else is in place, you now come to the question of how you are going to communicate and raise awareness about your provision, internally, to the wider community around your school, and the wider PE and educational community. You may even, by this point, have already implemented part or all of your curriculum, done your testing and reflection, adapted things a few times and trialled aspects of it. Now you're ready to go with your newly developed provision, it's time to celebrate and publicise the effort and quality of the work you have undertaken.

Promoting the success of your PE program will require a level of proactivity on you and your team's part. If you don't talk about what you are doing and have done, then you cannot expect anyone to be aware of it and leaving it to your pupils alone to tell everyone what a great experience they are having, is leaving things somewhat to chance.

You will need to think about a positive, proactive communication strategy that engages with colleagues, parents, other PE departments and the wider PE community. To ensure that the provision you have developed and the impact that it is having in different areas, you will need to think about a strategy and plan for getting that information out into the wider community.

Some of this will happen through the normal reporting and assessment analysis processes within the school, but other, more creative ways to disseminate information, can really build the profile of your department and the provision.

Communication with colleagues will inevitably be formed through a range of data and information sharing exercises. Using data from assessments and observations, feedback from pupils that demonstrates the positive impact and outcomes your provision is having on pupil learning, development, motivation and engagement is a key starting point. Collating pupil news and activities that highlight pupil success that could be attributed in whole, or part, to the PE provision is another great way of gathering information. So are assembly demonstrations or presentations, website or newsletter articles that can all play a part in this wider information sharing process and highlight the positivity surrounding your new curriculum provision.

Depending on your school's approach to CPD and your individual school's context, it might be possible to organise or contribute to professional development opportunities. Offering workshops or training sessions for non-PE teachers, teaching and learning assistants, coaches, parents or other stakeholders using some of the work from your curriculum project, can be an excellent way to showcase the approach and style of PE you are now offering to the pupils for whom they also provide support.

Finding ways to collaborate with other departments can be a really effective sharing process. Finding cross-curricular or knowledge transfer opportunities can highlight areas of excellence within both department curricula and can have the added benefit of consolidating or reinforcing learning for pupils at the same time. Finding ways to develop interdisciplinary learning experiences that connect physical education to other areas of the curriculum is a powerful bonus that we should be looking to achieve for the benefit of our pupils. We can all think of examples of subjects working with PE to really embed content and theory across different curricular areas. The increasing awareness of the transfer of knowledge across different disciplines means these cross-curricular engagements are more frequent and more powerful.

Finally, finding ways to recognize and celebrate achievements at individual and group level will support your wider public acknowledgement. Hosting PE award or end of term events, success celebration in assemblies, noticeboards, letters/emails home, positive notes on your pupil management systems will all help to develop that acknowledgement of the curriculum, the contributions colleagues have made to the programme, the impact the curriculum is having and the successes your pupils are receiving as a result.

Some good tips for developing ways in which communication and public visibility can be effective are to use visualisations rather than data. Create charts, images, infographics, displays, posters, all of which will be of far more interest to non-PE specialists and stakeholders alike. Try to use storytelling in your messaging. Tell people about the stories of your pupils that showcase your PE provision, share the impact and outcomes because of your positive new approach. Use technology, leverage social media, websites, write blogs or articles and other online mediums to share your message and success with the wider PE community and build partnerships with anyone and everyone who can supplement, support, develop or enhance your provision further. There are many exceptional PE communities across the world now, who will want to hear your stories, showcase your work and celebrate your successes, so seek them out and use them.

Most importantly, across all of these communication routes, try to be passionate and enthusiastic at all times. Your enthusiasm and belief in the importance of the PE that you are now providing will be contagious and will inspire others across your school, local and wider community, to support the program. By consistently implementing these positive messages, you can really emphasise the success and impact of your PE program, garnering support from colleagues and parents, and ultimately creating a thriving environment where all students can experience the joy and benefits of the programme that you have created.

CHAPTER 10 - NUTS AND BOLTS

## Changemaker Reflection: Hannah Crawley
*Head of PE, The British International School Budapest*

When I started at this school nearly four years ago, it was never my intention to come in and make drastic changes. We were just coming out of the Covid pandemic and our main priority, as with many schools, was to re-establish some normality and consistency.
I knew I was entering a well-established department with many members having worked at the school for a significant number of years, and so I was aware that if changes were to be made at that time, they would need to be:

1. Absolutely necessary
2. Beneficial for everyone involved
3. Supported by the entire department

The changes I implemented were not immediate, they were borne out of open and honest dialogue with the team. I invested time observing but more importantly, listening. Listening to their opinions, ideas, aspirations and frustrations. I knew that as the department's newest member of staff, I needed to build relationships and trust for changes to be successful.
I came to realise that we could benefit from a clearer assessment framework. However, if this was going to be developed then it would be an appropriate time to also update and ensure our curriculum complemented how we were going to assess. Therefore, based on the conversations with the team, I made the decision to move to a more holistic curriculum: an adaptation of the Head, Heart, Hands approach.

I carried out research about how to implement successful change with much of my guidance taken from Kotter's (2005) 8-step and the ADKAR models (Hiatt, 2006). I would recommend these as a useful place to start if considering leading change within a team.

I developed my vision and established a clear strategy, putting in much of the groundwork before communicating this with the team. I was explicit about why the change was needed and how it would benefit everyone. I wanted to ensure that the department did not feel overwhelmed by the changes, or that it would require a significant investment of additional work and time. However, it was important that the team contributed to the process to enable their opinions to be considered and ensure the final product was a collaborative effort. We needed a model we were all confident delivering, explaining and that we passionately believed in.

When working together throughout the process, I reminded myself of the importance of keeping everyone motivated. I hope my timely reassurance and appreciation for their efforts contributed towards creating a safe environment for them to share their thoughts without fear of judgement.

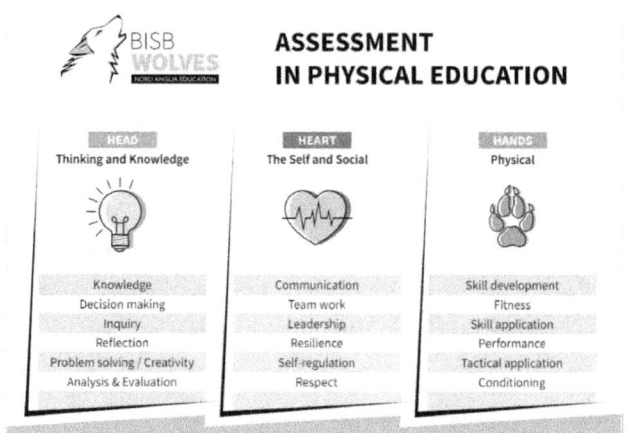

*Adapted from Frapwell, 2014*

Together we created a model, based around the Head, Heart, Hands model originally developed by Andy Frapwell (2014). It is a model that we all appreciate and values the skills and attributes important in today's landscape. We will continuously look for improvements, as this is by no means a final product, but we now have greater clarity and a shared vision. I also now have confidence that if I were to introduce new initiatives in the future, I would have the team's full support, due to the relationships and trust I have built leading them through this period of change.

This was quite a significant chapter within *Changemakers*, so well done for making your way through it!

As we said at the start of the chapter, not every context is the same and every school will have its own, often tried and tested approaches to curriculum design. Not every element discussed above will be relevant or required within your school and that's fine. To undertake, in detail, every element we've discussed, is a major time and effort commitment and you have to be absolutely sure that work you undertake will always make a positive difference to the teaching and learning your department provides. If it doesn't make a difference, then you must consider whether it is a priority. Ultimately, a well-designed, carefully crafted and considered curriculum set-up is always going to provide a better, more appropriate and meaningful learning experience for your pupils. This can be done in limitless ways, but the focus on teaching, learning and provision is key to the quality, value and benefit that comes from the project.

Curriculum design is both a challenge and an opportunity. If you go into this with a perspective of opportunity, and a passion to create and develop quality at every stage, then you are guaranteed to come out of the other side, with something you can be proud of, that will work, and that showcases the quality and commitment within your PE department or team.

From my own experiences, the time spent considering the individual aspects of your processes and documentation makes the difference between a well thought through and effective curriculum and a less impactful and disjointed one. Whilst this is never going to be a short and swift process, it is always going to be time well spent. If I reflect back to the start of my own journey leading change within a PE curriculum, the key aspects I would ensure I covered would always include:

1. Your vision and mission - If you are clear with your ambition and know what you want the final outcomes to look and feel like, you can always quality assure the work your team are doing, against those initial objectives

2. Know what elements of the overall curriculum documentation are going to have the most impact on teaching and learning and start with those. Rather than running down a list of documents you think you have to produce, order them in relation to the most beneficial and work together on those first.

3. Never assume that your first draft is the right draft. This book has gone through numerous iterations and editing processes and your curriculum design should be the same. Create, share, reflect, adapt should be a motto that resonates across your department. Share what you have created with specialists and non-PE colleagues alike, gather feedback and reflect together on the impact of your creations and never be afraid to change something that doesn't work. What you start with does not always reflect where you will end up, and that is a natural part of the transformative activity you are aspiring to undertake.

## Reflective Questions - Context

Your context is key to what you need to develop and design.
It's worth taking the time to really identify what your priorities are, by asking yourself and your department colleagues, the following questions:

- What are your absolute teaching and learning priorities?
- From this chapter, where do you see your opportunities for change?
- Will these opportunities impact positively on teaching and learning?
- How much time should you spend on each aspect?
- How can you split the work down to manageable volumes for each member of your team?

Could you use these reflective questions as the start of a departmental SWOT analysis, to really explore your strengths and weaknesses as a department and what opportunities and threats exist within the development of your curricular offering?

# Chapter 11 - Who And How?

## The Impact Of Change

**'The only limit to your impact is your imagination and commitment.'**
*Tony Robbins*

**Educational change is a fact of life for teachers across the world, as schools are subjected to constant and ubiquitous pressures to innovate.**
*Priestley, 2011*

Throughout recent decades, there have been significant studies conducted into the impact that organisational change has on the perception of 'smooth flow' within those mechanisms (Benford & Snow, 2000; Bouckenooghe, 2010; Pettigrew et al., 2001) and there is a generally held acceptance that the way that we react to change, is in part at least, determined by our cognitive and behavioural acceptance and response to an adaptation, as well as the level of understanding we have of the perceived expectations on us to accept and respond to change. (Al-Abrrow et al., 2019b; Peng et al, 2020)

As we discussed in an earlier chapter, change can be an unsettling or uncomfortable process for some people, whilst others can thrive and gain motivation through a change process.

The Kubler-Ross change curve was created by psychiatrist Elisabeth Kübler-Ross in 1969 to visualise the stages (grief, denial, anger, bargaining, depression, acceptance and eventually engagement) that individuals go through when exposed to a period of change within their personal or professional lives. Whilst not specifically designed for educational contexts it does represent a typical emotional cycle, we would expect individuals involved in our programmes to experience throughout the project.

## CHANGEMAKERS

It is important to recognise the different ways in which people react to change, and the process individuals go through when engaging with and being impacted by change, so that we can ensure we are supporting each individual in the best possible way, not only to help them but to increase the potential for success within the project as a whole.

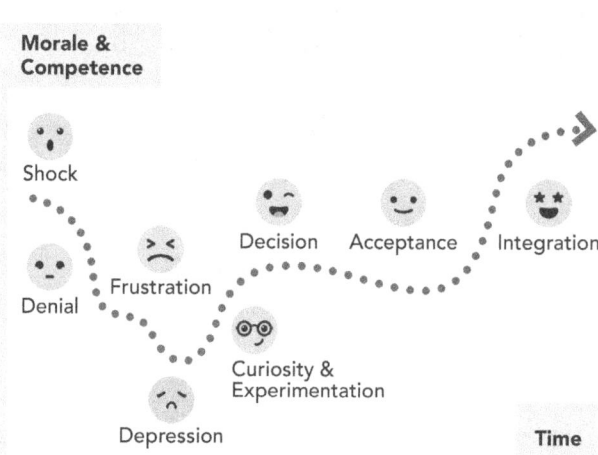

The Kubler-Ross Change Curve (1969)

---

### Changemaker Reflection: Ellie Woodcock
*Primary PE Teacher, Singapore*

Throughout my teaching career, I have contributed to the design and implementation of three distinct Primary physical education curriculums. While these experiences were inherently rewarding, they were not devoid of challenges and frustrations.

A key takeaway from my involvement in curriculum design is the absence of a one-size-fits-all approach. It is imperative to tailor the curriculum to the unique needs of the students in your school and the context that you are working in. Furthermore, I emphasise the collaborative nature of this process, highlighting that successful curriculum development is a collective effort where diverse perspectives converge to generate innovative ideas.

In one school that I worked at, we were fortunate to have considerable autonomy in adapting the curriculum to allow our students to thrive and flourish. This autonomy allowed us to leverage a broad spectrum of curricula and expertise, prompting thoughtful consideration of our department's intent, aspirations, and future objectives.

However, this journey was not without its hurdles. We grappled with questions about delivering content within spatial and time constraints, ensuring continued alignment with educational standards and the school's values, and how to effectively communicate our PE intent and rationale to children, parents, staff, and stakeholders. Additionally, devising a meaningful assessment system for tracking students' progress and achievements in PE posed a significant challenge and is still an area that we wish to further improve.

When redesigning our curriculum, the imperative of inclusivity weighed heavily on our considerations, especially given our school's composition with both mainstream and a Special Educational Needs and Disabilities (SEND) unit. Recognising the diverse needs across classes, we devised units of work with predefined learning intentions and outcomes, accompanied by a flexible bank of activities. This approach allowed teachers to adapt activities to suit the needs and abilities of their specific classes while ensuring that all students could meet the designated lesson objectives and achieve success.

## Mindful Leadership: Change for Teachers

Change, even positive change, can be unsettling. It can disrupt familiar routines and force us to adapt to new situations. This can lead to feelings of uncertainty, anxiety, and even fear. Our brains are hardwired to seek out predictability and stability. When things change, it throws us off balance and can trigger a fight-or-flight response. This is why we often resist or challenge change, even when it is demonstrated to be positive for us or the pupils we serve.

Teachers in particular can often struggle with change because our profession fundamentally functions through routines and structure, allowing us to effectively manage classrooms and deliver lessons. Change can disrupt this long established and deep-rooted approach, requiring us

- Change is a natural part of life
- Accept change in your life
- Focus on the present
- Ask for help managing change
- Be proactive with change
- Know that things don't always work
- Find meaning in the change

to adapt to new methodologies, resources, and expectations. This can be overwhelming and time-consuming, especially when it happens against a backdrop of pre-existing workload pressures. As teachers we often develop a sense of ownership and pride in our established teaching methods, making us hesitant to embrace new approaches that might be perceived to be challenging our expertise. If we're good teachers, why would anyone want us to do things differently? 'I've been doing this for years, and no one has ever wanted me to change before, look at my results'.

Often the fear of change is exacerbated by change without appropriate support and training or development. Asking us to do something new, without giving us the tools and resources and knowledge to be able to do it, can lead to anxiety and frustration. Some of the emotions that our colleagues could be facing include:

**Uncertainty:** When asked to step into new territory with a newly created curriculum, resources, and expectations can be daunting. It could potentially feel a little like navigating their way through a maze with no clear path forward. This uncertainty can lead to anxiety and a sense of being overwhelmed.

**Loss of control:** Moving away from established routines or familiar teaching methods can certainly provide a loss of control within the dynamic environment of our PE programmes. Change can disrupt our sense of control over our teaching, our classes or our approach, making us feel less confident and adaptable in the one area we already feel effective and competent.

**Resistance:** As PE teachers we have often developed a strong sense of who we are, why we do what we do and how we go about doing it. We develop this quickly when we first start off on our PE teaching career and that sense of pride and ownership over our teaching can be challenged by the suggestion we are going to do things in a different way. Facing this challenge to our pre-existing processes and approaches can trigger a natural resistance to change, especially if we feel that our expertise and experience is not being valued or considered.

**Loss of identity:** For some PE teachers, our teaching style and established programs are closely linked to our professional identity and personal values. Embracing systemic change to the way we deliver and perceive PE might require teachers to redefine themselves as educators, which can be an unsettling experience. If you have always taught PE through team sports, and suddenly you are told you can't, that could represent a significant sense of loss for you personally.

**Additional workload:** The process of implementing change inevitably requires additional time and effort on behalf of everyone involved. Training, planning, and adapting to new systems can all expend time and energy that previously was not required or was channelled into other aspects of a teachers' routine. This request or requirement on teachers to add to their existing workload can feel like unnecessary and unwelcome pressure leading to feelings of stress, pressure or anxiety.

**Lack of support:** Even the most organised and collaborative project can quickly unravel if the colleagues involved in the process do not feel equipped or supported to effectively undertake the activity, they are being asked to engage in. This starts with the process of developing the curriculum and will continue throughout the journey and will include practical and theoretical development in the new approaches and pedagogical framework you are offering. Without adequate training, resources, and ongoing support during the change process, PE teachers can quickly feel isolated and overwhelmed. Whilst they may not vocalise this, and instead keep their insecurity and vulnerability to themselves, it can lead to frustration, resistance, and a sense of being undervalued as an educator and colleague.

Navigating change from a department leaders' perspective is about clear and accurate communication, empathy and recognition of the anxiety that change could be causing, support and guidance where appropriate without seeming to be condescending or patronising. Collaboration with all the members of your department from the very outset will help but will not necessarily solve all the issues and so constant reflection and observation of the dynamics of individuals and relationships is critical throughout the process. Ultimately, we want to try to make all the members of our teams see the value in what we are doing, both from a personal and pupil perspective as well as support them to see the process as one that is including them, valuing their knowledge and expertise and utilising their ideas and vision as much as anyone else. If you can balance all of these things, then the likely outcome is that your team will get on board and make your project more effective, more efficient and easier to undertake.

When we create a positive, collaborative culture within our teams, related to the process of change we are looking to take our department on, we can emphasise the positivity within the project and the personal and professional benefits that each individual could experience as a result of the process they are going to go on with you.

**Professional growth:** There is no doubt that curriculum design is one of the most challenging but rewarding processes that any teacher can go through. We all desire that opportunity to create something unique and inspirational we can call our own. There is nothing better in PE teaching than being given a metaphorical 'blank sheet of paper' and being offered the freedom to create something from scratch. It's something that may only happen once in a teacher's career and therefore the opportunity to learn, develop and progress our skill set is one that should be grasped with both hands. Making our teams see the benefit to them as a professional and the wide depth of learning they will get throughout the project, can really help to inspire them to get on board and be positive about the process ahead.

**Learning to step outside of our comfort zone:** Stepping outside their comfort zones and embracing new ideas can stimulate creative thinking, improve teaching skills, and boost personal development.

**Increased Engagement with Pupils:** As we create new, fresh and innovative approaches to engaging with pupils within our PE spaces, we can energise, or re-energise students. When they are energised by our provision, they will increase their engagement in physical activities, in turn impacting positively on their sense of meaning within their PE lessons and their sense of personal worth when working physically. Ultimately this should help promote that lifelong love of movement that we are all striving for. Increasing our engagement levels will help with many aspects of teaching and learning, including developing those positive relationships with pupils that are so important to our programme's success.

**Improve our program effectiveness:** Ultimately when we develop something new or change something, it is with the goal of improving our practice, using evidence-based approaches and enhancing our provision as a result. The way we use our new PE curriculums to focus on our current pupil needs and outcomes, will lead to more effective programs that achieve better learning outcomes.

**Enhanced collaboration:** The opportunity to work within a project such as curriculum development is a great way to build a cohesive, supportive and collaborative environment within our teams, that will have many, positive, long-lasting benefits to individual teachers and the team as a whole. The opportunity to work in new ways, with colleagues, should always be seen as a positive outcome from any change project.

As the project or department leader, we can have a significant influence over whether our team perceives change in positive or negative ways. If we can support and encourage a positive attitude towards our curriculum development, we are far more likely to achieve the buy-in we really need to be successful. There are a few strategies we can adopt to really help us with this process, and increase our chances of engagement from everyone:

**Help our team to develop a growth mindset:** We need to regularly and clearly emphasise the opportunities presented to our team for learning and personal growth. If we can help our department members to see the challenge as an opportunity to develop new skills, improve their teaching practice, engage more effectively with their classes and be part of a significant collaborative project, they will increasingly see the benefits to them personally and hopefully embrace the change more positively.

**Keep them informed:** It's critical that every member of our team feels included. Just like we practise inclusive PE with our pupils, we must practise inclusive collaboration with our colleagues. Give them access to new information as soon as practically possible, inform them early about development or changes that are upcoming and really emphasise the positive impact these developments are going to have. Seek their input and give them responsibility for sharing their knowledge and findings as well. Make sure, at all times, the communication you are disseminating is backed by evidence or research. Whilst opinion is valuable, basing all of your communication on your own opinion can lead to disengagement from others.

**Build a strong supportive team:** By developing connections with colleagues, mentors, and administrators we can offer guidance and support when and wherever it is needed. The closer your team is professionally the less chance of frustration or disagreement there will be. Whilst debate and different viewpoints are important, the success or failure of your project could rest on the ability of your team to pull together to make it happen. Negotiating and mediation skills here, on behalf of the project leaders, will really be important and these are personal development opportunities for you as the leader of change, to enhance your own skill set and knowledge.

**Be adaptable and flexible:** Be willing to adjust your approach to the project as needed. If you are clear with your team that their opinions and ideas are valuable and you are willing to include those in the project where there is consensus, they will feel more engaged with the project as a whole and are more likely to adopt a positive approach to it.

**Maintain a positive attitude:** Not everything will go smoothly and when there are challenges or hurdles to be overcome, a positive attitude on your part can go a long way in helping everyone around you cope with change. Try to focus on the potential benefits of the changes and how they can improve your students' learning experience, as this will help keep your wider focus on positives and avoid dwelling on negatives.

**Practise self-care:** It's important that as well as considering the wellbeing and support of your team throughout the change process, you also take time to consider your own physical and mental wellbeing. Being on top of things is important but undertaking too much on your own or not giving yourself time away from the project to recuperate and recharge, can have a detrimental impact on your ability to maintain a positive approach to the process.

**Celebrate successes:** At every stage of your project, it is important to acknowledge and celebrate your own successes and the successes of your team. This can help maintain motivation and morale and keep the momentum of the project going. Look for things that happen, even if they are small, that can be recognised and celebrated along the journey, to break it up into more manageable elements.

**Mindful Leadership: Change For Children**
Anything that changes within a school can become a source of instability and stress for pupils. The social, educational and personal change that changes in school environments are sources of instability and stress for children. (Rose, 2016).

Adapting to change in schools can be challenging for pupils regardless of their ages. Whether it's moving to a new classroom, having a new teacher, or dealing with curriculum changes, change can disrupt their routine and sense of security. Just like adults, children can be unsettled, and this can have a detrimental impact on their learning and emotional wellbeing. We can also have a significant impact on their sense of security and safety within our PE provision, if we aren't clear on how the change is going to be perceived and managed by each individual pupil. It's really important, when embracing any form of change management project, that we consider every aspect from the perspective of the pupils being educated within that developing curriculum.

However, our pupils are inherently resilient to change and with careful consideration should not be negatively impacted by anything we undertake in relation to change within our curriculum or provision. There are a few key considerations that we need to reflect on when we are considering the impact of change within the pupils we teach.

Pupils respond better to clear and consistent provision and information. When we explain what is happening and why, in any context, pupils are more likely to understand and accept this. The same goes for anything that changes within their PE experience. If you are changing or adapting provision that pupils are going to experience, then explain why, how and what the outcome as a result might be. Obviously, we need to consider pupil age and needs here, and appropriate language and complexity is required, however generally the more open we are, the more included our pupils will feel within the process they are experiencing. Honesty is a key relationship building tool here as well. Being honest and upfront about the reasons behind something will bring a sense of inclusion on behalf of the pupils. If we are honest with them, they are more likely to feel positivity towards us as trustworthy adults.

### Helping children to cope with change

**Give them time**
Giving pupils time before change to understand, reflect and process change will support their emotional response.

**Listen to them**
Take time to address their questions and concerns during the process. Help them feel they are being considered throughout the change.

**Explore change**
Help them understand by exploring what change is and how they might react. Use age appropriate language and resources to support their understanding.

**Support routines**
Try and maintain as much consistency and routine as possible to help them manage their time, stress and emotion. Structure helps them feel safe and secure.

**Emphasise positives**
When talking and discussing change, try and emphasise the benefits and outcomes they can expect. Try and help them see the positive to them.

Always give your pupils the opportunity to feedback, discuss, and express an opinion in a safe and supportive manner. This is particularly important when we are 'testing' things out during our curriculum development. If you are going to 'trial' something with a group, make sure they know that it is happening, why it is happening and then give them the chance to give feedback to you on whether they felt it was effective. Just like we want to ensure our colleagues feel they have a voice in our project, we can do the same with our pupils, gaining even more trust, and positive relationship development as a result. Ultimately their voice is one of the most important as it is their experience we are looking to enhance, so listen to them and take on board their feedback.

Maintaining your basic routines and structures will help pupils to feel grounded and not overwhelmed by change. As long as the basic rules, expectations and routines remain constant, the pupils in your classes are far less likely to be confused or disrupted by curriculum change. Obviously if part of your change process is those rules, routines and structures then this becomes a harder task, however timing these so that they do not happen mid-way through a period of learning can help avoid any unsettling within the classes. Implement your new structures at the start of a new term, unit or year, rather than mid-way through. Ultimately, we want to maintain a sense of normality and predictability within our curriculum provision, so pupils aren't unduly stressed as a result of anything we do.

Remember your priority remains the same. Regardless of the type of style of curriculum you are building, the importance of positive relationships with pupils regarding PE, physical activity, sport and lifelong love of movement remain the same. If you can maintain these positive relationships and build around the connections you already have with your pupils, then the foundations upon which your curriculum provision is based will not falter. On top of this the structure can change but fundamentally we are always going to be trying to build that sense of positivity, personal meaning, value and self-worth, whatever way we go about it.

A really positive way to ensure pupil buy-in during periods of change is to offer your pupils the opportunity to get involved with the change itself. Can you set up student consultation groups or sessions? Can you engage with your student leaders or older pupils to get their perspectives and ideas? Can you use questionnaires and surveys to gather wider opinions and suggestions, and can you actually be explicit in showing your pupils you are listening to them and implementing the things they actually want? Giving pupils choice is a hugely important part of any modern PE programme. Whether it be pathways or options we know that giving pupils control over their learning works in terms of positivity and engagement. The same is true for curriculum change, the more the pupils feel included and valued the more likely they are to help spread your positive message and engage with your developments in supportive ways.

### Mindful Leadership: Change For Parents

Parents and guardians play a crucial role in supporting their children through change in schools. Whilst they may not be your primary focus, it is important to recognise and include parents in your communication related to any new approach to PE.

The important thing to remember when it comes to engaging with parents, in any capacity, is that their perception of PE is almost always linked to their own lived experiences. Their engagement with PE during their schooling is likely to be a significant factor in the way that they view provision for their children. The key to positive engagement with parents is to recognise these personal experiences and wherever possible highlight the differences between their experiences as pupils at school and those being afforded to their own children.

There are several different views that parents will have about PE within schools, and each will require a different approach when communicating about your own provision. Two critical aspects that are worth considering in your planning are the perception of PE as a negative experience, and the assumption that PE is the same as Sport.

**PE was a negative experience:** This is a particularly common attitude you will come across with parents. We recognise as a community that past iterations of PE weren't always the most inclusive or empathetic and as such there will be a significant number of adults for whom PE still remains something that brings anxiety or unhappy memories. They will be viewing your provision in relation to this and looking for reassurance that the experiences that their children are being given are more positive and inclusive than the ones they received themselves. In this instance the critical factor is to emphasise the positivity within your curriculum, the fact that you have worked with and listened to the pupils to develop the new curriculum and the change in approach from past versions of PE. Often showcasing your provision through open days, events, newsletters, parents' evenings or websites is a great starting point for showing the difference in the way that you are doing things and the approach you are taking within your own version.

**PE is all about Sport:** Depending again on the lived experience of parents, and the context in which they were educated, there will be parents within your community for whom the concept of PE and Sport being separate, distinct entities will not be immediately obvious or understood. The conversations and communication around this will, to some extent, depend on your own perception of this and whether you are creating/developing a curriculum that separates the two or retains those links. If you do intend to remove or lessen the link between PE and Sport within your curriculum then the messaging around this will need careful thought and planning. You will need to demonstrate what this means in practice, what experiences the pupils in your school are going to receive aside from traditional sport focused lessons and what the benefits of this approach are. These are messages that you will have to collaboratively decide on and develop a consistent and clear message around this before presenting it to your parent community. You will then need to ensure that all of your departmental members and associated colleagues are clear on the message, reinforcing this at every relevant opportunity. Ultimately you will know why you are creating the programme that you are, and as long as you can justify it, ideally with research and evidence to support it, then your message should be clear and understood. Just be prepared to answer lots of questions about it, as you cannot assume every parent will understand straight away.

Regardless of the message you want to disseminate to your parent community, there are no surprises that the key is to keep parents well-informed, with clear and simple communication in a timely fashion. Have detailed explanations ready for parents who want more information but try to keep your initial communication as brief, succinct and clear as possible, increasing the chances of it being read and digested.

Be ready to address the concerns and be welcoming of the questions. Whilst it is always tempting to close down any challenges or concerns, it is better to see these as raised with positive intent and if you are confident that your provision is meeting the needs of your pupils, their children, then do not be afraid to face these questions face on, in a positive and empathetic manner and always try to reach a position of agreement and understanding.

Be willing to engage in learning opportunities with your parents. Organising workshops or demonstrations to impart information and knowledge will not just provide parents with the opportunity to learn more about PE within your school's context but will foster that sense of collaboration, consideration and shared experience, all supporting a positive atmosphere around PE within your school and wider community.

There is nothing wrong with encouraging parents to share their feedback and suggestions about the changes and their own children's experiences. Your pupils are likely to be going home and talking about their school experiences and this is really beneficial information to gather when possible. This two-way engagement with parents gives you a different perspective on the way your curriculum is developing, and it also fosters collaboration and builds trust within your wider community.

### Reflective Questions - Stakeholders

- Who are you making the changes for?
- Do you know how your different stakeholders feel about your PE provision?
- Have you considered all your different stakeholders within your project?
- How are you going to continue to monitor and reflect on the impact across all the different impacted parties throughout your project and upon completion?

## Changemaker Reflection: Matthew Kelly
*Head of PE, Warrington*

Students without PE kit, students watching in uniform, low numbers at extracurricular, no sports teams, high numbers of students removed from lessons. This was a regular sight in the department. This comes as a result of working with students from low-income families, where physical activity outside of school was inaccessible to the majority. Regularly, students would ask, 'Why are we doing this?'. The curriculum that was offered to students, could not be transferred to life away from school, resulting in low engagement. Thus, our 'lifelong love of sport' rationale was falling short of the desired impact. Unfortunately, students cannot change their circumstances, therefore we needed to do things differently.

As a result, I researched further into the concept curriculum, with the idea of adapting this model to best support our students. Our new curriculum needed our children's circumstances and challenges at the core to allow for this to make an impact. To ensure this happened, we began to correlate ideas through pupil voice; PE kit and Curriculum as the main focal points. It was identified that the PE kit was not fit for purpose for the modern-day pupil and therefore needed a rebrand to ensure all students felt comfortable to engage in all styles of PE lessons. Students are now offered tracksuits, leggings and t-shirts as optional extras as opposed to the more traditional polo shirts and skorts. Although we now have these optional kits, they came at a price. For those students who could access this, it had a huge impact on lesson and extra-curricular engagement. Despite this, we could not expect all parents and students to be able to access this straight away. We were aware it would take a few years for all students to have equal access due to the context of our school.

As practitioners, we are expected to remove barriers to learning where possible. Books, stationery and uniform are provided to our families that need support to ensure students can access all areas of the curriculum. SLT supported the idea that PE kit should be included in this. Investment was made into our 'spare kit cupboard', however, we needed to ensure this was relatable to the modern-day student. Students are less likely to involve themselves in PE if they are offered unwashed, old and mismatched kits. To ensure that borrowing kit was more idealistic, we invested in clothes rails and washing machines that were seen by students. Once the kit had been used, students were to put this into the wash bag. Kits were washed daily, and although time consuming, this had a great impact on uptake in PE. Students recognised quickly that the kit was clean, ready to wear and available for all. Arguably, some students used this to their advantage and were reminded that

they own a kit and the expectation for this to be brought to each lesson. However, for the latter they experienced for the first time since joining our school; a warm, comfortable kit the same as their peers. Luckily, our community and staff further donated trainers and football boots. Our biggest barrier to learning has now been removed.

Next, we needed to ensure that this engagement was sustained. Our curriculum needed to ensure that more than the 5% of students that already enjoyed sport began to partake. We adopted the 'Know, Grow and Show' (KGS) assessment model and concept curriculum.

Having an outcome and focus for each strand, gave us a clear way to engage more learners. We could easily identify the learners we knew could benefit from each strand. Praise was a great factor in our new model.

Over the coming weeks, the model began to show its effectiveness. Students who had typically displayed negative attitudes towards PE, now accepted new challenges and volunteered independently. It became evident that this would result in praise for communication and confidence, not just their performance levels. Praise was offered for their knowledge of skills and tactics and the way they're articulated to each other. For those students that we had that were practically competent, we could stretch and challenge their 'grow' element of the assessment model. How can they lift morale, confidence and in turn team performance for their team? Arguably, we went too far. We were designing lessons and content that focused so much on concepts that we lost some practical development in our students. However, overtime we found that balance. Students knew their strengths. Students knew which strand they needed to work on, and they had that focus for every lesson. The focus moved away from their sole ability to pass a football, to how communication, teamwork tactics and basic passing principles can be applied to team-sports and eventually life.

The 'why' has always been to create opportunities for success. As much of the research suggests, some students' only exposure to sport, PE and physical activity is in PE lessons. Giving students a positive experience in our PE lessons is our why. As a result of these changes, we had our highest numbers in our KS4 options, students taking part in extra-curricular and fixtures. We only had one or two regular PE refusers in the whole school, and we had students taking part in our sports leaders' events that would never have volunteered previously. We had more students playing sports outside of school. We changed our focus, by putting students at the core of our curriculum. Hopefully, this has a long-lasting impact on attitudes towards physical activity both in and outside of formal education.

# Chapter 12 - Solid Foundations

The Challenge Of Project Management

*'Leadership and learning are indispensable to each other.'*
*John F. Kennedy*

Formal project management is not something that we usually identify with educational establishments, but when we really consider the dynamic, fluid nature of schools, we are almost always exposed to something that resembles a project during our working lives. There are always new initiatives, new proposals, development of aspects of our provision, changes in personnel or frameworks and these evolutions could each be seen through the lens of project management if we, as a teaching community, recognised this.

Rarely are teachers and staff within schools provided with formal project management training or exposed to the processes and structures used within project management elsewhere in industry. Perhaps we should be though, because when we break down the processes we go through with change within our schools, many direct comparisons can be drawn between what we are doing, and what it would look like within a more formulaic project management programme.

So, in this section, we are going to step away from educational contexts and look at the actual structures, procedures and frameworks for project management generally. We are going to explore potential structures and methods we could adopt within our project to formalise it within a recognised project management structure. I am going to introduce you, at a relatively basic level, to some of the most common project management approaches, and identify aspects we could replicate within our own curriculum development plans.

There are many recognised methodologies developed to support project management within industry. Some of these include the Waterfall Methodology, the Agile Methodology, the Scrum Methodology, the Lean Methodology, Six Sigma and PRINCE2. Most of these names will mean nothing to you and we rarely come across any of these during our teaching journey. Each one is an adaptation of a basic process of managing change and all are used heavily and interchangeably within business and industry, to structure our processes whenever a project is initiated.

Essentially, a project management methodology is a basic set of principles, techniques and resources we can use when we are going through a project management process. They are designed to help those involved and leading projects to structure their work, find efficiencies and effective approaches and to help lead stakeholders in positive, effective, collaborative ways.

There is no ideal project management methodology, and most have complementing or similar aspects to them. Each has positive and negative aspects to consider as well, and it's important when thinking about the methodology we are going to adopt, to evaluate its suitability within the context of an educational environment. Some are much more suited to use within schools than others, and there is no formal agreement about which is the most beneficial for use within our sector.

Each variety of project management methodology could fill a book in its own right, and as PE teachers who occasionally undertake projects, we probably do not need an encyclopaedic knowledge of all the different potential methodologies we could use, however it is worth understanding at the most basic level, how each works, so that you can decide which ones to explore in more detail.

(Remember when we are looking at potential methodologies to use, your context is critical. You do not need to implement every aspect or follow one to the letter. It's also important to remember that your methodology will help you define the approach to your project, not necessarily shape the actual project steps we've discussed earlier in this book).

**The Waterfall Methodology** (Royce, 1970) promotes an approach that is sequential and linear, like the flow of a waterfall. It is a well-known and traditional methodology that is structured and predictable (Sherrell, 2013)

The key principles of the Waterfall Methodology are that it is sequential and Linear, in that each phase of the project must be completed before moving on to the next. There is no room for going back or making changes. It forces you to set clear and defined requirements at the start of the project which are gathered, approved and documented at the beginning and are set and unchangeable throughout the project. It requires stakeholders to adopt a phased approach whereby the project is divided into distinct phases, each with separate deliverables and competition points. The Waterfall methodology focuses on planning and documentation and encourages the project manager and project team to formalise these at the very early planning stages, before any actual work begins.

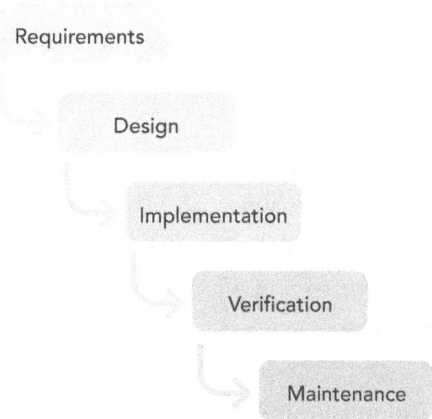

The Waterfall Methodology, 1956

There are five phases within the Waterfall methodology, these are:

**Requirements** - Identify and document in detail all your projects' objectives, scope, requirements and any technical aspects specific to your project.

**Design** - Here you will use the previously determined scope and requirements to design a project overview, including all the various elements we've previously discussed to formulate a comprehensive design overview

**Implementation** - This phase requires you to build the actual aspects of the project, testing each element to confirm effectiveness at each stage.

**Verification** - Rigorous testing in a variety of different situations to ensure that your design is fit for purpose and rigorously ensuring that it is meeting your original scope and vision set out in the requirements phase.

**Maintenance** - Starting once the newly designed programme is fully implemented, this phase requires continuous monitoring and evaluation of the effectiveness and appropriateness of each aspect, adapting and revising elements that are not meeting your original objectives.

The Waterfall methodology is simplistic and relatively simple to utilise, however each phase will require significant focus and likely to need to be broken down into smaller aspects to ensure you are comprehensively designing and implementing everything. You will find the Waterfall methodology particularly effective if you are only undertaking a relatively simple or light touch project, changing one aspect of your provision for example, rather than a more complex entire curriculum development.

Implementing change in schools presents various challenges, impacting teachers, students, parents, and the overall school environment. Here are some of the fundamental challenges:

**The Agile project management methodology** (PMI, 2017) allows for a much more flexible approach to project management, than the waterfall method. It is designed to be used in a collaborative context with many individuals contributing to a self-organised framework in which your project will progress. In other words, it is deliberately flexible without any specific phases set out, allowing you to design your project stages to suit your specific requirements. It focuses on the importance of adaptability, early implementation and constant evaluation and improvement. This allows for a more fast-paced, early implementation which could be particularly appropriate for a curriculum build as you can get it up and running quickly and then adapt it as you assess it in practice.

Whilst its positive aspects relate to the flexibility of approach, adopting this methodology can be challenging as you effectively have to design your project plan from scratch rather than following a predetermined set of stages. This is perhaps more appropriate for experienced curriculum designers who already have a good idea of what steps are required to take a project from initial concept to delivery and not so helpful for first time project managers.

**Agile Management, 2001**

**The Scrum Methodology** (Schwaber & Sutherland, 1991) is particularly popular within project management organisations currently and is being adopted widely in a wide range of different contexts. Originating from research done by Harvard University, it's ideal for small teams of very closely aligned colleagues and requires you to stick to rigid two-week cycles of project progress meetings, known as scrum meetings. It is led by the project manager, known as a scrum master and that individual will always have the final say in the next steps and the delegation of jobs and responsibilities. This seems to fit well with the normal dynamic of a PE department, but it can be challenging to keep pace with the strict timescales adopted by this methodology and can build pressure on individuals to ensure tasks are completed on time and effectively. Similar in approach to the agile methodology, there is a requirement on the 'scrum' and the 'scrum master' to ensure that the phases of the project are clearly designed and communicated to all parties and that

**Scrum Methodology**

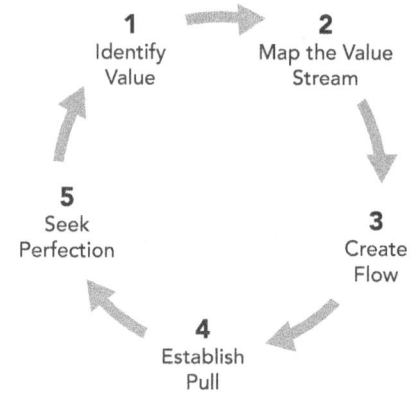

*Takeichi & Nonaka, 1986*

deadlines are clear and adhered to. If you are time-pressured and believe your team has the resilience to manage the pressure of those time frames, then the scrum methodology might be just the approach you are looking for.

**The Lean Methodology**, does exactly what its title suggests, giving the project team the primary focus of reducing or eliminating wasted time and wasteful activity to focus specifically and directly on the most important aspects of the project first (Womack & Jones, 1996) to get it up and running as quickly as possible. This will require careful consideration of any technique, technology or pre-existing resources or curriculum elements already existing within your programme, utilising whatever you can to save time and effort redesigning it. Originally championed by car manufacturer Henry Ford, the approach found a niche in the automotive industry but has now been adopted far more widely, including within education. This methodology requires you to decide, at the initial project planning stage, what you can reuse or retain, what are the most critical aspects of your project and how quickly you can get it organised, developed and implemented. This methodology is most suitable when you are revising rather than redeveloping a curriculum, or only changing specific elements of your provision rather than starting from scratch.

**The Six Sigma methodology** (Bill Smith, 1987) is a well-known and widely adopted project management approach, first used by Motorola in 1986. There are, however, many variations of it being used in different industries and as such it can be a confusing and complex methodology to try and apply. It is probably more suited to experienced project managers however the structure of the phases can be quite appropriate for the kind of curriculum design projects we are looking to implement. (Ilin & Nohlen, 2023)

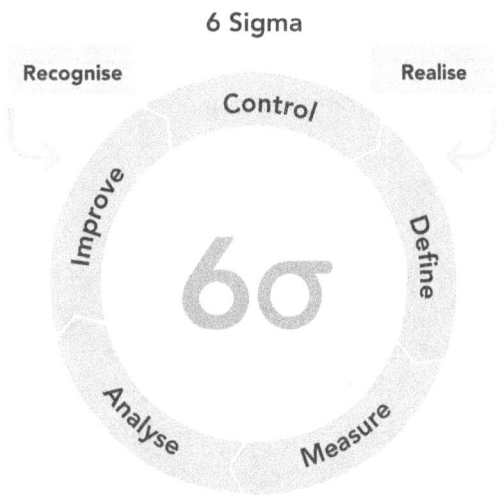

B.Smith, Motorola, 1986

Six Sigma aims to enhance quality by identifying any inefficiencies within your project management project. It has complex quality management and assurance structures that you can follow to ensure your developments not only meet your project objectives but are effective and efficient in practice. Often Six Sigma requires the engagement of skilled professionals from outside of your core team, with specific expertise in specific areas, but in most PE department projects these experts are brought in from within your own organisation rather than from outside. There are several external consultancy organisations who can bring specific curriculum or subject expertise to your project, but often at a cost.

Six Sigma sets out five key phases of your project, which is useful if looking for an easy to follow structure for your work:

**Define:** Initially, understand the problem, set your goals, identify the resources you have available to commit to the project, determine your project's scope, and establish a clear timeline. Make a project charter, including facts about the project, objectives, and team responsibilities. Keep this as it will be constantly referred back to throughout your project progression.

**Measure:** Establish a baseline for your project's effectiveness. What do you absolutely want/need your new curriculum to do and decide together on the definition of success in relation to your project. Now establish a method of monitoring, assessing and measuring your projects success against this baseline and decide how regularly you will evaluate your progress. It's important to understand that initially you are unlikely to meet your objectives as you will still be developing your curriculum, but you should be seeing progression towards your desired outcomes as the project progresses.

**Analyse:** Now you need to collaboratively reflect and identify potential obstacles that will delay or hamper the successful progression of your project. Once you have done this, drill down into each one to uncover the specific causes of these problems as well as the likely impact of each obstacle. Then focus your effort on finding potential solutions to the most critical obstacles so you can plan to avoid them delaying your project as you progress through it. Through this process of identifying your obstacles and resolving them you will naturally make progress through the design of your curriculum although how this design process actually happens is not defined by Six Sigma.

**Improve:** Once you have identified and resolved your obstacles and implemented your newly designed programme, you need to conduct a period of testing and refining of your provision to ensure it meets the objectives set out at the first project phase. Six Sigma focuses on data-driven evaluation and therefore you will need to ensure you are able to collect data to support your project evaluation. Creativity over your elimination of obstacles is encouraged but it is important to recognise this is unlikely to be a quick process and therefore adequate time must be allocated to this testing and improvement phase.

**Control:** To maintain the benefits of your project implementation you should create a control plan, to monitor and evaluate your programme once delivered. This plan should cover a significant period of time post implementation and should be updated regularly once you have confirmed that obstacles have been resolved. The constant identification of new obstacles and effective solutions to these should be part of the plan and you repeat the previous stages as many times as required until the implementation completely meets the objectives set out at the initiation of the project.

As we said previously. Six Sigma is a very comprehensive and potentially complex methodology and will take significant research and learning to utilise it effectively. There are many templates and resources available to support your use of the methodology however it is possibly not the simplest approach to take if you are inexperienced at project management or have a very complex and in-depth development planned.

**PRINCE2** is by far the most commonly used project management methodology, especially in the UK where it was first created to manage the very complex IT projects implemented by the government (Bentley, 2010) It is now the primary choice of process for many companies, popular predominantly because of its flexibility. It is not a 'one size fits all' methodology and as such can be adapted to suit the specific requirements and unique aspects of your own project.

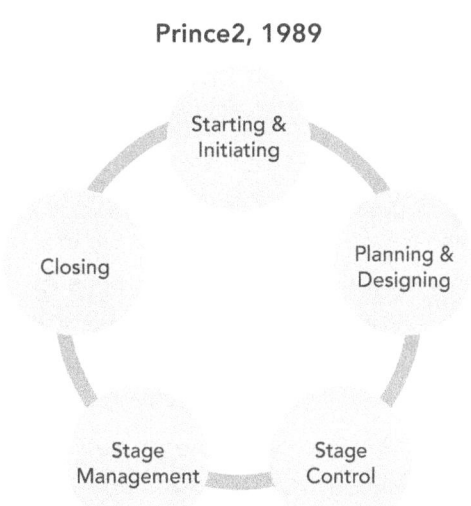

Prince2, 1989

There is a huge volume of resources available to support your use of the PRINCE2 approach, however this will require either someone in your team to have relatively in-depth knowledge of the methodology or a significant amount of training to use it effectively. It is worth considering whether you can afford this time within your project lifespan to undertake the development your team will need.

You can, however, take the basic principles of PRINCE2 and redesign the process to streamline it and make it more user friendly within your context. Whilst you may not follow the exact project management methodology, you can certainly adopt some of the principles to give your own variation a similar level of rigour.

The basic phases of the PRINCE2 approach are:

**Start Up the Project**, where you will determine whether the project is realistic and viable. To do so, you should create a project brief, a justification and a detailed stage plan or GANTT chart to scope out the timeframe and stages of the upcoming project.

You should also create a project initiation document, that will summarise the most important key aspects of the project. This is a really helpful document that can be shared with all stakeholders to help with your wider communication to leadership or managers. This project initiation document should be written in simple, clear terms that anyone could read and understand, without the need for specialist understanding of the jargon or terminology within our specific subject area. The more comprehensive your project plan is, the more time and potentially money you will save once the project starts, because it will help you maintain focus on the key objectives and not be distracted away from your primary purpose.

**Initiating the Project** requires you to detail all the aspects you've identified in the start-up phase, looking in greater depth at the scope, benefits, cost, timescales, obstacles or barriers, quality assurance and benefits. This should form an extension to your project initiation document to allow everyone involved to see the progression of the project and gain clarity on the development as you make progress.

**Direct the Project** is the phase where you decide on the process you are going to implement and the responsibilities for different aspects of the project. In full PRINCE2 methodology this requires you to develop and approve a project board who are accountable for the project and all decisions related to it, however in the context of departmental project management this is likely to be the members of the department and this phase becomes more about defining roles and responsibilities as you will share accountability for the final outcomes.

**The Control Stage** is the main implementation and development phase where individual team members are allocated or assigned tasks, deadlines and objectives and any issues are raised and reviewed at regular development meetings as your project progresses. Any significant issues that can hinder the delivery of the project should be highlighted immediately but smaller issues can wait until team or project meetings. Ultimately the project manager takes responsibility for resolving any issues raised by the team at this stage, as well as monitoring and evaluating the progress of the project and implementing any changes as required to keep the project on track.

**The Product Delivery stage** is the main delivery period, where your newly developed programme is rolled out, with the project manager in overall control of the quality and timing of implementation and execution of the project either in full form or in stages as work is completed.

**The Manage Stage** is the evaluation and feedback period, where evidence is gathered as to the effectiveness of the implementation and a review of the performance is undertaken, linked to the objectives set out at the initial phases of the project. At this stage, if a partial implementation has been done, then the next steps are identified and the PRINCE2 process effectively starts again. This cycle is repeated until every aspect of the project is completed and only at this stage do you move forward to the final stage.

**Closing the Project** occurs only once the cycles of project development have concluded, and every aspect of the project as set out at the very start, have been completed. Once this occurs and evidence has proven that the project has achieved its goals and objectives will the project manager confirm that the project has ended, and it is effectively 'handed over' to be delivered. At this stage a process of monitoring and evaluation begins, and the project can be re-initiated if additional work is required on any aspect of the programme.

As we already said, regardless of the approach and methodology you decide most closely fits your vision for the project, there is nothing to stop you creating an amalgamation of different aspects of these methodologies to design your own, bespoke project management plan. Indeed, it is very likely, and probably sensible that you and your team sit and discuss exactly what the project phases are going to look and feel like, what they are going to include, how you are going to monitor them and how they will be identified. Using some or all of the aspects of methodologies we've looked at, or indeed parts from the many other versions available, will definitely help give your work structure, keep you on your time plan and eventually lead to more effective outcomes for your team, and your pupils.

### Reflective Questions - Project management

- Have you ever heard of any of these Project Management approaches?
- Has anyone in your department got any experience of using one or more of them?
- Which one do you feel fits your approach best?
- Can you apply your project plan to a Project Manage model?
- Now, try writing down your project steps using one of the models or your own interpretation of a project management plan.

CHANGEMAKERS

### Changemaker Reflection: Anna Sheppard
*Head of PE, The Alice Smith School & Chair FOBISIA PE and Sport Executive Committee*

**'Insanity is doing the same thing over and over again and expecting different results.'**
*Albert Einstein*

**10 Steps for Successful Curriculum Change**
Anyone who has had anything to do with physical education over the last five years has seen change. PE teachers overnight became fitness instructors. We looked for ways to deliver a meaningful curriculum at home through the means of dance, martial arts and activities that did not require teams and did not need sophisticated equipment. It was the ultimate change period for PE. We were all in it without choice and found ourselves in a cycle of delivering, reflecting, and refining to ensure we could offer the best possible experiences for our children. With no fixtures and school sports, it also provided time. Time to read, reflect and consider the future of our subject.

Those who have worked with me will say I have always been 'non-traditional' in my approach to PE. A career in sport and physical activity prior to education has allowed me to view our subject through a different lens. Attempting to play catch-up with my own learning has enabled me to consider the many facets and approaches to PE without a particular bias on 'the way I was trained'.

However, I thank Lee Sullivan, author of 'Is PE in Crisis?' for the work he has done around change. His questioning of his own 'why' has supported teachers all around the globe to question why we do what we do. His bold move to develop a concept-based curriculum that no longer focuses on activities and fully promotes a holistic approach has prompted a change in the thinking of others.

Over the past academic year, my school in Malaysia has undergone a PE curriculum change. I would describe it as a journey, and the first step of any journey is knowing where you are going.

# CHAPTER 12 - SOLID FOUNDATIONS

1. **Who is on your PE bus?** Who is driving the change? Who can support the change, both in your department and out?

   In our PE Department, we were lucky to have a team of forward-thinking PE teachers who were well-read and ready for curriculum change. However, your team may not be as ready for change. You may need to provide CPD for change, show new methods of teaching, and share articles that support the change that you are looking for.

2. **Start with the finish.** Many begin their journey with the why or the purpose, however I agree with Greg Dryer, we need to begin with the Who.

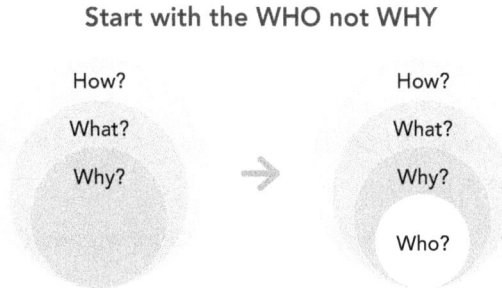

*Dryer, 2022*

What do you want alumni to have gained from PE if you were to see them in 5, 10, or 20 years? We considered their attitudes, skills, knowledge, and experiences. We were unanimous that we wanted them to still be physically active many years on.

3. **Ask your students!** Do you know your students? Do you understand your context? Use your student leaders and student voice to understand issues, trends, likes and dislikes.

4. **Define your purpose.** Why are you doing what you are doing? Does your department have a purpose? Does it align with your school's purpose, mission and vision? Be clear with your purpose.

Our PE Curriculum aims to nurture and develop student physical literacy.

Physical literacy is the motivation, confidence, physical competence, knowledge and understanding to value and take responsibility for engagement in physical activities for life.

5.  **Do your research.** Understand curriculum and speak to others. You will need a curriculum for your context. The PE Scholar Curriculum Design course (Stern, et al, 2021) was invaluable for supporting our process of curriculum change. You will never be able to read every piece of research, but you can read some! Perhaps an off-the-shelf curriculum will work for you; explore the options available to you and collaborate if you can.

6.  **Assessment - control your controllables.** Most PE departments need to fit into whole-school assessment and reporting, and very often, as a subject, we just don't fit. However, don't get confused by what you have to do and what you can do. Through designated department meeting times, we designed our assessment using examples from Heart, Head, Hands (Frapwell, 2014) and Me in PE (Tom Brush, n.d) to support our purpose.

### Competence Domains

| Cognitive Competence (Head) | Affective Competence (Heart) | Physical Competence (Body) | Social Competence (Connections) |
|---|---|---|---|
| Knowledge and understanding | Empathy | Movement with control | Collaboration |
| Decision making | Responsibility | Skill competence | Communication |
| Reflection | Perseverance | Fitness | Leadership |

7.  **Long-term planning - the scope and sequence.** What will your students learn over a year or key stage? Step back. What does that journey look like, and what does it include? At our school, we identified key concepts and anchoring concepts to underpin our curriculum. These concepts appear and reappear as students' progress through their learning journey. I love the Learning that Transfers work by Julie Stern. Her concept mapping tasks, and thinking have helped to provide our curriculum with significance, relevance and meaning for our students.

There is no right or wrong here. We considered so many factors. These included our facilities, our resources, trends in physical activity, our school sports offering and our expertise. This helped us decide which activities would be on our curriculum, in which year groups as well as the model for delivery. Models-based practice is embedded into areas of our curriculum in our quest to meet our departmental purpose.

8. **Medium-term plans - unit planning.** Our units are inspired by the work of Julie Stern, and Mihai Catrinar and attempt to facilitate opportunities for Learning that Transfers.

We have moved away from the scheme of work on a document or sheet and have all our units on visible Slides. This way, we can project in our teaching spaces and provide students with clarity. The key model in all our units is Acquire, Connect, Transfer (Stern, et al, 2021).

The following example is taken from our stand-up paddle unit. We look the ACT model from the Learning that Transfer methodology and added our own 'Why' to each aspect to try and contextualise it for our own environment.

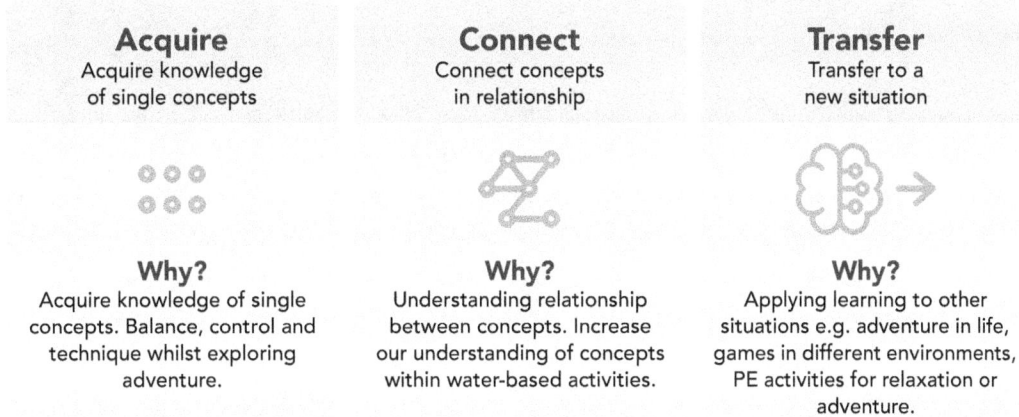

Stern, et al. 2021

9. **Short-term plan - Lesson Planning.** As educators, we continue to evolve our lesson planning by considering our movement and learning time within the lesson. How do we start and finish our lessons? How can this be consistent between teachers and activities? How do we use questioning to support students and develop higher-level thinking? How do we support students in making connections to transfer their knowledge, skills and attitudes in real-life situations? We continue to work on this together as a team, sharing experiences and expertise.

10. **Reflect and refine.** The best practitioners continue to reflect formally and informally. What worked well, and how will it be better? Curriculum work is never complete; there is always more you can do!

# Chapter 13 - How Change Happens In Your Context

'When you change your thoughts, remember to also change your world.'
*Norman Vincent Peale*

By now you will have a good understanding that change, whatever it looks like, is a complex and often challenging process within schools. It involves many moving parts and the engagement of many stakeholders working together to consider numerous factors and overcome significant challenges. All the way through the initial stages of deciding on change, the initiation of a project, with clear goals and objectives, the planning and development of an alternative to what you already have in place, the piloting and implementation of the new programme you have created and the subsequent evaluation and communication of the newly created provision, the process is complicated and often emotionally difficult. It is critical that you give yourself, and your team, the time, tools and knowledge you all need to manage and cope with the significant pressure that inevitably will come with such a major project.

By having a clear plan, and collaborative foundations within your department as well as an empathetic and supportive approach to working with each other, you can remove much of the potentially damaging stress that major projects can create; however it cannot be underestimated and consideration of everyone's well-being and emotional stability throughout the project is absolutely the most critical thing you will need to do as a project leader. Ultimately a newly developed curriculum will be utterly ineffective if your team is not fully prepared and energised to deliver it with enthusiasm, professionalism and motivation.

# CHAPTER 13 - HOW CHANGE HAPPENS IN YOUR CONTEXT

Your school's context is unique and there is no school exactly like yours. Therefore, it is reasonable to assume that no pre-existing model for change management is going to smoothly and efficiently fit directly into your plans. You will need to adapt the work of other people in terms of your project management methodology, and you will need to be flexible enough to change your approach as quickly as you recognise that something is not quite working within your context.

The most important things to remember are that your pupils' experiences and engagements with your PE curriculum must be at the absolute centre of everything you do. Whenever a decision needs to be made, it is vital you make your choice based on what is best for the pupils, rather than what's simplest, cheapest, quickest or what you think will make your lives as teachers the easiest. Never make a decision that could negatively impact on your pupils' experiences, otherwise you risk having to go through the whole process all over again when your programme fails to deliver.

Do not rush your project. Inevitably you will have time pressures to deliver, either internally within your department or from your leadership teams, but time spent on the development of genuine quality will inevitably lead to better outcomes. Any senior leader should understand that time spent on activity that will directly improve teaching and learning, is time well spent. Make sure you set your timeframes realistically and communicate these widely. Do not decide to implement a new curriculum with a few weeks to go before the start of a new academic year. Whilst we all want to get things going if we believe it will make pupil experience better, nothing is ever as effective or of quality, when it is rushed. Plan your project so it meets its deadlines by working backwards and give your team and yourself the time you need to make things work, without breaking yourselves in the process.

## Reflective Question - Context

- Ask all of your team to write down in one paragraph:
  What they think makes your school unique?
- Now compare notes and draw up an overview of your school's context
- Reflecting back on everything we've covered in Changemakers to this point, which aspects are most relevant to your school's unique context?

CHANGEMAKERS

## Changemaker Reflection: Alan Dunstan
*Deputy Head, BISR DQ and creator of the infinite Learners Podcast*

The most dangerous phrase in Education is 'We've always done it this way'. These words have been thrown at me on multiple occasions during the last 26 years of working in schools; much to my dislike! As a young teacher in the UK, I often questioned this phrase when there was a better way to do something and was usually sent on my way curtly by more experienced colleagues! I now understand why; change is often challenging and involves a great deal of work compared to keeping the status quo. As I became more 'battle hardened' and moved overseas, I quickly learned that if I offered a solution or proposed a different way that would benefit all stakeholders, then the possibility of change was more open to debate.

It is often the sense of fear that accompanies the concept of 'change' that has an emotional effect on people. As I have transitioned into senior management from being a Head of PE, firstly as an Assistant Headteacher in Primary School and now as a Deputy Headteacher in Senior School, I have experienced this emotional response to change. My response was fear; a real fear of being way out of my comfort zone or 'Habitus' as the French sociologist Pierre Bourdieu describes it.

Fear can control you if you allow it. Recently, the term 'imposter syndrome' has found traction in the podcasting world as many high profile CEOs, actors and sportspeople have started to show more vulnerability in talking about their fears. Physical education is my field, I am confident in that area and have presented and written about the subject internationally. On the other hand, I was both aware and fearful that I had pigeonholed myself as a PE expert. I frequently spurned opportunities to go for promotions as I was comfortable in my role and did not want to fail in a new role or get rejected in an interview. Covid-19 provided the seminal moment and the reflection opportunity to help me realise that I could contribute to a school in a different way, but I had to embrace that change and walk towards it rather than running away from it. I enrolled upon a Masters' degree in Educational Leadership, which I recently completed; this gave me both the professional and cultural capital to make me feel like I could belong in a school leadership team. From there on it was about learning to 'fly by the seat of my pants', utilising past experiences whilst rapidly taking in new ones. Every failure, conversation, interaction was a learning opportunity.

For me, the transition into senior leadership has been a real eye opener in dealing with the concept of change. I have come to realise it really boils down to two key themes:

You cannot please everybody all of the time.

It is okay to not know all the answers.

Both themes challenge the fixed mindset approach of 'we've always done it this way', and both require the establishment of a school culture that embraces failure and encourages innovation to help demolish the fallacy that change is a bad thing. Shifting the paradigm to a 'this is how we do things around here' culture recognises that 'change' is an integral component of working with young people who themselves are undergoing huge physical, mental and social changes. Education is no different to any other sector and change should be welcomed as long as it has the best intentions of the students at heart.

# Chapter 14 - Make It So

## How To Make Change Happen

**'Things are only impossible until they are not.'**
Jean-Luc Picard

So how do we make this all happen? Whilst it's great to sit and reflect on how exciting it would be to take a blank sheet of paper and build something new, exciting and meaningful for your pupils, actually making it a reality is a far scarier prospect. I believe we all have it in us to undertake a project, but we need to be absolutely clear with ourselves, as the individual leading the change, on what we are going to make happen.

The implementation or creation of something new really comes down to a few critical self-reflections and subsequent decisions. If we can be ruthlessly clear with ourselves on our motivations, values, perspectives, desire and ambition, and we can keep a clear picture in our head of where we want to end up, the design and development process can be a major professional and personal journey with a significant outcome, for not just your pupils and programme but for yourself as well.

**Remember the absolute strategic priorities when developing anything curriculum related are:**

**Identify the Need for Change:** Look at what you do currently, study the student data, review what is happening in your lessons and identify the areas you can have the most impact on.

**Decide on your priorities:** Identify the most important things to change and start with them. Recognise the positive elements that already exist within your provision, do not discount anything you currently do until you are absolutely sure you can do it better. Reflect with your team on their perspectives, talk to your stakeholders and most importantly your pupils. Define the scope of your activity and decide early who is going to be responsible for what.

**Gather feedback:** Conduct surveys, hold focus groups with everyone related to your PE provision. Understand their needs, concerns, desires and aspirations. Listen to your team's professional experiences and their ambitions and build a project structure that meets as many of these professional and personal goals as you can. Keep your pupils at the heart of every decision you make. They are your priority.

**Benchmark your practice:** Compare your PE program to others in your region. Engage with other individuals or teams who have been through a similar process. Look for expertise to complement your own and reach out to thought leaders to see how they can support you. Use this benchmarking process to develop the skills and knowledge within your department and make yourselves experts in project management and curriculum design. Test everything, all the time, look for weaknesses and be willing to acknowledge and accept them when discovered. Never be satisfied and always look for the next step or adaptation that can further enhance your provision.

**Build collaboratively:** Everything's better when shared. Enjoy the experience of working with others. Trust in the knowledge and professionalism of your team and embrace the differences of opinion that will inevitably exist. Pull together when things get challenging and support each other. Use the process to grow as a team, to look out for each other and to come closer together.

**Plan and document everything:** Leave nothing to chance. Build a plan and stick to it. Have regular check-in points built-in and use these to flex or adapt. Do not 'wing' it. Expect challenges and prepare for them. Identify potential obstacles early and think through the problems together. Use these to shape your next steps and see obstacles as learning opportunities. Embrace the chaos and retain your sense of humour!

**Communicate:** Do not work in Silos. Reach out and engage with stakeholders in all their forms. Be willing to publicise your progress and celebrate your success. Be the 'expert in the room' and look for opportunities to introduce or explain your process to the wider community. Be proud of what you are achieving and shout about it from the rooftops. Do not hide anything, especially when it presents a challenge. Seek support and guidance from those who are tasked with supporting you. Use other people's expertise whenever possible and trust in them. Do not be too proud to ask for help and do not take on everything on your own, even if it feels like the easiest option.

**Track your progress:** Keep a close eye on everything that is happening. Keep a record of your progress, your developments and your successes. This could be invaluable if you have to go through a similar process again. Journal your thoughts and feelings, keep a good eye on the wellbeing of your team, and yourself and pace your project so everything feels positive.

**Sustain your changes:** Once things are implemented or introduced, stick with them. Be confident in what you have created and give it time to settle and bed into your context. Do not assume everything will be perfect from day one and give yourself the chance to observe and analyse your developments before judging them. Accept that this is an extended piece of work that will not happen overnight, but ensure you are observing positive change within your pupils and your curriculum and if you aren't, discuss why with your team.

**Seek continuous improvement:** Foster a departmental culture that embraces change and ongoing learning. Never sit on your laurels. Assume there is always a next stage and look for those opportunities to develop even further. Never sit still. Embrace change as a natural part of your departmental development and be reassured by the fact you have already achieved so much and can continue to do so.

**Focus on your pupils:** Throughout your process, whatever it looks like and whatever it generates, remember that your absolute priority is the positive experiences your pupils deserve. Never do anything that limits your inclusive, supportive pupil-focused PE and be prepared to stop or adapt as soon as you think something is having a negative impact on any pupils in your programme.

**Have fun:** Whilst occasionally stressful, always challenging and often pressured, the process of designing and developing a curriculum can be one of the most rewarding activities you will engage in as a teacher. Whether you have a blank sheet of paper or a crowded one to simplify, you have an opportunity to make a long-lasting mark on your pupils, your department, your school and the wider PE community. Embrace the challenge and enjoy the process. Find time to laugh and enjoy the social aspect of collaboration, take time to relax and switch it off within your department and retain the unique, positive environment that already exists within your department.

## Changemaker Reflection: Gary Spink
*Director of Sport and physical education, Normanton, UK*

Over the past decades, the landscape of physical education (PE) curricula has undergone notable transformations, reflecting a nuanced response to evolving educational paradigms, societal trends, and scientific advancements. What was once grounded in hierarchical levels spanning Key Stage 3 (KS3) to Key Stage 4 (KS4), the intrinsic flaws within the guidelines for each assessment criterion fostered a notable disparity in interpretation across schools. Over recent decades, a discernible shift has occurred towards a more holistic approach, where PE is perceived not merely as a platform for physical activity but as an integral component fostering comprehensive well-being.

I was lucky enough to gain the role of head of the department early in my career, and capitalising on the absence of a well-defined curriculum structure, I was able to introduce what I perceived to be more holistic assessment models, resources, and pedagogies. My initiatives faced some resistance from the school's management, as they did not align with the institution's educational approaches. Still, over time we were able to position PE as a crucial part of a holistic offering that contributed as significantly as any other subject across the school.

When the DfE introduced the head, heart, and hands (Frapwell, 2014) assessment criteria into the suggested approaches for PE delivery, this gave a significant opportunity for schools like ours, which were already focusing on more than just a traditional sport-focused approach. However, the lack of comprehensive guidance and exemplification (WAGOLLS - What a Good One Looks Like) hindered wider adoption, with limited tools to implement these criteria effectively.

One noteworthy development pertains to the broadening conceptualisation of 'physical fitness' within PE curricula. The traditional emphasis on cardiovascular endurance and muscular strength has expanded to incorporate components such as flexibility, agility, and balance. This expansion aligns with contemporary research highlighting the multifaceted nature of fitness and the imperative to address diverse aspects of motor development.

Moreover, the integration of technology has become a hallmark of modern PE curricula. Wearable devices, augmented reality, and fitness apps are employed to enhance engagement, provide real-time feedback, and personalise physical activities. This incorporation of technology not only caters to the digital-native generation but also aligns with educational trends emphasising the intersection of traditional subjects with modern tools.

In tandem with these technological and pedagogical shifts, a growing recognition of the socio-emotional dimensions of physical education has also emerged. Our curricula now incorporate components fostering teamwork, communication skills, and emotional regulation. This acknowledgment of the interconnectedness between physical and mental well-being echoes contemporary educational philosophies emphasising the development of the whole child.

Furthermore, inclusivity has become a real focus point for all of us leading PE in schools today, with PE curricula increasingly designed to cater to diverse abilities and interests. Adaptive physical education programs aim to provide equitable opportunities for all students, irrespective of their physical or cognitive abilities.

These adaptations align with a contemporary understanding of education as a dynamic and holistic process that extends beyond the confines of traditional disciplinary boundaries.

This innovative curriculum approach accommodates diverse student backgrounds, addresses issues such as poor attendance, considers prior primary school experiences, and caters to individual interests in health and physical activity. Notably, it ensures gender equality by offering all our students the opportunity to engage in the same activities, fostering a fully inclusive educational environment. Our KS4 curriculum, focuses on students being active for long periods of time, as (like many schools) we have reduced lesson time from two hours to one hour. Therefore, we have taken out the assessment and instead focused on students sustaining physical activity through their informed choices from what activities and areas of the curriculum they enjoyed at KS3. We have also embedded ABC oracy to promote literacy and oracy skills, which is one of academies weaknesses, with reading ages around 3-4 years below their biological age.

A persistent challenge for us within the PE curriculum landscape arises from the regular modifications imposed by the policy makers, particularly regarding the inclusion of qualifications in school judgement. The dynamic nature of these alterations necessitates constant adaptation by heads of department, resulting in a fluctuating workload and the need to constantly and effectively develop and evolve provision to meet these newly imposed modifications. Our PE curricula are dynamic and fluid entities subject to constant recalibration, shaped by regulatory adjustments, communication challenges, and the ever-present spectre of scrutiny.

CHANGEMAKERS

# Chapter 15 - And Then

## What Happens After Change?

**'Things don't have to change the world to be important'**
*Steve Jobs*

The development of a curriculum, in any form, should be a positive experience, full of meaningful and effective moments, for us and our pupils. The process is long and at times challenging but seeing the impact that your project has on the curriculum you deliver, should make it all worthwhile.

There are unlimited variations on what a newly developed or implemented curriculum might look and feel like, depending on the context in which it is designed, but you should be looking at a newly launched programme that engages your pupils in really positive, inclusive and meaningful ways. Hopefully, at this stage, you are identifying increased engagement, motivation and enthusiasm. Still, you should also be seeing more quantitative developments in terms of improving attainment alongside more productive and accurate assessment. Your recording and reporting should be more effective, reflecting individual pupil progress and a better, more balanced assessment that includes wider holistic aspects of pupil development rather than just core movement or sporting capabilities.

Hopefully throughout the process you have seen the profile of your department increase and the engagement in conversation with stakeholders and external influences grow, you may be sought out to support other departments undertake similar projects and your team may have become the example of how curriculum design projects can happen within your school or wider school partnerships. You may be more visible on PE platforms locally, regionally or even globally. People may be asking you to comment, reflect, explain or present your project and outcomes and hopefully you are embracing this for your own personal and professional development. Almost always the development or redesign of a

PE (or any other subject) curriculum will lead to increased exposure for you as a practitioner within your field. If you look at social media around our subject you will see that many of the most prominent and influential voices are those who have developed something new, created a new way of doing things or redesigned something already in existence to make it even more effective. You could be the next big voice within PE because your experience and the expertise you have developed through your project are valuable to those within the wider community who are thinking about or embarking on change themselves. Embrace this opportunity as it can open doors and present opportunities that you may never have considered but could result in the next stages in your own professional journey.

Regardless of the 'noise' around your project and outcomes, it is important that your focus does remain on the provision itself and the impact it is having on your pupils. It can be easy to be distracted by the way in which your project has changed you personally and I have first-hand experience of how you can get wrapped up in the individual opportunities that such a successful undertaking can present, but fundamentally you must remember why you set out on this journey in the first place. Remember that you decided that you wanted to create something more positive or meaningful for your pupils, and whilst you may have gained many opportunities and had many experiences along the way, your primary driver was improving the experiences for your pupils. Make sure you give the programme the time it deserves, to be reviewed, to be observed in practice, to be discussed internally and to be continuously adapted and improved. No project ever really finishes in such a dynamic and fluid environment as PE; therefore, you cannot ever really assume that things are finished. As soon as you think you are nearing the finishing line or the completion point, something new will be discovered, some new research will come to light, a new and interesting observation will be made and before you know it, you'll be back in project manager mode, deciding on your next set of phases and developmental tasks!

### Reflective Questions - Now what?

- Are you finished? Are you sure?
- Have you already identified areas that you think you can develop further?
- Are you inspired to make those changes?
- How are you going to continue to monitor and assess your projects impact?

CHANGEMAKERS

## Changemaker Reflection: David Wallace
*Junior School PE Teacher, Bangkok*

Nurturing competition while encouraging participation has always been a delicate dance. A familiar story is that some students, despite their passion, do not quite make the cut for the school or house teams. Their enthusiasm dims, replaced by a disillusion that sport is just not for them.

As an educator, I firmly believe that every student deserves a chance to represent their school on the sports field, not just the most able athletes. However, PE teaching is multifaceted, and as a coach, I know that our top athletes need the challenge of top-level competitions, of which opportunities are limited. Two opposing forces, creating a familiar headache: the same faces dominating inter-school teams.

This is not a unique conundrum. Most teachers and coaches have grappled with team selection issues at some point in their careers. Some opt to give every student a turn to represent the school at inter-school competitions. However, this can result in negative experiences for students whose skill is significantly below that of the other players. Plus, for some larger schools, it simply is not possible to select every student for the limited number of competitions available.

It also needs to be considered that some schools, such as Kellett, carry a certain weight of expectation. As a prestigious institution, sporting prowess forms part of the school's identity. Performance on the sports field reflects upon the image of the school, and there is an expectation that the most talented students should be given the opportunity to play in top-tier competitions. That is when the Kellett 5s stepped in, bridging the gap between participation and competition, ensuring that every single student, regardless of skill level, feels the thrill and pride of representing their school in a developmentally appropriate competitive setting.

I believe that simplicity is the lifeblood to success for any new initiative. So, the Kellett 5s reflected this, and we kept things refreshingly uncomplicated. Five-a-side fixtures in netball, football, rugby, and (six-a-side) cricket – each aligning with their seasons. Local schools were invited to join us every week during our dedicated Games afternoons on Tuesday (Year 3 & 4) and Thursday (Year 5 & 6).

For some, this may seem underwhelming. But in its apparent simplicity lies the Kellett 5s' brilliance. Together with the school's Director of Sport, Kevin Paradise, we leveraged the resources, staffing, time and facilities that we already had and minimised disruption for all stakeholders to maximise the chance of buy-in:

- Using timetabled Games afternoons guaranteed access to all the sports facilities without clashing with the senior school or external providers.
- The Kellett Games kit doubles up as the inter-school sports kit, so all our students were already dressed and ready to play.
- Staying on-site eliminated the need for parental consent or travel arrangements.
- Visiting schools could select a date that suits them and play against a team that closely matches the skill level of their students – ensuring developmentally appropriate challenges and positive experiences.

Initially meeting with modest enthusiasm from other schools- attributed partly to post-COVID reluctance for inter-school sports- we persevered. The inaugural term of the Kellett 5s saw one school visit, then three, and now it's a regular fixture for Kellett and many of the neighbouring schools. This initiative not only provides Kellett students with additional avenues for competitive sports but also serves as a lifeline for smaller schools lacking formalised competitive leagues.

Although I have now left my role as Head of Prep PE at Kellett, the legacy of the Kellett 5s continues. A simple concept that empowers teachers and coaches to select students for inter-school competitions with the knowledge that every Kellett student, regardless of skill level, can experience the joy of competitive sports tailored to their abilities and developmental needs.

# Chapter 16 - So What?

## How To Assess Change

**'If you do not change direction, you may end up where you are heading.'**
*Lao Tzu*

So here you are, the project has been fully implemented, your pupils are experiencing and engaging with your newly created or adapted PE curriculum and all the signs are that it is having positive, meaningful and enriching benefits across all your cohorts and in individual pupils within them, but how do you know? How can you be sure that the outcomes you set out to achieve are actually happening? Where is your evidence to support your conclusions that you've done what you set out to do, and really made the change you were looking for?

Traditionally, project managers used something called 'The Iron Triangle' to assess the impact of their project. This looked specifically at three factors, Cost, Time, and Quality, to assess whether a project outcome could be deemed successful. (Prostejovska and Tomankova, 2017)

'The Iron Triangle' however, cannot provide a definitive picture of the outcomes of a project in a dynamic and multifaceted environment such as education and therefore we need to consider a broader spectrum of success criteria when assessing the perceived success of a project in our sector. Whilst it is critical to assess the effectiveness of our programmes we must understand and accept the challenge and difficulties in doing this through a formulaic structure across a whole curriculum design project (Dagenais, Hawley & Lund, 2003). Assessment though, as challenging and complex it can be, is critical if we are to learn the lessons, highlight the accomplishments and build on the practice we have undertaken and achieved during our project.

Ultimately you cannot ever assume things are working as designed or planned unless you really ensure that a rigorous and carefully crafted assessment of the project is undertaken. Just like we assess the progress and achievements of our pupils within our provision, we need to assess the project through a similar lens.

This isn't just about assessing the impact on pupils either, as you could have outstanding outcomes but have created absolute chaos in the process across your school. To improve and adapt any future curricular development projects, you need to actually assess the way in which you conducted your project in the first place and identify the things you and your team did well, and the things that you could improve on second time around.

To be clear on your outcomes and your successes, you need to go right back to the start of your project, before you had started designing resources, or schemes of work, or indeed anything formal at all. Think back to those initial reflective conversations and thought processes, when you were deciding that you wanted to make a change and what you were deciding that change might look like. What were your original, overriding and strategic objectives that drove you and your team to engage in such a time-consuming and potentially exhausting process in the first place? These are your ultimate success criteria, and this is what you should be judging your project against.

Have you achieved what you set out to achieve? Are your pupils getting an experience within their lessons that looks and feels like you really wanted it to? Are the lessons that are being delivered daily, meeting the objectives of what you decided PE should look like within your context at that particular time? Can you see meaningful PE being delivered consistently, effectively and responsibly all around you?

How have the dynamics within your team improved as a result of the process? Are you all working more collaboratively? Do you feel closer as a group of individual teachers and is there an increased sense of purpose and value amongst the team members? Have you all really bought into your new approaches and processes? Is there enthusiasm across your team for what you are doing now?

Did you enjoy the process? Which bits were most challenging or stressful, where were the biggest obstacles and how did you overcome them. Are there things you would do differently and if so, why? Do you think you were effective in your delivery plans, did you use your time efficiently, was there wasted effort or loss of focus at any point and how could you do this in a different way next time?

What are your biggest personal successes? How has the project changed you? Are these the same successes as other members of your team can identify? Have you grown as an educator, a leader or an academic practitioner? Has the project re-energised you and your love for PE curriculum development or are you exhausted? How well did you manage the workload personally and within your team and what ways did you protect and manage your own wellbeing and the wellbeing of those within your team?

Would you do it again? Have you learnt how to manage a project in a new or different way? Did the process help you develop new skills and knowledge that you can use in different ways in the future? What can you do with all of that newly acquired capability to support further development, either within your own department or across the wider school? Has it led to opportunities for you or your team to take on wider school roles and responsibilities and have you made progress professionally during the process? Where do you want to go next, and how can you achieve your personal, professional goals and help those around you achieve theirs?

What's next? Are you enthused by the idea of continuing your project? Are you already looking for new ways to develop things further? Have you still got ideas swirling around in your head and do you have the energy and bandwidth to take on the next challenge?

As much as data-driven analysis of the outcomes of your project in relation to the attainment, achievement, motivation and progress of your pupils are important, you will have hopefully considered these key questions and built them into your assessment processes. This final reflective activity is more about how the project itself has progressed and what has been achieved as a result. Taking the time to really think about the positives, and negatives of the process you have just undertaken is a huge learning opportunity for you personally and for the wider cohesiveness of your team. This was your project, and you deserve the opportunity to really reflect on the successes of it and how it has helped you personally and professionally grow. So, make sure you do this, and celebrate what an exceptional outcome you have created as a result.

CHAPTER 16 - SO WHAT?

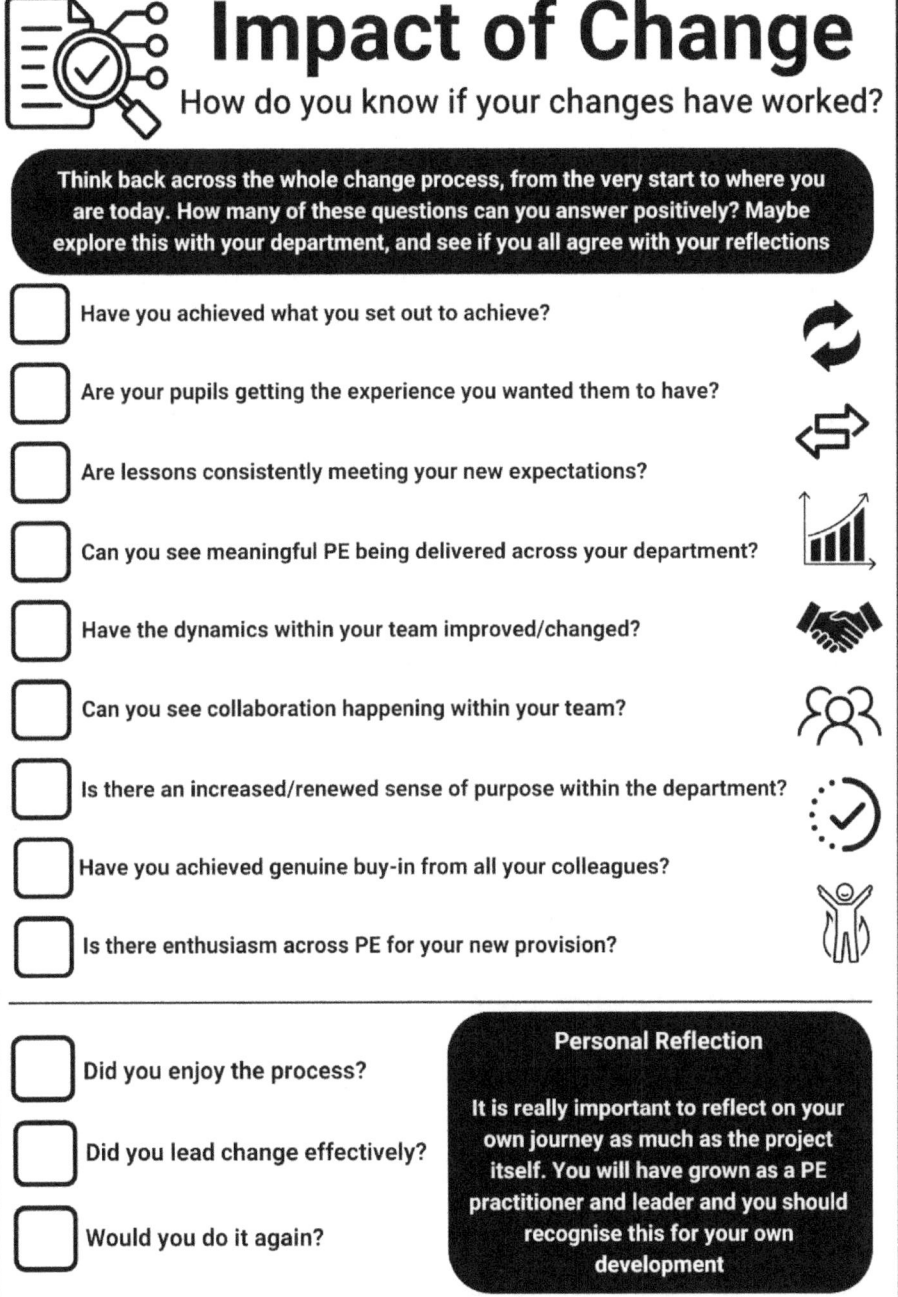

## Changemaker Reflection: Lee Sullivan
*Head of PE, Upton Court Grammar School, UK*

Picture the physical education department I took over – a space dominated by a sports-centric, elitist approach, oblivious to the significant impact it had on student disengagement. I was made aware prior to taking the post I was being brought in to drastically change the PE delivery at the school and I realised within a day exactly why. It was a challenging landscape to navigate, but I knew that to lead meaningful change, I had to foster self-reflection within my resistant team and introduce perspectives that would collide with their preconceived notions.

In my quest to transform the PE experience, I initiated a process of introspection by encouraging each staff member to reflect on their 'why.' Why were they PE teachers? What contribution did they aspire to make to physical education, and what impact did they genuinely wish to have on their students? Unveiling a shared aspiration to provide a positive PE experience, nurture movement competence in all students, and instil a lifelong commitment to physical activity, the staff had articulated their collective 'why.'

This set the stage for a more profound inquiry. I asked them to question whether their current practices aligned with their 'why.' Some remained stubborn in their conviction that they were on the right track, necessitating a more compelling revelation.

To substantiate the misalignment between intention and reality, I turned to a source that held undeniable credibility in the eyes of my team – the students. Armed with the results of a comprehensive student voice survey, I laid bare the unfiltered opinions of those at the receiving end of our educational efforts. Students, renowned for their brutal honesty, had spoken, and their sentiments were impossible to dismiss.

The survey outcomes painted a stark picture: many students did not value PE, failed to derive enjoyment from it, and perceived the learning as inconsequential to their lives.

The revelation became a pivotal moment – an awakening that compelled the team to confront the uncomfortable truth. There is no going back from awareness.

# CHAPTER 16 - SO WHAT?

Armed with the undeniable reality of student dissatisfaction, I leveraged this newfound awareness to guide the team toward a collective reconsideration of our true intent. The subsequent journey involved a comprehensive review of research, practitioner insights, and alternative perspectives. We deconstructed our curriculum, scrutinised our assessment methods, and even addressed teacher behaviour to align every facet with our renewed commitment to creating a positive, inclusive PE experience.

A team united by a shared purpose is inherently more motivated to attain its objectives. This shared vision not only offers clarity but also imparts purpose to every decision and conversation within the team. It establishes accountability, guiding everyone towards a common goal. Such a vision not only gives the 'what' and 'how' of PE delivery genuine value but demands steadfast dedication from the team to fulfil its intent. Use it to review the totality of the student experience within PE and share it with everyone. The strongest teams remain true to their collective 'why'. It should drive everything.

The transformation was not immediate, nor was it without its challenges. However, the collision of self-reflection, student voices, and a commitment to our shared 'why' laid the foundation for meaningful change. As the leader of this change, I understood that true impact went beyond merely altering structures – it involved reshaping attitudes, fostering empathy, and, above all, rekindling the flame of passion for physical education in both educators and students alike.

*If Lee's story and message resonates with you, and you would like to know more about the journey he took and the reflections that came about as a result of his exploration of what PE meant to him and his pupils, then I would strongly recommend you read his book 'Is PE in Crisis' or follow him on social media.*

# Chapter 17 - Be The Change

## Being Part Of Change

**'Be the change that you wish to see in the world.'**
*Mahatma Gandhi*

We can discuss at length whether change in PE is a good thing, but the volume of evidence recognising the health and social benefits of PE are irrefutable (HHS, 2015, 2018) and, we know, through long accepted findings of multiple research projects that pupil engagement within PE is a primary factor in wider school success (Fredricks, Blumenfeld & Paris, 2004). We also know that meaningful and appropriate PE looks and feels different to pupils in different contexts, so it's fair to surmise that a PE curriculum that addresses the engagement and attainment of the specific pupils it is delivered to, needs to be a fundamental objective of any PE provision. That is why change within PE is such a critical and ongoing process. We have to adapt, and we have to flex within our provision to meet the needs of a changing pupil demographic within our schools, we have no choice. To stick rigidly to a programme that was designed at a time when our pupils were different is not just limiting our potential impact but possibly detrimental to the experiences our pupils receive within their PE programmes. If we are to break the cycle of negative perception within the adult population when reflecting on physical education within schools, then we must adopt a willingness to change to meet the needs of the pupils currently within our schools rather than those already passed through.

Our programmes can improve student outcomes, whether these are fitness, skill, engagement, enjoyment or more holistic in their focus. We can introduce pupils to newly designed, modern and exciting opportunities to move and participate. We can adopt practice and approach based on research and evidence to enhance the potential benefits of our provision, we can make PE more relevant and motivating, more inclusive and accessible, more accepting, supportive and equitable. We have the power to change pupils' perceptions of what PE is, and their relationship with movement for their whole school, and adult lives. We must never lose sight of the responsibility we have to develop young people who have a genuine love for movement, in all its forms, and therefore we must welcome change as a natural part of our departmental, curricular world.

If you want things to change, then you have to be part of the process of making it happen. Whether you are the curriculum lead, head of department or a member of the team, you have the power to initiate the conversations and challenge the status quo. Whilst this sometimes feels like a significant and scary thing to do, especially for younger or less experienced teachers, a supportive and collaborative department will be willing to listen. You might just say the one thing that sparks a revolution within your school and changes your pupils' school lives for the better.

There will always be steady progress towards improved schooling whether or not we consciously plan to that end. Change is ultimately inevitable, and we can either accept and embrace this as a positive contributor to our schools' progress, or choose to be intimidated, disengaged, disruptive or disingenuous towards the change, but it will happen anyway. I would argue it is always better to be part of something than to watch it from the outside and not be able to contribute towards it. It is far more productive and positive for you professionally to see and seize the opportunities that a curriculum design and development can offer you rather than let it pass you by and ultimately you will still have to deliver the curriculum designed by someone else, which is potentially a more challenging and negative experience than engaging from the start.

Of course, your experience when engaging with the process of change will be an individual one, depending on a whole load of personal, contextual, value-based factors and there is no way to really tell someone how the process will feel or progress for you. All we know is that the potential benefits of being part of something as big and significant as redeveloping the provision that generations of your pupils will receive, experience and benefit from are numerous and lasting.

> Change will change you, change will challenge you and change will stay with you for the rest of your academic career.

The experience of being involved with the process of changing something will lead to personal and professional growth like few other experiences will. The opportunity to learn, develop, practice, reflect and expand as a teacher, a leader and an educator is one that everyone should experience and benefit from and eventually, when your curriculum is fully implemented, your pupils are engaged in it and you can see it in full flow within your classrooms, your sports halls and fields, you will be able to sit back and reflect on not just the achievement of making it happen, but the lasting legacy you have helped create.

Be part of it, embrace it and enjoy it. **We are all** *Changemakers*. The journey is one like no other and I cannot wait to hear of what you create for your pupils, within your programmes, within your curriculums, within your schools. Good luck!

### Reflection Questions - Final thinking

We said, at the very start of *Changemakers*, that we would revisit our initial thinking, to see if our perspectives and visions have changed. Here we are, at the end. So, what do you think now?

Try to think about something that has changed for you recently, either professionally or personally:

- How do you feel about that experience?
- What went well. Do you think others would agree?
- What could have been better? Do you think others would agree with that too?
- What could you have done differently?
- If you had to describe, in only a few words, what time of Changemaker you think you are now, at the end of the book, and possibly, at the end of your project, what would you say?
- Write those words down, place them somewhere visible and let them be your call to action or validation every day

# CHAPTER 17 - BE THE CHANGE

# References

Al-Abrrow, H., Alnoor, A., & Abbas, S. (2019). *The effect of organizational resilience and CEO's narcissism on project success: Organizational risk as mediating variable.* Organization Management Journal, 16(1), pp. 1-13.

Maguire, A. (2016). *Illustrating Equality VS Equity* "Interaction Institute for Social Change [online] Available at: https://interactioninstitute.org/illustrating-equality-vs-equity/

Banville, D., Marttinen, R., Kulinna, P. H., & Ferry, M. (2021). *Curriculum decisions made by secondary physical education teachers and comparison with students' preferences.* Curriculum Studies in Health and Physical Education, 12(3). pp. 199–216.

Beckey, A. (2021). Meaningful PE as a metaphor for teaching PE. In T. Fletcher, D. Ní Chróinín, D. Gleddie & S. Beni (Eds.), *Meaningful Physical Education.* pp. 52–63. Routledge.

Benford, R. D. and Snow, D. A. (2000). *Framing Processes and Social Movements: An Overview and Assessment.* Annual Review of Sociology, 26(1), pp. 611-639.

Beni, S., Fletcher, T. and Ní Chróinín, D. (2017) *'Meaningful Experiences in Physical Education and Youth Sport: A Review of the Literature'*, Quest, 69(3), pp. 291–312.

Bentley, C. (2010). PRINCE2: *A Practical Handbook* (3rd ed.). Routledge.

Booth, Josephine N., et al. (2022) *The Impact of the Daily Mile™ on School Pupils' Fitness, Cognition, and Wellbeing: Findings from Longer Term Participation.* Frontiers in Psychology 13

Bouckenooghe, D. (2010). *Positioning Change Recipients' Attitudes Toward Change in the Organizational Change Literature,* The Journal of Applied Behavioral Science, 46(4), pp. 500–531.

Brown, Daphne, (2014) *Negative Experiences in Physical Education Class and Avoidance of Exercise.* Master's Theses. 55. Available at https://scholars.fhsu.edu/theses/55

Brush, T (n.d) *Me in PE.* Available at: https://tombrush1982.blogspot.com/

Caspersen, C.J., Powell, K.E. and Christenson, G.M., (1985). *Physical activity, exercise, and physical fitness: definitions and distinctions for health-related research.* Public Health Reports, 100(2), pp.126-131.

Casey, A. and Kirk, D. (2021) *Models-based practice in physical education.* Abingdon: Routledge.

Cespedes, D.J., Montaña, A.D., & Autodirigido, M.E. (2014). *Ipsative Assessment of Essay Writing to Foster Reflection and Self-Awareness of Progress.* Handbook of Research on Assessment Literacy and Teacher-Made Testing in the Language Classroom.

# REFERENCES

Dagenais, ME, Hawley, D & Lund, JP. (2003). Assessing the effectiveness of a new curriculum: Part I. *Journal of Dental Education* 67(1), pp. 47–54.

Datnow, A. (2002). *The Gender Politics of Educational Change*. Routledge.
De Bono, E. (1985). *Six Thinking Hats*. London: Penguin Books.

Dishman, RK, Sallis, JF & Orenstein, DR. (1985). *The determinants of physical activity and exercise.* Public Health Reports (Washington, D.C.: 1974) 100(2), pp.158–171.

Donaldson, G., 2016. *A systematic approach to curriculum reform in Wales.* Wales Journal of Education, 18(1).

Doolittle, Sarah. (2007). *Is the Extinction of High School Physical Education Inevitable?* Journal of Physical Education, Recreation & Dance. 78, pp. 1-58.

Durden-Myers, L (2022). Social Justice in PE. [online] Available at: https://www.pescholar.com/insight/social-justice-in-pe-some-key-terms-and-resources/

Earl, L, Hargreaves, A & Ryan, J. (2013). *Schooling for Change*. Routledge.

Ekberg, J. E. (2021). *Knowledge in the school subject of physical education: a Bernsteinian perspective*. Physical Education and Sport Pedagogy, 26(5). pp. 448–459.

Ennis, CD. (2015). *Knowledge, transfer, and innovation in physical literacy curricula.* Journal of Sport and Health Science 4(2), pp.119–124.

Ennis CD. (2017) *Educating Students for a Lifetime of Physical Activity: Enhancing Mindfulness, Motivation, and Meaning.* Research Quarterly in Exercise and Sport. pp 241-250.

Fletcher, T, Chróinín, DN, Gleddie, D & Beni, S (eds). (2021). *Meaningful physical education: An Approach for Teaching and Learning.* 1st ed. Abingdon, Oxon; New York, NY: Routledge, 2021.

Fletcher, T, Chróinín, DN, Gleddie, D & Beni, S. (2021). *The why, what, and how of Meaningful physical education.* In Meaningful physical education. 1st ed. Edited by T Fletcher, DN Chróinín, D

Gleddie & S Beni. Abingdon, Oxon; New York, NY: Routledge, (2021). Series: Routledge focus on sport pedagogy: Routledge, pp. 3–19.

Frapwell, A. 2014. *A practical guide to assessing without levels: Supporting and safeguarding high quality achievement in physical education.* Worcester, UK: Association for Physical Education.

Fredricks, JA, Blumenfeld, PC & Paris, AH. (2004a). *School Engagement: Potential of the Concept, State of the Evidence*. Review of Educational Research 74(1), pp. 59–109.

Fredricks, JA, Blumenfeld, PC & Paris, AH. (2004b). *School Engagement: Potential of the Concept, State of the Evidence*. Review of Educational Research 74(1), pp. 59–109.

Fullan, M. (1998). *The Meaning of Educational Change: A Quarter of a Century of Learning.* In International Handbook of Educational Change. Edited by A Hargreaves, A Lieberman, M

Fullan & D Hopkins. Dordrecht: Springer Netherlands, pp. 214–228.

Fullan, M., & Quinn, J. (2020). *Coherence: The right drivers in action for schools, districts, and systems.* Corwin.

Green, D. (2016). *How Change Happens.* First edition. Oxford: Oxford University Press

Greiner, LE. (1967). *Antecedents of Planned Organization Change.* The Journal of Applied Behavioral Science 3(1), pp. 51–85.

Gutierrez, L. (2014). Cognitive science: adult training and development. Available at: http://freshapproachlearning.wordpress.com

Hargreaves, A & Fullan, M. (2000). *What's worth fighting for out there?* Nachdr. ed. New York, NY: Teachers College Press.

Harold W. Kohl, III, Cook, HD, Environment, C on PA and PE in the S, Board, F and N & Medicine. (2013). *Physical Activity and physical education: Relationship to Growth, Development, and Health.* In Educating the Student Body: Taking Physical Activity and physical education to School. National Academies Press (US).

Harris, BM. (1985). *Supervisory behavior in education.* 3. ed. Englewood Cliffs, N.J. Prentice-Hall.

Hiatt, J. (2006). ADKAR: A Model for Change in Business, Government and Our Community. Prosci Research.

Singer. S. (2021) *I Love Teaching, But…* https://www.badassteacher.org/bats-blog/i-love-teaching-but-by-steven-singer (Accessed 14 January 2024).

Ilin M, Bohlen J. Six Sigma Method. [Updated 2023 Jan 9]. In: StatPearls. Treasure Island (FL): StatPearls Publishing; Available from: https://www.ncbi.nlm.nih.gov/books/NBK589666/

Iqbal, MdH, Siddiqie, SA & Mazid, MdA. (2021). *Rethinking theories of lesson plan for effective teaching and learning.* Social Sciences & Humanities Open 4(1)

Jaeschke L, et al (2017). *Socio-cultural determinants of physical activity across the life course: a 'Determinants of Diet and Physical Activity' (DEDIPAC) umbrella systematic literature review.* Int J Behav Nutr Phys Act.

Johnson, S. (1998). *Who moved my cheese? an amazing way to deal with change in your work and in your life.* New York: Putnam.

Kirk, D. (2010). *Physical education Futures,* London: Routledge

Kirk, D. (2021). *Precarity, the health and wellbeing of children and young people, and pedagogies of affect in physical education-as-health promotion* [Online] Available at: https://pure.strath.ac.uk/ws/portalfiles/portal/131075429/Kirk_ED_2021_Precarity_the_health_and_wellbeing_of_children_and_young_people_and_pedagogies_.pdf [Accessed 25 Oct 2022)

Kotter, JP & Rathgeber, H. (2005). *Our iceberg is melting: changing and succeeding under any conditions*. New edition ed. New York, New York: Portfolio/Penguin.

Kübler-Ross, E. (2009). *On death and dying: what the dying have to teach doctors, nurses, clergy and their own families*. London: Routledge.

Lamb, C.A., Teraoka, E., Oliver, K.L., Kirk, D. (2021). *Pupils' Motivational and Emotional Responses to Pedagogies of Affect in physical education in Scottish Secondary Schools*. Int. J. Environ. Res. Public Health 2021, 18, 5183.

Lewin, K. (1951). *Intention will and need. In Organization and pathology of thought: Selected sources*. New York: Columbia University Press, pp. 95–153.

Lorenzi, Nancy & Riley, Robert. (2000). *Managing Change: An Overview*. Journal of the American Medical Informatics Association: JAMIA. 7. pp. 116-24.

Lunenburg, FC. (n.d). *Approaches to managing organizational change*. International journal of scholarly academic intellectual diversity, 12(1), pp.1-10.

McLaughlin, C. (2008). *Emotional well-being and its relationship to schools and classrooms: a critical reflection*. British Journal of Guidance & Counselling 36(4), pp. 353–366.

Mclaughlin, Milbrey & Mitra, Dana. (2001). *Theory-based Change and Change-based Theory: Going Deeper, Going Broader*. Journal of Educational Change. 2. 301-323.

Meyer-Looze, C, Richards, S, Brandell, S & Margulus, L. (n.d). *Implementing the Change Process for Staff and Student Success: An Instructional Module*.

Mitra, D.L., (2009). *Amplifying student voice*. Engaging the whole child: Reflections on best practices in learning, teaching, and leadership, pp.242-252.

National Academies of Sciences, Engineering, and Medicine. (2019). *The Promise of Adolescence: Realizing Opportunity for All Youth*. Washington, DC: The National Academies Press

Orr D. 1992. *Ecological Literacy: Education for a Postmodern World*. Albany, US: State University of New York.

Peng, J, Li, M, Wang, Z & Lin, Y. (2021). T*ransformational Leadership and Employees' Reactions to Organizational Change: Evidence from a Meta-Analysis*. The Journal of Applied Behavioral Science 57(3), pp. 369–397.

Pettigrew, AM, Woodman, RW & Cameron, KS. (2001). *Studying Organizational Change and Development: Challenges For Future Research*. Academy of Management Journal 44(4), pp. 697–713.

*Physical Activity Guidelines for Americans Midcourse Report: Strategies to Increase Physical Activity Among Youth*. Washington, DC: U.S. Department of Health and Human Services, (2012).

Priestley, M. (2011). *Schools, teachers, and curriculum change: A balancing act?* Journal of Educational Change 12(1), pp. 1–23.

Project Management Institute. 2017. *Agile Practice Guide.* Newton Square, PA: Project Management Institute.

Prostějovská, Z & Tománková, J. (2017). *Project Management: How To Assess a Project's Success.* Business & IT VII (1), pp. 2–7.

Rose, T. (2016). *The end of average: how we succeed in a world that values sameness.* First Edition ed. New York: Harper One.

Sallis, JF, Prochaska, JJ & Taylor, WC. (2000). *A review of correlates of physical activity of children and adolescents: Medicine & Science in* Sports & Exercise (May), pp. 963–975.

Satcher, D, Marks, JS, Bales, VS, Daily, LA, Speers, MA & Trowbridge, FL. (1996). *Physical Activity and Health: A Report of the Surgeon General:* (305102003-001).

Schöttle, Annett & Tillmann, Patricia. (2018). *Explaining the Benefits of Team Goals to Support Collaboration.* pp. 432-441.

Schwaber, K. and Sutherland, J. (1991) *The Definitive Guide to Scrum: The Rules of the Game.* www.scrum.org

Shen, Y. (2008) *The Effect of Changes and Innovation on Educational Improvement* in International Educational Studies 1(3), pp. 1

Sherrell, L. (2013). *Waterfall Model.* In: Runehov, A.L.C., Oviedo, L. (eds) Encyclopedia of Sciences and Religions. Springer, Dordrecht.

Sinek, S. (2011). *Start with why: how great leaders inspire everyone to take action.* London: Portfolio Penguin.

Singer, S. (2021) *I love teaching but.* Badass Teacher Association. [online] Available at: https://www.badassteacher.org/bats-blog/i-love-teaching-but-by-steven-singer

Sipos Y., Battisti B., Grimm K. 2008. *Achieving transformative sustainability learning: Engaging head, hands and heart.* International Journal for Sustainability in Higher Education. 9.

Stern, et al, (2021). *Learning That Transfers: Designing Curriculum for a Changing World*, Corwin Press

Sullivan, L, (2021). *Is physical education in Crisis? Leading a Much-Needed Change in physical education.* Scholary.

Sport England, (2014). *The Challenge of Growing Youth Participation in Sport.* Sport England [online] Available at: sportengland-production-files.s3.eu-west-2.amazonaws.com

Sport England, (2020). *Under the Skin.* Sport England [online] Available at: https://sportengland-production-files.s3.eu-west-2.amazonaws.com/s3fs-public/youth-insight_under-the-skin.pdf

# REFERENCES

Tamadoni, A., Hosseingholizadeh, R., & Bellibaş, M. Ş. (2024). *A systematic review of key contextual challenges facing school principals: Research-informed coping solutions.* Educational Management Administration & Leadership, 52(1), pp. 116-150.

Toshalis, Eric; Nakkula, Michael J. (2012). *Motivation, Engagement, and Student Voice* in Education Digest; Ann Arbor Vol. 78, Iss. 1. pp. 29-35.

Tripp, D. (1993). *Critical Incidents in Teaching: Developing Professional Judgement.* London: Routledge.

U.S. Department of Health and Human Services. (2015) Strategies to improve the quality of physical education [online] Available at: .www.cdc.gov/healthyschools/pecat/quality_pe.pdf.

U. S. Department of Health Human Services. (2018) *Physical Activity Guidelines* Advisory Committee Scientific Report.

Waddell, S., (2016). *Change for the Audacious: A Doer's Guide.* Networking Action Publishing.

Wang, C., Berry, B., & Swearer, S. (2013). *The Critical Role of School Climate in Effective Bullying Prevention.* Theory Into Practice. 52. pp. 296-302.

Welsh Government (2020a). Introduction to Curriculum for Wales guidance - Hwb. [online] Available at: https://hwb.gov.wales/curriculum-for-wales/introduction-to-curriculum-for-wales-guidance/.

Welsh Government (2020b). Developing a vision for curriculum design - Hwb. [online] hwb.gov.wales. Available at: https://hwb.gov.wales/curriculum-for-wales/designing-your-curriculum/developing-a-vision-for-curriculum-design/#curriculum-design-and-the-four-purposes.

Welsh Government (2020c) Area of Learning Experience: Health and Wellbeing. [Online] Available at: https://hwb.gov.wales/curriculum-for-wales/health-and-well-being/ [Accessed 4 November 2022]

Womack, James & Jones, Daniel. (1996). Lean Thinking: Banish Waste and Create Wealth in Your Corporation. 10.1038/sj.jors.2600967.